THE INSATIABILITY OF HUMAN WANTS

THE INSATIABILITY

OF HUMAN WANTS

ECONOMICS AND

AESTHETICS IN

MARKET SOCIETY

REGENIA GAGNIER

THE UNIVERSITY OF CHICAGO PRESS
CHICAGO AND LONDON

Regenia Gagnier is Professor of English at the University
of Exeter. She is the author of *Idylls of the Marketplace:
Oscar Wilde and the Victorian Public* and *Subjectivities:
A History of Self-Representation in Britain, 1832–1920*
and the editor of *Critical Essays on Oscar Wilde.*

The University of Chicago Press, Chicago 60637
The University of Chicago Press, Ltd., London
© 2000 by The University of Chicago
All rights reserved. Published 2000
Printed in the United States of America

09 08 07 06 05 04 03 02 01 00   1 2 3 4 5

ISBN: 0-226-27853-0 (cloth)
ISBN: 0-226-27854-9 (paper)

Library of Congress Cataloging-in-Publication Data

Gagnier, Regenia.
    The insatiability of human wants : economics and
aesthetics in market society / Regenia Gagnier.
        p. cm.
    Includes bibliographical references and index.
    ISBN 0-226-27853-0 (alk. paper)—ISBN 0-226-
27854-9 (alk. paper)
        1. Culture—Economic aspects. 2. Aesthetics—
Economic aspects. 3. Economic history—19th century.
4. English literature—19th century—Economic
aspects. I. Title.
HM548. G34 2000
330.1—dc21   00-030231

CONTENTS

■ ■ ■

ACKNOWLEDGMENTS

■ ■ ■

As the last chapter indicates, this book is the result of more than a decade of research and reflection on the place of the humanities in market society, and I gratefully acknowledge support from the following: the Doris McNamara Scholarship Fund, the Marta Sutton Weeks Faculty Scholarship in the Humanities, the Marilyn Yalom Fund of the Institute for Research on Women and Gender, and the Office of Technology Licensing Research Incentive Fund at Stanford University; the Modern Language Association of America's Conference Travel Fund; the John Simon Guggenheim Memorial Foundation; the Research Committee of the University of Exeter; and the Arts and Humanities Research Board. The book began in the 1980s with my perception that the subject matter I customarily taught as a professional Victorianist provided a valuable supplement to contemporary public economic debate. It also began in the United States, a country that, as Mill predicted in 1848, has gone substantially further than others in deliberately cultivating economic liberalism. Having emigrated in the course of writing, I have debts spanning at least two continents as well as two decades to more experts and intellectuals than I can name here, although most of them appear in the notes.

Also at Stanford I'd like to acknowledge the Cultural Studies Group, the Feminist Studies Program, the Program in Modern Thought and Literature, and the English Department, the two latter for providing me with graduate students to die for. Not all of them were around when this particular book took shape, but those who were and who contributed to it through their ideas, learning, and commitment were Helen Blythe, Kenneth Brewer, Jason Camlot, David Cantrell, Jeffrey Erickson, Ross Forman, Sung-Hee Kim, Stephanie Kuduk, Diana Maltz, Richard Menke, Victoria Olsen, Gail Perez, Amit Rai, Brian Rourke, J. B. Shank, Eric Schocket, Ardel Thomas, and Tim Wandling.

At the University of Exeter, I'm just beginning to know those who will fill their role.

Also at the University of Exeter I'd like to acknowledge in the School of English my colleagues Colin MacCabe, Duncan Petrie, Angelique Richardson, Jane Spencer, and Helen Taylor for comments on the manuscript and thank extramurally Barry Barnes in the Department of Sociology, Mark Blaug in the Department of Economics, Susan Hayward in the Department of French, and Alan Munton at the University of Plymouth. On both sides of the Atlantic, Isobel Armstrong, Joseph Bristow, Steven Connor, Sally Ledger, Scott McCracken, and John Sutherland have befriended and advised me.

I'd also like to acknowledge the Society for Critical Exchange, especially Martha Woodmansee, Mark Osteen, and Max Thomas. Since 1991, the SCE's project on culture and economics has been the major forum for research in the area. And I am grateful to a few editors of scholarly journals who have encouraged dialogue between the disciplines: Diana Strassmann and Myra Strober of *Feminist Economics;* David Ruccio, Jack Amariglio, and Stephen Cullenberg of *Rethinking Marxism;* Ruth Towse of *The Journal of Cultural Economics;* Herbert Tucker of *New Literary History;* John Maynard and Adrienne Munich of *Victorian Literature and Culture;* and Peter Euben of *Political Theory.*

My greatest debt of gratitude is to John Dupré, who has collaborated with me over the years on the history and philosophy of economics as well as the division of labor in raising our children. Economists like to talk about the inefficiencies of family "governments": conflict spillover, high tolerance of inefficient personnel (that is, children), inability to realize economies of scale, and so forth. My partner is evidence ("anecdotal") to the contrary.

Thus for my debts. Now my credit or gift. Representing as it does their mother's store of "human capital," or as feminist economists call it, her "fund of goodwill," that will be transferred to them, this book is dedicated to my sons, Gabriel and Julian Gagnier Dupré. I cannot do better than to reiterate the dedication of Olive Schreiner's *Woman and Labour,* cited in chapter 2:

> You will look back at us with astonishment[.] . . . You will marvel at the labour that ended in so little. But what you will never know is how it was, thinking of you and for you, that we struggled as we did and accomplished the little which we have done. It was in the thought of your larger realisation and a fuller life, that we found consolation for the futilities of our own.

The Chartist William Lovett called his autobiography *The Pursuit of Bread, Knowledge, and Freedom* (1876) and claimed that it was also the biography of the nineteenth century: the pursuit of material well-being, scientific knowledge, and political emancipation.[1] When J.-F. Lyotard in *The Postmodern Condition* (1979) characterized the West's "master narratives" one hundred years later, he included the last two, knowledge and freedom, but omitted bread.[2] The culture that had not seen beyond the horizon of scarcity and struggle in the face of nature dissolved toward the end of the nineteenth century, as Western society saw surplus and excess. It became possible to contemplate abundance and the capacity of human industry to control nature. Although economics still was called the "science of scarcity," scarcity was no longer a material obstacle but a recognition of society's ability to create unlimited new needs and desires as its productive capacity and leisure time increased. Bread and the labor that produced it no longer dominated the consciousness of individuals. This is why Lyotard let the concept drop from his description of the postmodern condition.

Economically, Lyotard was premature: much of the world still needs bread, and political economy would tell us, rightly, that the rest of the world is interdependent with the West. Conceptually, however, Lyotard probably *over*complicated his case. Knowledge and freedom in market society may be reducible to a single dominant narrative about the total actualization of individual pleasure. Is freedom in market society anything more than the capacity to exercise choice in the marketplace? Is knowledge more than the ability to maximize these choices in the most

1. William Lovett, *Life and Struggles of William Lovett in His Pursuit of Bread, Knowledge and Freedom*, 2 vols. (1876; reprint, London: G. Bell, 1920).
2. Jean-François Lyotard, *The Postmodern Condition: A Report on Knowledge*, trans. Geoff Bennington and Brian Massumi (Minneapolis: University of Minnesota Press, 1984).

efficient way? Each of these narratives may be but a part of a deeper contemporary narrative of Individuation. The postmodern emphasis on the irreconcilability of differences, its breakup of unified master narratives, may be the culmination of Individuation.

Viewed in this way, the disappearance of "bread" is understandable: material well-being is a means to increasing individuation, not an end in itself. Freedom and knowledge are also means rather than ends. Increasing individuation was the *telos* in Herbert Spencer's social evolutionism, as it is in contemporary neoliberalism, whose object is not Truth or Freedom, modernity's master narratives, but each individual's abstract right to choose, based not on knowledge but on an abundance of "information." Lyotard calls this move from knowledge, or Truth, to information one of the many "little narratives" of the postmodern condition. Economic "Man" today—the scare quotes designating the gender analyses developed below—may be more acquisitive than productive, first and foremost an individual whose aesthetic, or taste, is revealed by the choices he (or she) makes, however much those choices are conditioned by mass consumption. This book is about modern man and woman as producers and consumers, creatures of labor or pain and pleasure, in their pursuit of bread, knowledge, and freedom in market society.

Or, as one economist put it, the book is a *Picture of Dorian Gray* of modern Economic Man, a prize-fighter who gets bigger and meaner, dominating more and more of our cultural life, as he ages.[3] His managers keep promising that he will be redeemed by success and start to mellow but to date that has not happened. I have tried to create a moving picture of him through the lens of literary and cultural critique, comparing his progress with that of his coeval Aesthetic "Man." In tracing the progress of Economic Man and Aesthetic Man, I have also tried to keep a place for the opportunities they passed by.

The second half of the nineteenth century saw a shift from notions of Economic Man as producer (Smith, Ricardo, Mill, and Marx) or reproducer (Malthus) to a view of Economic Man as consumer. Chapter 1 describes in detail the turn from classical political economy to neoclassical economics and the related turn in aesthetics in the last quarter of the nineteenth century. Its function is to clarify for both specialists and nonspecialists the cultural significance of this shift. To a culturalist, one of the most important insights of classical political economy was that the division of labor was the source of differences

---

3. I owe this description to an anonymous reader of the manuscript at the University of Chicago Press; only an economist would have put it in precisely these terms.

between people. People may or may not identify with a social or economic class; in Britain in the nineteenth century they often did; in the United States today they typically do not. But as Smith showed in the early chapters of *The Wealth of Nations* (1776), most people's subjective and objective identities are centrally related to whether they make nails, automobiles, books, contracts, breakfast, hotel beds, music, speeches, or babies. The fact that the division of labor also reflects major social divisions of race, gender, and ethnicity, and internationally reflects relations of domination and subordination between nations, is also crucial in establishing individual and collective identities, as Smith and the other political economists of the Scottish Enlightenment well knew.

Second, the political economists were concerned about the negative consequences of the division of labor. Mixing mechanistic and organic metaphors, Smith proposed government structures to ameliorate British workers' deterioration in what he called the social, intellectual, and martial virtues. Mixing market and virtue ideology, Mill feared that competitive individualism would drive out sympathy and altruism. And Marx and Engels, who criticized political economy while adopting some of its fundamental categories, put alienation and atomism at the centers, respectively, of working and bourgeois life. Despite their penchant for economic laws and the abstraction of a self-interested maximizer of material advantage called Economic Man, the political economists also believed that economic systems made kinds of people and that the division of labor, as John Ruskin said, also divided people from one another.

Third, the political economists, being typically *progressive* rather than *developmental*, did not believe that markets were the end of history. Markets were taken as one stage of growth, but economic growth was no more an end in itself than Beauty was to their contemporaries in aesthetics. Smith thought that free trade, if it ever happened (which he thought unlikely), would lead to world peace (the so-called Doux-commerce thesis). Mill thought that once production reached a certain level, society's primary concern should be more equal distribution; indeed, he believed that the appropriate level of production had already been reached in 1871, a view that inclined him toward socialism late in his life. Political economy entailed a theory of social relations in a world in which scarcity was perceived to be a relation of productive forces to Nature, and markets were appropriate to but one stage of the development of those productive forces. Once society had *developed* its productive forces, humanity could *progress* ethically and politically.

Around 1871, economic theory began to shift its focus from the social relations of population growth, landlords, entrepreneurs, work-ers, and international trade to the individual's subjective demand for goods. The labor theory of value, which had seen the human body and human labor as the ultimate determinants of price, was abandoned in favor of consumer demand. Value no longer inhered in goods them-selves—whether the goods were grain or human labor—but in others' demand for the goods. Political economy's theory of the productive relations between land, labor, and capital thus gave way to the statisti-cal analysis of price lists or consumption patterns. One of the corollar-ies of marginal utility theory, as it came to be called, was that consumer choice ceased to be a moral category: it did not matter whether the good desired was good or bad, just that the consumer was willing to pay for it. Value ceased to be comparable across persons: it became individual, subjective, or psychological. The theory of economics be-came more psychological than sociological.

The psychological bias transformed the modern concept of scarcity. For Malthus and the political economists, scarcity was a relation of productive forces to the earth, as in population growth and diminish-ing returns from agriculture. Under marginal utility theory, scarcity was relocated in the mind itself, as a consequence of the insatiability of human desires. Stanley Jevons, Carl Menger, and the other early theorists of consumption saw that as the basic needs of subsistence were satisfied, humankind's desire for variety in shelter, food, dress, and leisure grew limitlessly, and thus the idea of needs, which were finite and the focus of political economy, was displaced by the idea of tastes, which were theoretically infinite.

All this amounted to a noticeable shift in the concept of Economic Man. Under political economy, Economic Man was a productive pur-suer of gain; for Jevons and Menger, on the other hand, Economic Man was a consumer, ranking his preferences and choosing among scarce resources. Significantly, *modern* man would henceforth be known by the insatiability of his desires, and the indolent races of savages—whether Irish, African, or native American (key examples throughout Victorian political economy)—needed only to be inspired by envy to desire his desires, imitate his wants, to be on the road to his progress and his *civilization*. His nature, insatiability, was henceforth human nature itself. His mode, consumer society, was no longer one stage of human progress but its culmination and end, the end of his-tory. And here we begin to see the displacement of ideas of *progress*, which implied moral and political progress as well as economic growth, by ideas of development, which implied, by way of increasingly biological or organic analogies, only an inevitable trajectory toward high mass consumption. These distinctions between Progress and Development are central to chapter 3, on modern individualism and the economic aspects of the "civilized" Man of Taste.

This history of economic thought must be qualified by competing theories, for the reduction of Economic Man to an individual consumer maximizing his self-interest did not go unchallenged. The traditions of democratic socialism and feminism, from the Ricardian and Owenite socialists to the Cooperativists and the Labourites of the first half of the twentieth century, show in eloquent detail that although the narrower production and consumption models became dominant or hegemonic at key moments, there were always broader economic visions that saw humans as both producers and consumers, workers and wanters, and as both individuals with individual needs and capacities and as members of social groups whose material conditions could be constitutive.[4] One purpose of this book is to recall social visions that challenged modern market society, visions that under current conditions of mass communications are in danger of being erased from cultural memory. Consequently, chapter 2, "Is Market Society the *Fin* of History? Market Utopias and Dystopias from Babbage to Schreiner," presents some of the early views about market society, from technophiles such as Charles Babbage and Andrew Ure, who thought that social relations could progress as mechanically as technology, to the fin de siècle socialists and feminists whose notions of social progress, while including full aesthetic visions, were heavily influenced by mid-Victorian biological and evolutionary theory. In these varying perspectives on market society, productivist models vie with models of pleasure and—the Victorians' own term—hedonics. The discussions in chapters 2 and 3 are supplemented by an appendix on taste, sex, and social class.

It is necessary to remind ourselves of the ways in which developments in economic thought were contested in the past because we find now that economism—the tendency to interpret all phenomena in market terms—is widespread and influential. Thus in *The Economic Approach to Human Behavior,* the Chicago economist and Nobel lau-

---

4. These have been recently represented in *Democratic Socialism in Britain: Classic Texts in Economic and Political Thought 1825–1952,* 10 vols., ed. David Reisman (London: Pickering and Chatto, 1996). See also *The Corn Laws: The Formation of Popular Economics in Britain,* 6 vols., ed. Alon Kadish (London: Pickering and Chatto, 1996). Frequent reference will also be made throughout the work to feminist critics of economics.

reate Gary Becker claimed that the "economic approach" was the only legitimate or fruitful approach to the study of human behavior.[5] Twenty years later, his claims are more specific: "The rational choice model provides the most promising basis presently available for a unified approach to the analysis of the social world."[6] In recent years rational choice theory has colonized anthropology, biology, political science, social psychology, and sociology, forging a chasm, especially in the United States, between political *science* and political *theory*. Inverting nineteenth-century humanistic attempts to model the market on familial relations of trust and responsibility, the Chicago School has modeled the home on market relations of efficiency and maximization. The "New Home Economics" are best illustrated in Becker's *Treatise on the Family* (1981).[7] The Chicago School economist Robert Pollack has further developed Becker's insights in "A Transaction Cost Approach to Families and Households." This approach recognizes the disadvantages of family "governments": conflict spillover, the toleration of inefficient personnel (that is, children), inappropriate ability match, inability to realize economies of scale, and so forth.[8]

Extending economism to law, in *The Economic Analysis of Law* (1977) the Chicago law professor and later a U.S. Court of Appeals Judge Richard Posner considered markets in childbearing and children, thereby applying the sweeping commodification that has accompanied neoclassical economism. That there are people who are capable of bearing children but who do not want to raise them, and other people who cannot produce their own children but want to raise them, suggested to Posner the possibility of a market in babies, especially since the costs of production by the biological parents are typically much lower than the value that many childless people attach to the possession of children. In the same volume, Posner experimented with a cost-benefit analysis of rape, calculating whether the cost to the victim exceeded the "benefit" to the rapist. In *Contested Commodities* (1996), the legal theorist Margaret Jane Radin analyzed Posner's "market rhetoric," showing how the "pleasure" and "satisfaction" of maintaining the rape victim's bodily integrity are commensurate for Posner

5. Gary S. Becker, *The Economic Approach to Human Behavior* (Chicago: University of Chicago Press, 1976).
6. Gary S. Becker, *Accounting for Tastes* (Cambridge: Harvard University Press, 1996), 156.
7. Gary S. Becker, *A Treatise on the Family* (Cambridge: Harvard University Press, 1981), 153. For a feminist critique, see Marilyn Waring, *If Women Counted: A New Feminist Economics* (San Francisco: Harper and Row, 1988), esp. 37–38.
8. Robert Pollack, "A Transaction Cost Approach to Families and Households," *Journal of Economic Literature* 23 (June 1985): 581–608.

with the "pleasure" and "satisfaction" of the rapist who invades it and who can only take "pleasure" and achieve "satisfaction" in sex when his partner is coerced.[9]

Radin's point is that the victim's and the rapist's claims are incommensurate, that Posner's hedonic calculus is irresponsible in reducing all values to one metric. In a more recent work Posner and the economist Tomas Philipson propose an economic approach to the epidemiology of AIDS.[10] In their universe of self-interested, maximizing "sex-traders," voluntary testing is likely to increase the spread of the infection. A trader in the sex market contemplating risky sex will estimate the benefits of the activity and subtract the costs of contracting a fatal disease, discounted by the probability of contracting it. That probability will depend on the prevalence of infected persons in some relevant class and the likelihood of contracting the disease even from an infected person, both of which are quite low in most circumstances. But for someone who has been able to determine by means of a reliable test that he or she is already infected with HIV, the costs of a sexual transaction are zero, and they will be much more likely to engage in risky sex, thereby spreading the infection.

Philipson and Posner do acknowledge that there may be some altruists in the population, or people for whom infecting a sexual partner with a fatal disease would involve some disutility. But the fact that the proportion of altruists is unknown is sufficient to show that the actual effect of widely available voluntary testing remains an empirical issue. Nonetheless, it is clear throughout the book that Philipson and Posner are strongly inclined to believe that the effect of testing will be deleterious. It is a common theme of economism, probably deriving from the cosmic irony of Smith's Invisible Hand, that altruism has perverse effects. Since altruists, who would prefer not to infect their sexual partners, will generally be less active in the risky sex market, the market will have a higher proportion of self-interested maximizers and therefore be all the more dangerous. This inclination fits into a pattern of skepticism about government interventions of various kinds that is characteristic of proponents of unfettered markets. In another critique of this kind of economism, the philosopher of science John Dupré has come to much the same conclusion as Radin: that a taste for altruism or ethical behavior and a taste for fast cars—the sex "market" and

9. Margaret Jane Radin, *Contested Commodities* (Cambridge: Harvard University Press, 1996), 86.

10. Tomas Philipson and Richard Posner, *Private Choices and Public Health: The Aids Epidemic in an Economic Perspective* (Cambridge: Harvard University Press, 1993).

nonhuman markets—are incommensurable.[11] One need not be a Lukacsian to be skeptical of a social science that conceives of, and articulates, social life and social policy in this way. Yet if commodification is not yet universal, market rhetoric is. In chapter 2, I refer to a lexicon of fetishism, commodification, and reification formerly associated with the Frankfurt School of cultural critique, who analyzed the classic form of the novel as "the transposition on the literary plane of everyday life in the individualistic society created by market production."[12] In later chapters such critical concepts are extended to social policy.

As Radin amply demonstrates, today policy inclines toward privatizing—that is, marketing—everything from education to body parts to the air we breathe. The goal of environmental policy, for example, is to allocate financial responsibility for pollution in such a way that pollution for the sake of profit is seen as an economic rather than an ethical or political problem. Modeling the atmosphere's finite capacity to absorb toxic waste, economists are now implementing a market in licenses to pollute.

Probably the best-known colonization of ethics by economism is the philosopher David Gauthier's *Morals by Agreement* (1986), in which Gauthier announced that it was "neither unrealistic nor pessimistic to suppose that beyond the ties of blood and friendship, which are necessarily limited in their scope, human beings exhibit little positive fellow-feeling. . . . One of the problems facing most human societies is the absence of any form of effective and mutually beneficial interaction among persons not linked by some particular bond."[13] Gauthier's solution to the problem of modern anomie was not ethical or political humanity, which he calls "the residue of an image of human beings that we have rejected," but market relations *tout court.*

> The superiority of market society over its predecessors and rivals is manifest in its capacity to . . . direct mutual unconcern to mutual benefit. If human interaction is structured by the condition of perfect competition, then no bond is required among those engaged in it, save those bonds that they freely create as each pursues his own gain. The impersonality of market society, which

---

11. John Dupré, "Against Scientific Imperialism," *PSA 1994* (1995): 2:374–81. For a fuller critique of economic reductionism, see Dupré's *The Disorder of Things: Metaphysical Foundations of the Disunity of Science* (Cambridge: Harvard University Press, 1993), esp. ch. 2, "Reductionism," 85–169.

12. Lucien Goldmann, introduction, *Towards a Sociology of the Novel,* trans. A. Sheridan (London: Tavistock, 1964), 6.

13. David Gauthier, *Morals by Agreement* (Oxford: Oxford University Press, 1986), 101.

has been the object of wide criticism, and at the root of charges of *anomie* and alienation in modern life, is instead the basis of the fundamental liberation it affords. . . . Those who hanker after the close-knit relationships of other and earlier forms of human society are in effect seeking to flee from the freedom to choose the persons in whose interests they will take an interest. (102)

The players in Gauthier's very abstract market society—and we shall see that one of the triumphs of modern economism has been its valorization of abstraction—are individuals rather than social groups. Even allowing that Gauthier does not clarify how we are to arrive at the utopian position of "perfect competition" given both the natural and socially entrenched positions of inequality in which we live our lives, the claims for market society are clear. Like Smith, but without Smith's strong qualifications and caveats ("unless government takes some pains to prevent it . . ."), Gauthier and other free marketeers claim that the market frees people. Mill himself argued repeatedly that only by making women equal participants in the market would they be released from the servility and brutality of the Victorian home, and Marx thought (notoriously) that anti-Semitism ("The Jewish Question") would dissolve as all society became more market-oriented. But while arguing that the market was better—or in classical terms, a higher stage of Progress or development—than slavery and bigotry, few of the political economists were prepared to say, as free marketeers have been boasting especially since Soviet communism has collapsed, that it was the highest form of society, or the end of history. Indeed, historians of "the idea of Progress" frequently point out that the idea of progress in our fin de siècle typically refers merely to economic progress, or economic growth as progress, and its sole supporters seem to be economists and advocates of economism (see chapter 3). Now that the failures of unfettered markets seem as luminous as those of central planning (see again postcommunist Russia as well as the discussion of the 1980s in chapters 6 and 7), it may be salutary to reconsider some of the historical claims for both planning and markets that were more richly put than those of the public rhetoric of the 1980s and 1990s. Some of these concern the aesthetic life as an activity rather than objects with value or price.

Until very recently it was a principle of mainstream economic thought that tastes were exogenous to economic models. Economists had only to do with "revealed preferences," or what people actually bought, not with why they bought one thing (crack cocaine) rather than another (an edition of Flaubert). They left the construction of taste to sociologists and called evaluative distinctions between different tastes "paternalism." Very recently, however, the colonization of other areas of thought by rational choice arguments has spread to aesthetics. In *Accounting for Tastes* Gary Becker acknowledges that a lack of attention to social interaction due to "excessive attention to formal developments [that is, mathematical modeling] has made it impossible for economists to discuss why people have the tastes they do."[14] This newfound interest on the part of economists in the endogeneity of preferences, or the social construction of taste, begins with what Becker calls the personal and social "capital" an individual inherits from the past. In *Aesthetics and Economics* Gianfranco Mossetto has used Becker's earlier concept of "addiction" to explain why, unlike the declining marginal utility of most goods, the consumption of literature and other cultural products increases with use: as with heroin, the more cultural exposure one has, the more one wants.[15] (And, of course, the reverse: the less people are exposed to cultural phenomena, the less they want them, total lack of exposure leading to total lack of demand, or even to hostility.) Against the generalized and abstract analyses of Becker and Mossetto, this books makes the claim that literary and other cultural critics may make a particular contribution to economic knowledge by showing how people come to "choose" what they do, by showing how tastes and choices develop and, just as important, are constrained. This intervention opens toward a broader conception of aesthetics than economists, with their emphasis on price rather than value, currently imagine. Just as "taste" means more than neutral "choice," so aesthetics means more than the market price of artistic commodities.

Just as nineteenth-century economics derived from broad and practical perceptions of people as producers, creators, laborers, and consumers, or creatures of taste and pleasure, so did aesthetics derive from these same perceptions. That is, the aesthetics of market society developed concurrently with the economics. In J. S. Mill's inaugural address to the University of St. Andrews (1867), the topic of which was the content and purpose of a university education, Mill proposed science, ethics, and aesthetics, or the True, the Good, and the Beautiful. He specifically defined *aesthetics* as the education of the feelings through the culture of poetry and art. Mill claimed that "commercial money-

14. Becker, *Accounting for Tastes*, 194.
15. Gianfranco Mossetto, *Aesthetics and Economics* (London: Kluwer, 1993).

getting" caused Britain, unlike Europe, to undervalue the arts.[16] It was the British character to be moral in small things but to lack a noble purpose and a larger vision. An aesthetic education was needed that would inspire exalted feelings and the kind of idealism that would lift the British toward richer lives and a more harmonious whole than "the business of getting on" had to that point allowed.

The function of aesthetics, then, was to provide aesthetic feeling, to soothe the mind and to harmonize humankind's multiform needs and capacities as they became increasingly subjected to the demands of the marketplace. Further, the shift in economics actually privileged subjective psychological factors on the part of the consumer that a science of aesthetics was best placed to explain. Yet Mill's Schillerian view of aesthetics was just one among others. Chapter 4 deals with production, reproduction, and pleasure in Victorian aesthetics and the turn from the substantive aesthetics of the self-styled "political economists of art" to the preoccupation with the formal aspects of art and literature that came with physiological aesthetics at the end of the nineteenth century. Ethical aesthetics arose with industrialism and was concerned with the creation of self-regulating subjects and autonomous works; aesthetics of production were concerned with producers or creators and the conditions of creativity and production; aesthetics of taste or consumption, often with a physiological base, became dominant by the end of the nineteenth century, largely through the ascent of psychology in academic institutions; and aesthetics of evaluation, best evoked today under the name of Matthew Arnold, were historically linked with the idea of national cultures and races (remembering the range of meanings these terms encompassed in nineteenth-century Britain). These aesthetics had a number of points of contact or overlap, but their promoters often had very different motivations. The approach to aesthetics below will be pragmatic, showing how different aesthetic formulations functioned within market society. Readers whose interests are primarily in aesthetics might want to begin with chapter 4 and then read other chapters in light of its findings.

Employing the aesthetic criteria traced in chapter 4, in the last three chapters I develop a concept of practical aesthetics that asks, What are the pragmatics, or practical functions, of aesthetics in everyday life in modern market society? A number of recent works have considered the divergences and convergences of aesthetics and economics since the

16. John Stuart Mill, *Essays on Equality, Law, and Education*, vol. 21 of *Collected Works of John Stuart Mill* (University of Toronto, 1984), 215–58, esp. 253.

eighteenth century.[17] Although this book focuses on the shift in both from production to consumption after the 1870s, and on models of consumption and taste unavailable in earlier periods, it also explores moments when aesthetic knowledge has provided alternatives to the forces of mechanization, commodification, and brutalization. In historicizing how the great aesthetic categories—the Beautiful, the Sublime, the Creative Genius or Poet, the Man of Taste, and so forth—functioned in market society, the book is also an intervention into current debates about cultural historicism versus aesthetic evaluation, making cases for both the historical limits of aesthetics and the practical value of aesthetics in criticizing, and providing alternatives to, the market. Chapter 5 provides detailed examples of such practical aesthetics in Frederick Rolfe's *Desire and Pursuit of the Whole* (1909), Oscar Wilde's long letter from prison to Alfred Douglas known as *De Profundis* (1897), and some of the New Woman literature that was critical of "unproductive" male leisure. Conceptions of the Beautiful in philosophical aesthetics have specifically excluded consideration of self-interest and private property. Taste, understood as evaluative distinction, has had everything to do with property and individualism, whether in the sphere of practical or philosophical aesthetics.

If notions of value were contested in the history of economic thought, they were equally contested in the history of aesthetics. The economist Arjo Klamer recently edited a collection called *The Value of Culture* in which he (though not the other contributors) opposes a romantic idea of cultural value to economic value.[18] Klamer uses aesthetic value to criticize the reduction of all value to price; yet the history of aesthetics shows models of production, consumption, and value contemporary and often compatible with economic models. There are models of production, reproduction, and creativity that posit Aesthetic Man as producer or creator and that elucidate the conditions of creativity; models of consumption that posit Aesthetic Man as hedonic and that concern themselves with the calculation of pleasure, the pursuit of happiness, and distinctions of taste. And there are both absolute and relative conceptions of aesthetic value, as there are in eco-

17. See, e.g., Patrick Brantlinger, *Fictions of State: Culture and Credit in Britain, 1694–1994* (Ithaca: Cornell University Press, 1996); James Thompson, *Models of Value: Eighteenth-Century Political Economy and the Novel* (Durham: Duke University Press, 1996); and Gillian Skinner, *Sensibility and Economics in the Novel, 1740–1800: The Price of a Tear* (London: Macmillan, 1999). Many more examples will be discussed below.

18. Arjo Klamer, "The Value of Culture," in *The Value of Culture: On the Relationship Between Economics and Arts* (Amsterdam: Amsterdam University Press, 1996), 13–28.

nomics. The technically Beautiful, as in Kant or Wilde below, is a product of civil bourgeois society, perhaps its highest product; other aesthetics have taken as their object something more like the perception and expression of the True, or what Adorno called in a characteristically complex formulation "the self-consciousness of the truth content of what is radically temporal." [19]

In the following quotations from the modern history of aesthetics, which will be discussed in detail in the chapters below, we see a movement from an ethical, to a productivist, to a consumption aesthetics, informed by the social appurtenances of gender, or race, or class. [20]

> Now I maintain that the Beautiful is the symbol of the morally Good; and only because we refer the Beautiful to the morally Good does our liking for it include a claim to everyone else's assent.

Probably the most famous statement in Western aesthetic philosophy, Kant's referral of the Beautiful to the Good in *The Critique of Judgment* (1790) is a statement of absolute value; it is universal; it refers to a freedom from desire or self-interest that harmonizes the self and the self in relation to society. The Kantian aesthetic arose with industrialism and concerned itself with disinterested subjects and autonomous works: it was self-regulating, mechanistic, and bourgeois, like Smith's market. The Kantian aesthetic is not about the object or its producer but about a process that occurs between the perceiving subject and the object; it is not about pleasure ("mere liking") but a system of equilibrium between the good, the true, and the beautiful.

John Ruskin's "The Nature of Gothic" from *The Stones of Venice* (1851–53) provides a classic application of the labor theory of value:

> Go forth again to gaze upon the old cathedral front, where you have smiled so often at the fantastic ignorance of the old sculptors: examine once more those ugly goblins, and formless monsters, and stern statues, anatomiless and rigid; but do not mock at them, for they are signs of the life and liberty of every workman who struck the stone.

The object has value because of the labor mixed in it. A purely economic labor theory of value, as in Locke or Smith, traces value merely to labor as the scarce transformer of natural resources into goods. Ruskin, like Marx, has a deeper account of the value in human labor, so

19. Theodor W. Adorno, draft introduction to *Aesthetic Theory,* trans. and ed. Robert Hullot-Kentor (London: Athlone Press, 1997), 357.

20. Full bibliographical information on the quotations from the history of aesthetics will be supplied in the chapters in which they are discussed below.

that ultimately the value of goods is determined by the quality of life of the producer.

In his autobiographical notebooks, *Mon Coeur mis à nu* (1863; published 1867), Charles Baudelaire presented his critique of productionism, including biological reproduction, in the form of an attack on the socialist-feminist George Sand:

> Women cannot distinguish between soul and body, whereas the dandy creates a more and more perceptible divorce between the spirit and the brute. . . . The more a man cultivates the arts, the less often he gets an erection. . . . Only the brute gets really good erections. Fucking is the lyricism of the people.

Baudelaire preferred the more voyeuristic pleasures of the connoisseur *flaneur* to the active life of production and reproduction, indicating a shift in aesthetics from the producer to the consumer of the arts.

A comic version of the same critique of productionism is in Max Beerbohm's preface to his *Complete Works* (1896):

> I shall write no more. Already I feel myself to be a trifle outmoded. I belong to the Beardsley period. Younger men, with months of activity before them, have pressed forward since then. *Cedo junioribus.*

Published when he was twenty-four years old, Beerhohm's inscription illustrates some common upper-class stances toward the economy at the fin de siècle: boredom with production but love of comfort, insatiable desire for new sensation, and the fear of falling behind the competition.

Wilde's famous definition of a cigarette from *The Picture of Dorian Gray* (1891) also defines the perfect commodity: "A cigarette is the perfect type of a perfect pleasure, because it leaves one unsatisfied." The cigarette is the perfect commodity because it is addictive, it creates the desire for more. Here Wilde continues the emphasis on pleasure, consumption, insatiability, and desires (rather than needs), or what the turn-of-the-century economist Vilfredo Pareto would call "ophelimities." In the next quotation, women are no longer producers, as above in Baudelaire, but themselves resemble the cigarettes, or commodities, that feed the insatiable desires of George Moore's hero Mike Fletcher (1889):

> More than ever did he seek women, urged by a nervous erithism which he could not explain or control. Married women and young girls came to him from drawing-rooms, actresses from the-

atres, shopgirls from the streets, and though seemingly all were as unimportant and accidental as the cigarettes he smoked, each was a drop in the ocean of the immense ennui accumulating in his soul.

In Olive Schreiner's "The Woman Question" of 1899, the productivist feminist replies to the male consumer. Here the woman as wage earner despises the idle consuming pleasure-seeking man, a tension we shall discuss in detail in chapter 5. The parasitic female, on the other hand, *produces* the consuming male. The image is one of consumption as decay or decadence, a fall from production:

> Only an able and labouring womanhood can permanently produce an able manhood; only an effete and inactive male can ultimately be produced by an effete and inactive womanhood. The curled darling, scented and languid, with his drawl, his delicate apparel, his devotion to the rarity and variety of his viands, whose severest labour is the search after pleasure; . . . this male whether found in the late Roman empire, the Turkish harem of today, or in our northern civilisations, is possible only because generations of parasitic women have preceded him. More repulsive than the parasitic female herself, because a yet further product of decay, it is yet only the scent of his mother's boudoir that we smell in his hair.

Schreiner's emphasis on creative production can be compared with that of other New Women, like the novelist Sarah Grand, whose productivism made her pathologize all French literature as "vain, hollow, cynical, . . . *barren*."[21]

A final quotation, from Arthur Symons's *London: A Book of Aspects* (privately printed 1909), may be contrasted with Ruskin's valuing of laborers above: here the people going to and from work are only valued for the consumption of the aesthete. Unaesthetic in themselves, they supply the pleasures of condescension to the discerning aesthete, a "utility" that resurfaced in particularly barbaric ways in the 1980s (see chapter 7):

> As I walk to and fro in Edgware Road, I cannot help sometimes wondering why these people exist. Watch their faces, and you will see in them a listlessness, a hard unconcern, a failure to be interested. . . . In all these faces you will see no beauty, and you

21. Angelique Richardson, "The Eugenization of Love: Sarah Grand and the Morality of Genealogy," *Victorian Studies* 42 (1999–2000): 227–55, 244.

will see no beauty in the clothes they wear, or in their attitudes in rest or movement, or in their voices when they speak. They are human beings to whom nature has given no grace or charm, whom life has made vulgar.

Economic models thus informed both practical and philosophical aesthetics in conceptions of humans as producers or creators; as consumers or creatures of taste, pain, and pleasure (hedonics); and as arbiters of value. Similarly, aesthetics informed economics. There were always economic visions that were less crude than our millennial economism, and many economists have offered comprehensive and accessible moral, political, and aesthetic visions. When Adam Smith explicitly discussed scientific method in "The History of Astronomy" (1750, published 1799), his standard was not truth but beauty.[22] He analyzed how the heavenly systems as conceived from Copernicus to Newton were increasingly "fitted to soothe the imagination" and how each system was more aesthetically satisfying than the previous one.[23] Bernard Shaw's powerful jeremiad "The Economic Basis of Socialism" establishes disgust as a motive for redistribution—the aesthetic basis of economic distribution; and most of the *Fabian Essays* of 1889 share its, at base, aesthetic impulse.[24] The architect Arthur Penty left the Fabians when they "substituted engineering for architecture, mechanics for aesthetics."[25] In 1905, A. R. Orage, the editor of *The New Age: A Weekly Review of Politics, Literature, and Art,* began to promote a "socialism of taste," writing that "Socialism as a means to the intensification of man, is even more necessary than socialism as a means to the abolition of economic poverty."[26] In *In Place of Fear* (1952), Aneurin Bevan, a former miner from Wales who established the National Health Service and a comprehensive net of welfare benefits, appealed directly to poetry and the senses, invoking his compatriot Dylan Thomas on the fact of empathy.[27] Today Douglas Jay's critique of markets, *The Socialist Case* (1938), seems astonishingly timely as it

22. Adam Smith, "The Principles Which Lead and Direct Philosophical Enquiries: Illustrated by the History of Astronomy," vol. 3 of *Essays on Philosophical Subjects of the Works and Correspondence of Adam Smith,* ed. W. P. D. Wightman and J. C. Bryce (Oxford: Clarendon, 1980), 33–105.

23. See Deborah A. Redman, *The Rise of Political Economy as a Science: Methodology and the Classical Economists* (Cambridge: MIT Press, 1997), 220–24.

24. Bernard Shaw, "Over Population," in *Fabian Essays,* vol. 4 of *Democratic Socialism in Britain,* 20.

25. Arthur Penty, *Old Worlds for New,* vol. 5 of *Democratic Socialism in Britain,* viii.

26. A. R. Orage, *Old Worlds for New,* vol. 5 of *Democratic Socialism in Britain,* xii.

27. Aneurin Bevan, *In Place of Fear,* vol. 10 of *Democratic Socialism in Britain,* 199–200.

grapples with the "efficiency principle" of contemporary economic theory and the problem of inheritance of cultural capital, or taste, and the *reproduction* of class as culture.[28] Between Smith and Jay fall most of the writers discussed in this book. Against the grain of the rationalization of knowledge each refuses to decouple the satisfaction of our needs and desires (economics) from their perception and expression (aesthetics). Because competing models of humankind as producer and as consumer have figured so prominently in our conceptions of modernity after 1870, chapter 6 ("On Heroes, Hero-Worship, and the Heroic in the 1980s," on high finance) and chapter 7 ("Homelessness as an 'Aesthetic Issue,'" on California's Theatre of the Homeless), bring the relations of production and consumption up to the present, focusing on the redistribution of wealth and poverty since the 1980s and its implications for the aesthetic life.

A word about the last two chapters in relation to the historical argument. The historical argument constitutes the most detailed account to date of how an aesthetics of taste, pleasure, and consumption arose with a conception of Economic Man as maximizer of individual choice. A number of explanations for the shift from producer and labor or creativity to consumer and taste will be discussed in the pages that follow, as will the particular distinctions of postindustrial, post-Darwinian forms of taste and consumption. Yet while I propose the historical argument as a contribution to our knowledge of aesthetics and culture in market society, I have wanted to retain the motivation for the research in the last two chapters. The competitive individuals who were the imaginative centers of the popular culture of the 1980s, whether wearing the face of wealth and glamour or the face of poverty and crime, have been sanctioned in economic and aesthetic theory since the second half of the nineteenth century. Competitive individualism and aesthetic individuation through taste, choice, and preference have certainly liberated us, but they have also served as the justification of our indifference toward others and as an ideological cover for institutional manipulations of power. Chapter 6 shows how myths of heroic individuals masked legal, financial, and political manipulations of wealth. Chapter 7 shows the way that questions of taste and preference mask social indifference and apathy. The most recent examples happen to be American, but it would be naive and perhaps optimistic to think that they are parochial. One of the threads running through this book is the historically much-debated relation of British and European capitalism to that developing in the United States and to its North Ameri-

28. Douglas Jay, *The Socialist Case*, vol. 8 of *Democratic Socialism in Britain*, 277.

can corollary, competitive individualism. Predictions since Hegel of economic rather than political (or military) hegemony and of global consumer cultures may not have been entirely fulfilled, but they have not been entirely off the mark, either.

In one of the earliest but still one of the best critiques of neoclassical economics, *Economic Thought and Language* (1937), L. M. Fraser described the narrowing of economic thought that occurred from 1871 to the 1930s, which has only become narrower, more abstract, and more mathematical since he wrote: "Almost every essential characteristic of the older economics has disappeared. From being philosophical and humane, the theory of value has become scientific and abstract; it has abandoned its claim to prescribe remedies for economic ills or to act as a defence of one economic system against another: it has withdrawn from the problems of social welfare into the pure atmosphere of mathematical speculation. . . . But the process of purification has not as a rule been accompanied by a corresponding adjustment in terminology," Fraser continues with reference to the discipline's semantic confusion. "Old words have been employed in new senses without wholly losing their familiar associations and overtones: the revolution in thought has been concealed behind a veil of linguistic continuity."[29] Fraser, a logician, persuasively analyzes four distinct kinds of "value" in economic theory, each with numerous subsets (106). He analyzes "more nearly forty than four" meanings of the word *capital* (370). Yet since the 1980s a popular economic discourse of growth, productivity, value, and choice has dominated social policy and cultural life with similar confusion. Fraser in 1937 thought that the narrowing of economics was a sign of the discipline's "modesty," and most contemporary economists would see it that way. Yet the explosion of economism in public rhetoric and social policy at the end of the twentieth century looks more like imperialism than modesty. Hegel derived the aesthetic impulse from the fact that it is in our nature for humans to represent ourselves to ourselves and thereby to construct our identities.[30] If any readers doubt the centrality of modern economic thought to modern self-representation, modern aesthetics, and modern culture generally, they may begin with the last two chapters and then return to the history for understanding.

29. L. M. Fraser, *Economic Thought and Language: A Critique of Some Fundamental Economic Concepts* (London: Black, 1937), 373.

30. G. W. F. Hegel, *Introductory Lectures on Aesthetics*, trans. Bernard Bosanquet, ed. Michael Inwood (London: Penguin, 1993), 34–35.

ONE

On the Insatiability of Human Wants

Economic and Aesthetic "Man"

When Fraser wrote his chapter on capital in *Economic Thought and Language* (1937), he apologized for its "monstrous length . . . it got completely out of hand,"[1] whether ironically with reference to capitalist growth itself or parodically in relation to Marx's magnum opus it is not clear. Although it covers some ground that has been covered elsewhere in the history of economic thought, this longish first chapter has had to cover it in a way that emphasizes cultural implications, that relates it to the history of aesthetics, and that will serve as the foundation of the chapters to follow. To these ends I have decided to lay the foundations solidly, aiming for elegance in subsequent chapters.

This chapter on the concept of "Economic Man"[2] describes in detail the turn from classical political economy to neoclassical economics in the second half of the nineteenth century and the related turn in aesthetics during the same period. In the political economists from Smith to Mill there is a tension in the concept of Economic Man. The concept represents both man as such, that is, universal human nature, and a particular kind of man, the product of a particular economic class and race at a particular historical moment in global market relations. This tension between universal economic man and historical economic man functioned critically. For example, the historical conception allowed

An earlier version of this chapter appeared as "On the Insatiability of Human Wants" in *Victorian Studies* 36.2 (winter 1993): 125–54, published by Indiana University Press.

1. L. M. Fraser, *Economic Thought and Language: A Critique of Some Fundamental Economic Concepts* (London: Black, 1937), x.

2. As the feminist economists discussed below, among many other feminist critics in other disciplines, agree, rational Economic Man is typically that, a man having the freedom and autonomy to pursue his self-interest, even a particular kind of man with respect to class, race, and place. When referring to the typical construction of political economists, then, I shall use the traditional term. When referring to humankind, I use the term *humankind* or other non-gender-specific terms.

the political economists (including their critic Marx) to express their reservations concerning the advances of "civilization" (defined as technological superiority and a complex division of labor) and to compare "civilization" to "barbarism," occasionally in "barbarism's" favor. It also allowed the political economists (including Marx) to see economic man as simply one stage in human history or progress—the stage characterized by technological superiority based on the division of labor. Under neoclassical economics, here represented by the theorists of the so-called marginal revolution that began in the 1870s, Stanley Jevons and Carl Menger, the social relations central to political economy were replaced by a theory of the individual consumer and his wants. Labor was reduced to merely one commodity among others, and intersubjective comparisons of utility and thus welfare (as opposed to "wealth") were prohibited. Economic man became modern man as such, the universal man of insatiable consumer desires. Under neoclassical theory, economic man loses his critical function and represents the end of history itself, the end to which all other classes and races of men aspire. Capitalist markets are not one stage of human progress but the final stage.

Although always present in the Malthusians, scarcity became the dominant feature of economic man's environment only when the economy seemed ostensibly to shift from scarcity to abundance. Only multiple consumer choice made people aware of their relative scarcity. In the course of discussion of economic man a new kind of man was created: one who was civilized by virtue of his technology and whose advanced stage of development was signified by the boundlessness of his desires. He must choose from a universe of goods on display, and his status, his level of civilization, his "taste," are revealed by his choices or preferences. The terms are the terms of twentieth-century economics—rational choice, revealed preference—and so are the methods: methodological individualism, subjectivism, behaviorism. The characters are the man and woman of late Victorian economics and aesthetics, from Pater's discriminating consumer of the art object, to the characters who people Wilde's spectacular stages, to Conrad's corporate colonizer, Kurtz. They are insatiable.

Others have argued that in the early industrial "take-off" period, when the economy was incapable of significantly ameliorating poverty, poverty was viewed as an inevitable condition of life. Since the economy then required a high level of production, political economy, like its cultural counterpart, the "industrial" or "social problem" novel, gave priority to production and its interpersonal and objective values:

work, action, cooperation, abstinence. Later, as industrialism matured and productive capacity increased, a high level of consumption became more important, with its corresponding values of leisure, privacy, and subjectivity (choice), constituting modern individualism.[3]

ECONOMIC MAN AS HISTORICAL PRODUCER AND PRODUCER OF HISTORY: CLASSICAL POLITICAL ECONOMY

In *The Theory of Moral Sentiments* (1759) and *The Wealth of Nations* (1776), Smith provides one account of human nature as rational, self-interested, and acquisitive, but lazy—man hates to work. So why does man work? He works to acquire property, not because it is valuable in itself but because through it he will achieve status, the admiration and even subordination of his fellows. Ideally he would earn these tributes by virtue of his wisdom, but wisdom is notoriously harder to discern than wealth, so most of the world judges by appearance: yet in so judging and in so working to possess the wealth of others the world is wrong. Of the poor man's son, "whom heaven in its anger has visited with ambition" and who "looks around and admires the condition of the rich," Smith writes that if in the extremity of old age he should at last attain to wealth he will find it to be in no respect preferable to the humble security and contentment that he had abandoned for it. In the last dregs of life, his body wasted with toil and diseases, his mind galled and ruffled by the memory of a thousand injuries and disappointments that he imagines he has met with from the injustice of his enemies or the perfidy and ingratitude of his friends, he will find that wealth and greatness are no more adapted for procuring ease of body or tranquillity of mind than ingenious toys or gadgets. Like gadgets, they are more trouble than they are worth. On our deathbeds, we shall

3. Although I have contributed the emphasis on particular values associated with the two modes here, Gertrude Himmelfarb summarizes elements of this argument of Calvin Woodward, with whom she disagrees, in *Poverty and Compassion: The Moral Imagination of the Late Victorians* (New York: Knopf, 1991), 304. Himmelfarb herself dismisses Jevons as not "laying claim to any radical revision of political economy" (282) and turns to Alfred Marshall, whose *Principles of Economics* (1890; reprint, London: Macmillan, 1920), she believes, sanctioned the welfare state. Marshall, a Kantian, did attempt to restore normative content to economics and, although a finer mathematician than the avowedly mathematical economists of his time, resisted its mathematization; but with the exception of the Welfare economists (discussed in the text), economists then and later largely ignored his ethical purposes and used his formal analyses to justify laissez-faire (whose limitations he showed). He himself argued that price was determined by both demand and supply, that this had been understood by the classical political economists, and that the "marginal revolution" never happened.

realize that we were wrong in our pursuit of wealth and that we have wasted our lives.[4]

Yet this "deception" is for Smith ironic; it is a happy deception.[5] In his wrong-headed pursuit of the wealth he covets in others, the poor man's son will make the world more comfortable for us all:

> It is this deception which rouses and keeps in continual motion the industry of mankind. It is this which first prompted them to cultivate the ground, to build houses, to found cities and commonwealths, and to invent and improve all the sciences and arts . . . and made the trackless and barren ocean a new fund of subsistence, and the great high road of communication to the different nations of the earth. (263)

In this passage, on our sympathetic identification with the rich and our desire to imitate them in their acquisitiveness, is the convergence of Smith's two principal works. The first shows how agents learn to be moral through their relations with each other, the second how agents pursuing individual interests achieve social order and the wealth of nations. In their errant pursuit of wealth, which they will regret on their deathbeds, the wealthy sons of poor men "are led by an invisible hand . . . without intending it, without knowing it . . . [to] advance the interest of the society, and afford means to the multiplication of species" (265).

In *The Wealth of Nations,* Smith intervenes between the self-interested rationality of the Hobbesian contractarians and the altruism of the civic humanists by proposing social order without either a Leviathan state or altruism. The model posits, after Hobbes, that we are desiring creatures but averse to drudgery. We want to get what we want but not to work hard. Fortunately, as an inevitable consequence of lan-

---

4. Adam Smith, *The Theory of Moral Sentiments* (London: George Bell, 1907), 259–63.

5. In a 1991 MLA address titled "The New Economics," the economist Donald (now Deirdre) N. McCloskey claimed not only that the self-interest obsessively clung to by economists had been first popularized by the novelists Defoe, Richardson, and Austen, but also that the *figure of irony* in the form of unintended consequences was political economy's greatest contribution. While Ruskin and Marx saw only the unsubtle stories of families and communities breaking down under the cash nexus, McCloskey claims that the supersubtle political economists saw the irony of the invisible hand: that selfish individuals can make an altruistic society, that individualism is a basis for social understanding, that saving can be good for the individual soul but bad for society at large, that the pursuit of profit can be an ethical failing in an individual but on the social level lead to good.

guage use, we learn to truck, barter, and trade.[6] We efficiently divide tasks, or create divisions of labor. Specialization gives rise to markets, which give rise to equilibrium of supply and demand and to the accumulation of stock, or capital. This accumulation, or wealth, is productive, leading to more wealth, which leads to social order. For in Smith, civil government and private property develop concomitantly (see books 3 and 5), and law is "instituted for the defense of the rich against the poor, or those who have some property against those who have none at all" (*Wealth*, 674).

Like the delusion of the poor man's son, the great system of wealth and social order is a delusion for most of society. "Improved and civilized" society brutalizes the majority of the population but offers variety of employment and thereby great wealth. "Barbarous" societies, on the other hand, give individuals the capacity to perform all socially necessary tasks, but the number of employments and hence wealth are much diminished. Thus the wealth that matters is not individual wealth, or the welfare of individuals (today, standard of living), but aggregate wealth (today, GNP). In a famous passage in book 5 Smith contrasts the brutalizing and divisive effects of the division of labor, the source of national wealth, with the simple but pleasant equality of barbarous societies.

The man whose whole life is spent in performing a few simple operations generally becomes as stupid and ignorant as it is possible for a human creature to become. . . . His dexterity at his own particular trade seems, in this manner, to be acquired at the expence of his intellectual, social, and martial virtues. But in every improved and civilized society this is the state into which . . . the great body of the people, must necessarily fall, unless government takes some pains to prevent it. It is otherwise in barbarous societies . . . [where] invention is kept alive, and the mind is not suffered to fall into that drowsy stupidity, which, in a civilized society, seems to benumb the understanding of almost all the inferior ranks of people. (734)

Smith further muses on the fact that the elite few who do benefit from "civilization" by way of understandings "both acute and comprehensive" may not contribute any benefits to society at large.

6. In addition to Smith's comments about language in book 1 of *The Wealth of Nations* (New York: Modern Library, 1965), see "A Dissertation on the Origin of Languages," appended to *The Theory of Moral Sentiments* (1759; reprint, London: George Bell, 1907), 505–38.

The varied occupations [of "civilization"] present an almost infinite variety of objects to the contemplation of those few, who,
being attached to no particular occupation themselves, have leisure and inclination to examine the occupations of other people.
The contemplation of so great a variety of objects necessarily exercises their minds in endless comparisons and combinations,
and renders their understandings, in an extraordinary degree,
both acute and comprehensive. Unless those few, however, happen to be placed in some very particular situations, their great
abilities, though honourable to themselves, may contribute very
little to the good government or happiness of their society.
(734–36)

The elites' intellectual powers are materially—literally—expanded
by their contemplation of the wealth created through the division of
labor. The entrepreneurs of *The Theory of Moral Sentiments* and *The
Wealth of Nations* promote their own security and profit (*Wealth*,
423). Yet at no point in either work do the great body of the people
benefit themselves proportionately. Rather, they have no choice but
to become drudges in the division of labor that produces for self-
interested "undertakers" (entrepreneurs) the great profit that is the
wealth of nations and for an intellectual elite myriad objects for ingenious contemplation that materially expand their mental faculties.

In book 3 Smith gives a historical narrative of the establishment of
market economies in Europe that goes far toward producing culture-
specific psychologies that constrain his abstract theory of rationality
in book 1. Civilizations normally develop agriculture, then manufacture, then foreign commerce. In Europe, this progress was inverted:
commerce developed first, then manufacture, then agriculture. In the
town, however, freedmen who became merchants employed their
money in profitable projects. By (1) providing a market, (2) purchasing
land in the country and improving it, and (3) introducing order and
good government to a countryside previously living in fear of rival
lords, the merchants pursued their own interests while improving their
own countryside and foreign countries to boot. As long as the great
lords of the countryside were vulnerable to each other and the king,
they maintained large armies but accumulated no luxuries. Nor did
their vassals work hard, having no opportunity to own personal property. While their technology improved the land that the allodial lords
had left fallow, the merchants inadvertently contributed to the down-
fall of the lords as proprietors. With their objects of trade and manufacture, which Smith calls ornaments and baubles, they created new

wants. With no bounds to their expense, because there were no bounds to their vanity, the great proprietors squandered away their money on baubles and thereby lost their retainers, vassals, and ultimately power to the alliance of king and burghers.

Whereas books 1, 2, and 4 provide an abstract theory of rationality—human beings as such pursue their rational self-interest, which leads to economic optimality and market equilibrium for society in general—book 3 shows only one group, merchants from the town, who are so motivated. The vassals and retainers are lazy and content to be dependent on their lords, and the great proprietors themselves are motivated to their demise by their vain desires for ornaments and baubles. In anachronistic terms, the merchants are producers, the lords are doomed and self-consuming consumers, and the vassals and retainers are dependents, or parasites. These culture-based psychologies— which elsewhere in political economy were transposed onto other national or racial participants in the global market (see below)—are generally interpreted as reflecting Smith's primitive understanding of the three social classes (landlords, laborers, and capitalists) then coming to consciousness of their conflicting interests.[7] Yet even if one does not accept Smith as fully anticipating Marx, the cultural limits on the abstract individual's pursuit of self-interest are firm enough in Smith.

The class or cultural biases in fact compromise the free market system itself. In book 4, economic growth can be impeded by individuals, classes, or nations that put their particular interests above the efficient workings of the market. In the case of monopolies, self-interest leads to the formation of groups that impede the growth of all. Smith recognizes that self-interest appearing in the formation of class or cultural identities effectively limits the possibilities of free trade and corrupts the institutions of government.

To expect, indeed, that the freedom of trade should ever be entirely restored in Great Britain, is as absurd as to expect that an Oceana or Utopia should ever be established in it. Not only the

7. Ronald Meek argued that Smith's contribution lay in grasping the world-historical significance of profit from capital as a new generic type of class income for which the employment of wage labor was the essential condition. Merchants had made profits by buying cheap and selling dear, rents generated profits, as did interest on money. But Smith's association between profit and wage labor, and his recognition that the profit-making constituency would be the leading order of society, or the basic mainspring of the economy, cleared the way for the full development of classical political economy and its corresponding models of humankind. Ronald L. Meek, "Adam Smith and the Classical Theory of Profit," in *Economics and Ideology and Other Essays* (London: Chapman and Hall, 1967), 18–33.

prejudices of the public, but what is much more unconquerable, the private interests of many individuals, irresistibly oppose it. . . . The monopoly which our manufacturers have obtained against us . . . has so much increased the number of some particular tribes of them, that, like an overgrown standing army, they have become formidable to the government, and upon many occasions intimidate the legislature. The member of parliament who supports every proposal for strengthening this monopoly, is sure to acquire not only the reputation of understanding trade, but great popularity and influence with an order of men whose numbers and wealth render them of great importance. If he opposes them, on the contrary, and still more if he has authority enough to be able to thwart them, neither the most acknowledged probity, nor the highest rank, nor the greatest public services, can protect him from the most infamous abuse and detraction, from personal insults, nor sometimes from real danger, arising from the insolent outrage of furious and disappointed monopolists. (437–38)

In sum, in Smith economic rationality is not equal but always limited by the individual's social or class position, and markets are not free but subject to the manipulations of power. (See chapter 6.)[8]

By the time of Ricardo's *On the Principles of Political Economy and Taxation* (1817), the "classes" of landlords, laborers, and capitalist-manufacturers are fixed categories, and Ricardo is only concerned to analyze how rent, wages, and profit are distributed among them. Claims about human nature are only local and implicit: due to the diminishing utility of labor and capital as applied to land, the capitalist's profits will decline and landlords will be fat, idle, and rich. Laborers may well be deficient in desire altogether, as in chapter 5, "On Wages," in which, in a Malthusian attack on the Poor Laws, Ricardo and James Mill insist that the remedy for the Irish poor "who prefer present ease and inactivity . . . to a moderate degree of exertion with

8. Jacob Viner listed the flaws in the natural order of laissez-faire in a classic 1926 article, "Adam Smith and Laissez Faire," in *Adam Smith, 1776–1926* (1928; reprint, New York: Augustus M. Kelley, 1966), 116–55, esp. 134–36. There are four rich volumes of *Adam Smith: Critical Assessments,* ed. John Cunningham Wood (London: Croom Helm, 1983–84), and, in addition to the classic collection *Adam Smith, 1776–1926,* there is the superb *Essays on Adam Smith,* ed. Andrew S. Skinner and Thomas Wilson (Oxford: Clarendon, 1975) and the more recent *Wealth and Virtue: The Shaping of Political Economy in the Scottish Enlightenment,* ed. Istvan Hont and Michael Ignatieff (Cambridge: Cambridge University Press, 1983), for readers unfamiliar with the range of scholarly interpretation of Smith.

plenty of food and necessities" is "to stimulate exertion, to create new wants, and to implant new tastes."[9] Ireland as well as "many countries of Asia" and "the islands of the South Seas" produce little evidence of economic rationality. Thus in Ricardo as in Smith, and in most of the political economic writings through John Stuart Mill, economic man is limited by his social class and place in the empire. As Marx pointed out a half-century later, the early political economists wavered between positing a self-interested, maximizing, work-shy "human nature" and positing social types derived from their socioeconomic status. While reviving economic rhetoric from the classical political economic period, twentieth-century free-marketeers—who reject the notion of social class in favor of methodological individualism—have ignored the limitations on the laissez-faire system implied by the conflict between the social groups analyzed by the political economists.

ECONOMIC MAN AS PRIMITIVE: JOHN STUART MILL AND KARL MARX

John Stuart Mill published his *Principles of Political Economy* in the eventful year of 1848, and it became the nineteenth century's most influential text in economics, only yielding to the effects of the marginal revolution by the twentieth. Although the list of Mill's contributions to and qualifications of Ricardian economics is long and appreciated by historians of economic thought, of most interest here is his shifting the discussion from the laws of production to the customs of distribution. Despite his virtuosity in theoretical work, Mill himself told a friend regarding his *Principles,* "I regard the purely abstract investigation of political economy . . . as of very minor importance compared to the great practical questions which the progress of democracy and the spread of socialist opinion are pressing on."[10]

In "Preliminary Remarks" Mill tells his own story of how markets were established in ancient Europe, a story entailing considerably more physical force and corruption than Smith's but one equally based in class and imperial ideology. Small communities around ports "early acquired a variety of wants and desires, which stimulated them to extract from their own soil the utmost which they knew how to make it yield; and when their soil was sterile, or after they had come to the end of its capacity, they often became traders, and bought of the pro-

9. David Ricardo, *On the Principles of Political Economy and Taxation* (1817; reprint, Cambridge: Cambridge University Press, 1986), 100.

10. See "John Stuart Mill," in Mark Blaug, *Economic Theory in Retrospect,* 4th ed. (Cambridge: Cambridge University Press, 1988), 179–224. The quotation is on 220.

duction of foreign countries, to sell them to other countries with a profit."[11] Given the scarcity of land, after a time all of these communities were either conquerors or conquered. Mill writes in cautionary terms about the rise and fall of the Roman, or any, empire: rather than the pursuit of wealth leading to the enrichment of all, the great monopolies of wealth swallowed up the smaller, the government became corrupt, and the infrastructure decayed, until the poor barbarians from the north destroyed the empire altogether. Within each succeeding European country arose "two distinct nations or races, the conquerors and the conquered: the first the proprietors of the land, the latter the tillers of it" (24). After paying what they owed their lords, the serfs used the surplus to buy their freedom and access to town. They banded together against landholders, and "feudal Europe ripened into commercial and manufacturing Europe" (24). "As these bourgeoisie were a saving class, while the posterity of the feudal aristocracy were a squandering class, the former by degrees substituted themselves for the latter as the owners of a great proportion of the land" (25).

As the national wealth is distributed unequally among saving, squandering, and dependent classes, international wealth is distributed unequally among desiring and industrious northern populations and indolent southern populations with minimal wants, those, that is, who are insufficient in desire. In book 1, chapter 7, Mill mentions the customary causes of productivity: natural advantages of land and climate; the level of workers' skill, knowledge, and technology; and the division of labor. Of most significance, however, is the "greater energy of labour" that comes from a cold, hostile climate that makes industry a necessity for survival in many cases but also, elsewhere, appears endemic to certain populations. In pointing out the two extremes to be avoided, Mill contrasts the English and the Anglo-Americans "who have no life but in their work," and are "too deficient in senses to enjoy mere existence in repose," with the North American Indian, who rarely exerts himself for a distant object (81). English and Anglo-Americans consequently need to develop talents for enjoyment and reflection while the less energetic group, to whom Mill adds freed Jamaican slaves, need incentives to work harder, and Mill recommends baubles: "To civilize a savage, he must be inspired with new wants and desires" (81). Here the economics of British market expansion meet the goals of civilizing, in the colonial creation of new wants and desires. The colonizer-capitalist is the kind of man who uses "his will to employ his

11. J. S. Mill, *Principles of Political Economy* (London: Routledge, n.d.), 22–23.

commodities productively" (50), rather than, like the rentier descendants of feudal lords, wasting them on luxury items. Capitalists, that is, are driven by will and purpose, while landed gentry may suffer from apathy, and savages and workers may suffer from impoverished wants and low levels of desire. Furthermore, given the apparent psychological fixity of the different groups and the fate of the landed aristocracy, who squandered their wealth on baubles, there is no reason to believe that the creation of new wants in barbarians would lead to anything but their stupefied exploitation.[12]

Yet in the final two books of the *Principles*, Mill shows that economic man, a product of a particular economic class, nation, and moment in history, is himself but one stage in human progress. In book 4, on the "influence of the progress of society on production and distribution," he unequivocally condemns the abstract goal of expanding growth, arguing that economic man's competitive struggle for accumulation and self-interest itself are merely part of one stage—the industrial stage—toward progress, by no means the end.

Because his view that market society is not permanent but part of the flow of history is either forgotten by subsequent economists or associated solely with a discredited Marxism, Mill is worth quoting at length:

> I confess I am not charmed with the ideal of life held out by those who think that the normal state of human beings is that of struggling to get on; that the trampling, crushing, elbowing, and treading on each other's heels, which form the existing type of social life, are the most desirable lot of human kind, or anything but the disagreeable symptoms of one of the phases of industrial progress. It may be a necessary stage in the progress of civilization, and those European nations which have hitherto been so fortunate as to be preserved from it may have it yet to undergo. . . . But it is not a kind of social perfection which philanthropists to come will feel any very eager desire to assist in realizing. Most fitting, indeed, is it, that while riches are power, and to grow as rich as possible the universal object of ambition, the path to its attainment should be open to all, without favour or partiality. But the best state for human nature is that in which, while no one is poor, no one desires to be richer, nor has any reason to fear being thrust back, by the efforts of others to push themselves forward. . . . I know not why it should be matter of congratula-

12. Chapter 3 develops these themes of the global market.

tion that persons who are already richer than any one needs to be, should have doubled their means of consuming things which give little or no pleasure except as representative of wealth; or that numbers of individuals should pass over, every year, from the middle classes into a richer class, or from the class of the occupied rich to that of the unoccupied. It is only in the backward countries of the world that increased production is still an important object: in those most advanced, what is economically needed is a better distribution.[13]

By Mill's time, the myriad objects of created wealth were less productive of intellectual stimulation than "representative" of mere conspicuous consumption, indicative less of productive process than of wasteful distribution.

Here and elsewhere in the *Principles*, the United States is Mill's chief illustration of failure to progress beyond accumulation. He expresses his distaste for its national materialism with a characteristic disapproval of growth in the reproductive sphere as well (Mill was an obsessive defender of family planning): "They have the six points of Chartism, and they have no poverty: and all that these advantages seem to have done for them is that the life of the whole of one sex is devoted to dollar-hunting, and of the other to breeding dollar-hunters" (113–14 n; or 496). He concludes that he does not share political economy's fear of the stationary state that will follow on international competition, and, like Smith, questions whether industrial technology (that defined civilization for technophiles such as Babbage and Ure) in fact contributed to the greater happiness of the greatest number. It is the only passage in Mill that Marx ever praised, and it speaks of "the art of living" that would follow on "the art of getting on." The former depends on the abridgment of burdensome labor and the cultivation of leisure: "Hitherto it is questionable if all the mechanical inventions yet made have lightened the day's toil of any human being. They have enabled a greater population to live the same life of drudgery and imprisonment, and an increased number of manufacturers and others to make fortunes. They have increased the comforts of the middle classes. But they have not yet begun to effect those great changes in human destiny, which it is in their nature and in their futurity to accomplish" (116–17; or 498). Thus Mill, like Smith, had no faith that either tech-

13. J. S. Mill, *Principles of Political Economy* (London: Penguin, 1988), 113–15. Because unabridged and inexpensive editions of Mill's *Principles* are out of print, I cite from the Penguin edition when possible. In the edition used in the previous note, see 496–97.

nological growth or market activity alone would result in social or political progress.[14]

Mill does, however, outline the progressive program that will trans-
form the nature, including the gendered nature, of economic man.
Once women are liberated to participate freely in market relations and
thus be self-supporting, and the poor are educated to take their gover-
nance into their own hands, wage-labor itself ought to ease in favor of
workers' control of markets (what today we would call market socialism), and nuclear families ought to give way to associations of common interest. Regarding the *family* wage, Mill writes:

> Something better should be aimed at as the goal of industrial
> improvement, than to disperse mankind over the earth in single
> families, each ruled internally, as families now are, by a patriar-
> chal despot, and having scarcely any community of interest, or
> necessary mental communion, with other human beings. The
> domination of the head of the family over the other members, in
> this state of things is absolute; while the effect on his own mind
> tends towards concentration of all interests in the family, consid-
> ered as an expansion of self, and absorption of all passions in
> that of exclusive possession, of all cares in those of preservation
> and acquisition. (128)

Thus "proletarianization," or the division of humankind into waged
and unwaged labor, was predicated on the household that subordinated women to "nonproductive" labor, that is, labor that produced
no surplus to be appropriated by the employer. Mill saw that the corre-
lation of unwaged or "nonproductive" work and home devalued the
work of women and gave men false senses of autonomy and possession.[15]

He predicted the end of the family wage. "The speculations and
discussions of the last fifty years, and the events of the last thirty, are
abundantly conclusive on this point. . . . [T]he relation of masters and
workpeople will be gradually superseded by partnership, in one of two
forms: in some cases, association of the labourers with the capitalist;
in others, and perhaps finally in all, association of labourers among
themselves" (128–29). Mill further predicts that laborers will associate
"on terms of equality, collectively owning the capital with which they

14. Mill did, however, strongly believe that a "free market of ideas" was progressive.
See *On Liberty* (1859; in *Three Essays* [Oxford: Oxford University Press, 1975]). His
criticisms of the "stationary state" of China in book 3, "Of Individuality," of *On Liberty*
refer to its overwhelming traditionalism. See also chapter 3 on theories of progress.

15. See Immanuel Wallerstein, *Historical Capitalism* (London: Verso, 1983), 22–25.

carry on their operations, and working under managers elected and removable by themselves" (133). They will share profits—not equally but, after all have achieved subsistence, according to work done, the only hired laborers being "workpeople whose low moral qualities render them unfit for anything more independent" (129). For Mill the great incentive for production is workers' share in the profit. Regarding common fears for loss of incentive, he pointed out that communism supplied at least as much personal incentive as salaries or wages (communism, for example, also provided benefits).

One might pause here to consider how the discourse has changed, not simply in the abandonment of Mill's hopes for a cooperative and decentralized market socialism but even in the notion of incentive. For Mill, workers' incentive was *decreased* by wages; only by receiving a share of the profits could a worker hope to rise in the world, and hope of rising was the basis of Mill's progressivism. Today incentive in economic discourse is more frequently located in two opposite domains. Under "supply-side" economics, all discussions of incentive focus on *capitalist* incentive (low capital gains tax, deregulation, and so on). If there is incentive on the workers' part, it is negative: workers' *fear of falling* (into a residuum of the unemployed or uninsured or homeless— see the aestheticization of these in chapter 7, as in Mayhew's representations of London's poor creating a catharsis of pity and fear for middle-class readers). Mill's hope of rising on the part of the many defined his progressivism, while fear of falling on the part of the many and hope of maintaining the status quo on the part of the few define ours. Such a shift follows from the decoupling, fundamental to neoclassical economics, of wealth and welfare. Capitalist incentive may contribute to GDP ("wealth" or "growth") without affecting distribution (welfare, or the relation between the economic interests of individuals and those of the community). In writing of workers' incentive, Mill was as concerned with welfare as wealth.[16]

16. Our contemporary proponents of worker-control capitalism have the same concern for distribution. The political philosopher D. W. Haslett believes that "despite the fall of socialism" deep feelings of discontent with capitalism are as strong as ever, particularly with respect to inequalities of wealth and opportunity. In *Capitalism with Morality* he proposes for the former an antipoverty policy based on the abolition of minimum wage; a national income–related, cost-sharing preschool program; and share economies (D. W. Haslett, *Capitalism with Morality* [Oxford: Clarendon, 1994]). He also argues, like Mill, for a limitation on inheritance. Yet Haslett's moralization of capitalism goes beyond poverty containment and redistribution. One of capitalism's strengths over socialism, he argues, is its conduciveness to political freedom. Although socialism gives better access to necessities and equal opportunity, as well as to more overall social freedom, capitalism is better for entrepreneurial freedom, consumer freedom, freedom of

Mill described how the transition from private ownership of the means of production to market socialism would take place, a plan predicated on the eradication of "narrow selfishness":

As [workers'] associations multiplied, they would tend more and more to absorb all work-people, except those who have too little understanding, or too little virtue, to be capable of learning to act on any other system than that of narrow selfishness. As this change proceeded, owners of capital would gradually find it to their advantage . . . to lend their capital to the associations; to do this at a diminishing rate of interest, and at last, perhaps, even to exchange their capital for terminable annuities. In this or some such mode, the existing accumulations of capital might honestly, and by a kind of spontaneous process, become in the end the joint property of all who participate in their productive employment: a transformation which, thus effected, (and assuming of course that both sexes participate equally in the rights and in the government of the association) would be the nearest approach to social justice, and the most beneficial ordering of industrial affairs for the universal good, which it is possible at present to foresee. (140–41)

Mill concludes "On the Probable Futurity of the Labouring Classes" by distinguishing himself from socialist theorists. The distinction is not, as some historians have claimed,[17] that he was against the redistribution of wealth or socialized ownership of the means of production, but rather that he was for competition. Socialists, and many political economists, of the time typically saw competition as war: worker against worker, firm against firm, nation against nation. Mill sees competition as (as yet) the best stimulus to progress. "To be protected against competition is to be protected in idleness, in mental dul-

---

speech, and consequently, political freedom. In order to protect political freedom while enhancing substantive freedom, he proposes worker-control capitalism. Worker-control capitalism is better than traditional capitalism because under it managers will be accountable to workers, whereas now they are accountable to shareholders. He proposes that we implement worker-control in a mixed economy, so that workers' enterprises would compete with traditional capitalist enterprises.

Such late-twentieth-century liberal views may be contrasted with David McNally's socialist views in *Against the Market*, which, like Mill's, went beyond concern for inequality of wealth and opportunity in favor of quality of life as measured by the way workers actually spend their time (David McNally, *Against the Market* [London: Verso, 1993]).

17. See Blaug, *Economic Theory in Retrospect*, 220.

ness; to be saved the necessity of being as active and intelligent as other people" (142).

Since Mill, socialist critics of market socialism like David McNally have argued that workers' control, whether socialist or capitalist, is not possible in a situation in which groups of workers continue to relate their labor and its products to those of other workers by means of the market, or competitive accumulation.[18] What is crucial to capitalism is not a specific form of ownership of the means of production but the incessant drive to develop and expand them, so that workers are subjected, or, in the case of worker-control, subject themselves, to the pressures of accumulation in order that the producing unit can survive in the world of commodity exchange. McNally's description of how market competition drives labor to accumulation as an end in itself in order to maintain the market viability of the firm clarifies why even proponents of worker-control nonetheless give productivity priority over workers.[19] Wealth for the worker, on the other hand, in McNally's view, is disposable time, a view that also has its roots in nineteenth-century, more aesthetic, versions of socialism that led William Morris to call his Utopia "an Epoch of Rest" and that led Mill to say that his real "work" (as a public intellectual) began at home, after a day in his office at the East India Company.[20]

For Mill, it remained to be seen whether private or common property would be the better distribution of wealth. Distilling from the work of a number of socialist theorists—Blanc, Fourier, Condisérant, and Owen—he distinguished between socialism, which permitted private ownership of the articles of consumption but required public ownership of the instruments of production, and communism, which was dedicated to equal distribution or distribution according to need. Mill thought that remuneration according to work done was just only when the amount of work done was a matter of volition rather than of differential abilities. He agreed with socialist critics that current institutions of private property did not conform to the principle that justified it, which was to guarantee to individuals the fruits of their own labor and abstinence, and in book 2 ("Distribution") of the *Principles* and in his very late, posthumously published, writings on socialism, he considered at length the perversions of capitalism under current conditions and the promise of socialism.

Throughout these deliberations, Mill was constant on two points.

18. See note 16 above.
19. See discussion of Haslett in note 16 above.
20. J. S. Mill, *Autobiography*, ed. Jack Stillinger (Boston: Houghton Mifflin, 1969), 51–54. "An Epoch of Rest" is the subtitle of Morris's *News from Nowhere*.

First, the notion of property was not absolute and should be altered when needful for the public good. Although the laws of production partook of the character of physical truths, distribution was a matter of human institutions only, and it was therefore subject to change and, it was hoped, improvement in the direction of equality. Since land, for example, was the product neither of an individual's labor nor abstinence, it could only be privately owned when it was expedient for the general good, and the state should appropriate or redistribute it at will. Similarly, Mill argued that there should be a limit placed on the amount any one person could inherit in a lifetime.

The second point on which Mill was firm was that to be successful, socialism required a high standard of moral and intellectual education in all members of the community and that this education would not be available under capitalism: "Only a communistic Association can effectually train mankind for communism."[21] He predicted that, despite its democratic promise, the United States would not progress beyond dollar-hunting and that its democratic institutions and educational goals would fail due to its unchecked pursuit of individual and national profit. He also predicted that communist revolutions would fail when their populations were uneducated, because aligning self-interest with the social good—that is, "enlightened self-interest"—was a matter of cultivation. For a society of both liberty and equality, people needed a level of comfort sufficiently high to be educated and the kind of education that a society based on self-interest could not provide. The welfare economists of the early twentieth century would hold similar views.

Notoriously progressive in his own views of the probable futurity of the laboring classes, Marx said that the chief fault of the bourgeois science of political economy lay in treating capitalism as the final form of social production, instead of as a passing historical phase of its evolution. In the style of political economists, Marx also tells an *histoire moralisé*, in the concluding part of *Capital* (1867), "The So-Called Primitive Accumulation." He begins by parodying Smith et al.: "In times long gone by there were two sorts of people; one the diligent, intelligent, and above all, frugal elite; the other, lazy rascals, spending their substance, and more, in riotous living."[22] But Marx says that this "idyll" of primitive right and labor as the sole means of enrichment masks the actual history, one of "conquest, enslavement, robbery, mur-

21. John Stuart Mill, *On Socialism*, with an introduction by Lewis S. Feuer (Buffalo: Prometheus, 1987), 131.
22. Karl Marx, *Capital* (New York: International, 1967), 1:713.

der, briefly force" (714). For Marx, the so-called primitive accumulation of capital stock was in reality the historical dispossession of the producers. In England in the fifteenth and sixteenth centuries, a combination of the break-up of bands of feudal retainers, the usurpation of common arable lands and their transformation into sheep-walks or pasturage, and the dissolution of the monasteries under the Reformation forcibly tore landed peasantry from their means of subsistence and hurled them onto the labor market as "free" and "unattached" proletarians, thus creating wage labor as the "free contract" into which the dispossessed might enter. Chapter 28, "Bloody Legislation Against the Expropriated, From the End of the 15th Century," is one of the most painful and outraged in Marx: "Thus were the agricultural people first forcibly expropriated from the soil, driven from their homes, turned into vagabonds, and then whipped, branded, tortured by laws grotesquely terrible, into the discipline necessary for its wage system" (737). Wages, the working day, and trade unionism were regulated in due course to benefit the capitalist class. The industrial capitalist himself rose to power not on the just fruits of his labor and abstinence, nor on free trade, but on the colonial system, the national debt, heavy taxes, protectionism, commercial wars, and "a great slaughter of the innocents" (757), or child slavery: "the discovery of gold and silver in America, the extirpation, enslavement and entombment in mines of the aboriginal population, the beginning of conquest and looting of the East Indies, and turning of Africa into a warren for the commercial hunting of black-skins" (751).

Thus differing from Smith in much of his perspective on the source of the wealth of nations (Smith had simply said that it was "to no purpose" to discuss what might have been if the produce of labor had been left to the laborer [*Wealth,* 65]), in the final pages of *Capital* Marx nonetheless approves of Smith's suggestion that the self-interest of capitalists in the form of monopolies will lead to the failure of capitalist production itself. As capital becomes more centralized and concentrated in fewer and fewer hands, the mass of misery, oppression, degradation, and exploitation will grow. In time, the exploited will rebel, and the expropriators will be expropriated.

It is too obvious to belabor here that in Marx as in the political economists the basic categories are the productive relations between the three real or imagined classes of their time (landowners, workers, and capitalist entrepreneurs) and their commodified objects of exchange (land, labor, and capital), resulting in rent, wages, and profits in domestic and colonial markets. These are also the basic categories of mid-Victorian cultural production. Nineteenth-century Britain was the great era of the novel as a form, and the fiction of Jane Austen, Mary Shelley, Elizabeth Gaskell, George Eliot, the Brontës, Charles Dickens, William Thackeray, Anthony Trollope, and the rest was the fiction of social relations between landed aristocrats, entrepreneurs, and wage earners. Whether the aristocrats were represented as stable pillars of the community (as in Trollope) or lazy and decadent (as in Bulwer-Lytton), whether the entrepreneurs were energetic (as in Gaskell) or cruel (as in Dickens), whether the wage earners were docile and dependent (as in Eliot) or angry and seditious (as in Disraeli) depended on the political perspective of each novelist. But there is no doubt that the great novelists saw the world in terms of social groups in contact and often in conflict, in which no private life, as George Eliot said, was not determined by a wider public life.[23] Their view of socioeconomic relations extended considerably beyond that of the political economists, who refused to acknowledge the arena of unpaid work, like much housework and care of dependents, or widespread but illegitimate work, like prostitution. The novelists did not have a limited view of the economy. To the contrary, even the fiction of greatest psychological depth, like Charlotte Brontë's *Villette* (1853), finds economic relations constitutive of the psyche. Or, again as George Eliot said, "[T]here is no creature whose inward being is so strong that it is not greatly determined by what lies outside it."[24]

Political economy informed both philosophical and literary aesthetics. Social and psychological as well as physical landscapes—genders, crowds, leaders, and appropriate forms of response to them—were embedded in Edmund Burke's classic distinction between the Sublime and the Beautiful of 1757:

> Sublime objects are vast in their dimensions, beautiful ones comparatively small; beauty should be smooth, and polished; the great, rugged and negligent; beauty should shun the right line, yet deviate from it insensibly; the great in many cases loves the right line, and when it deviates, it often makes a strong deviation; beauty should not be obscure; the great ought to be dark and gloomy; beauty should be light and delicate; the great ought to be solid, and even massive. They are indeed ideas of a very different nature, one being founded on pain, the other on pleasure. . . . There is a wide difference between admiration and love. The sublime, which is the cause of the former, always dwells on great

23. George Eliot, *Felix Holt, The Radical* (Middlesex: Penguin, 1982), 129.
24. George Eliot, *Middlemarch*, ed. Gordon S. Haight (Boston: Houghton Mifflin, 1968), 612.

objects, and terrible; the [beautiful] on small ones, and pleasing; we submit to what we admire, but we love what submits to us.[25]

In Elizabeth Gaskell's *North and South* (1854–55), a classic in its own right among "industrial" or "social problem" fiction of the mid-nineteenth century, the aesthetic categories were unconsciously but indelibly mapped on to both economic types and geographical—in fact, political economic—locations. Margaret Hale, the heroine from the south, is described with the standard aesthetic adjectives corresponding to the beautiful and is more preoccupied with pleasure than with pain or labor. She exists to love and be loved, and the epithets that describe her might have been transferred from her teacups: "light-coloured," "pink," "round," "ivory," "pretty," "noiseless," "daint[y]."[26] In the next passage, the northern manufacturing entrepreneur Mr. Thornton is contrasted explicitly as the sublime, not only to Margaret as the Beautiful but also to her effeminate southern father, Mr. Hale, a tutor. Mr. Hale's face and figure are "slight," "soft and waving," "undulating," "trembling," "fluctuating," "arched," "languid," "feminine," and "dreamy." Thornton, on the other hand, through Margaret's eyes, is described in terms of the Sublime: "straight," "unpleasantly sharp," "penetrating," "lines," "carved in marble," "severe and resolved," "ready to do and dare everything" (80).

In the chapter called "Men and Gentlemen," the gentleman appears as an ephemeral social category associated only with present pleasure, whereas a man is associated with labor or pain and seen as sublime in relation to "life—to time—to eternity." Men, or as Carlyle called them, "Captains of Industry," are associated with the literary prototype of the autonomous entrepreneur Robinson Crusoe and, presciently, with the "animal spirits" that Keynes, taking the phrase from Blake, would attribute to investors.[27] The contrast between the sublime energy of the northern entrepreneurs and the parasitism of the southern gentry is epitomized in the distinction between Oxford ("Oxford men don't know how to move" [330–31]) and the northern industrial town of Milton, "Darkshire" ("It's the bustle and the struggle they like. . . . I don't believe there's a man in Milton who knows how to sit still" [ibid.]).

Elsewhere in the novel, the contrast is explicitly tied to pleasure and

25. Edmund Burke, *A Philosophical Enquiry into the Origin of Our Ideas of the Sublime and the Beautiful*, ed. James T. Boulton (Notre Dame: University of Notre Dame Press, 1986), 113, 124.

26. Elizabeth Gaskell, *North and South* (Oxford: Oxford University Press, 1982), 79.

27. John Maynard Keynes, *The General Theory of Employment, Interest, and Money*, vol. 7 of *The Collected Writings* (London: Macmillan, 1974), 161–64.

pain, the almost orientalized life of leisure, serene enjoyment, and the senses that Thornton associates with Mr. Bell and Oxford and that of Sublime action, exertion, and surmounting of difficulty he associates with Milton:

> We are of a different race from the Greeks, to whom beauty was everything, and to whom Mr. Bell might speak of a life of leisure and serene enjoyment, much of which entered in through their outward senses. I don't mean to despise them, any more than I would ape them. But I belong to Teutonic blood; it is little mingled in this part of England to what it is in others . . . we do not look upon life as a time for enjoyment, but as a time for action and exertion. Our glory and our beauty arise out of our inward strength, which makes us victorious over material resistance, and over greater difficulties still. We are Teutonic up here in Darkshire. (334)

In his admiration of the Sublime, Burke had written of the evils of indolence and of "how pain can be a cause of delight, absolutely requisite to make us pass our lives with tolerable satisfaction: Labour is a surmounting of difficulties, an exertion of the contracting power of the muscles; and as such resembles pain" (Burke, 35). In contrast to Milton, which is always associated with action and movement, the southern countryside is typically presented as civil, already congealed, leisurely, ordered—again the qualities that elsewhere were associated with "oriental" stasis and luxury.[28]

Ultimately the countryside disappears, except as a memory, a psychological condition of timeless youth and beauty, to be replaced by Milton and "progress." The village remains associated with a lost life in common, with the commons that had disappeared, and with the mother, whom Burke had made the original source of feelings for the Beautiful (Burke, 111; Gaskell, 401).

The critic John Barrell has associated landscape painting, aesthetic theory, and social class, arguing that panoramic views were understood to be fully grasped only by elites with wide experience, who simultaneously represented the interests of landed ownership and the public good.[29] By Gaskell's time the panoramic view had been replaced, at least in literature, with the linear view of Progress, in which the countryside was inert, abject, before the energies of the industrial

28. See Gaskell, *North and South,* 342, and chapter 3 of this book.
29. John Barrell, "The Public Prospect and the Private View," in *The Birth of Pandora and the Division of Knowledge* (Philadelphia: University of Pennsylvania Press, 1992), 41–61.

towns and in which the "total" views once encompassed by gentlemen were obscured by conflicting perspectives of social groups (north versus south, laboring, productive men versus serene, "nonproductive" women).

Both literatures, the novels of sublime industry transforming the beautiful land and the science of political economy, were motivated by their capacity to intervene in social debates, to resist anarchy or exploitation, to bring understanding of both sides of the wealth-welfare distinction. Smith showed that by acting out of self-interest entrepreneurs could perform the social good but that the self-interest of capitalists would make it unlikely that they would do so; Marx, that by its own growth capitalism would liberate those it had victimized; and Mill, that political economy itself was merely a primitive stage of human development: once humankind was raised out of a condition of scarcity, the happiness of the many would be in a just distribution and no-growth state. Political economy was thus a substantive, normative theory of social relations. As Marx said, "capital is not a thing, but a social relation between persons. . . . [A]s Wakefield discovered in the Colonies, property in money, means of subsistence, machinery, and other means of production, do not yet stamp a man as a capitalist if there be wanting the correlative—the wage-worker" (766). Political economy was also historical and progressive: it seized as its domain the distant past as well as the distant future. And it was realist. The economic theory that succeeded it denied its own normativity and claimed to be the end of history. By the mid-twentieth century (under Milton Friedman), there was a movement to abandon its claims to realism.[30]

THE END OF HISTORY, OR ECONOMIC MAN AS CONSUMER: THE MARGINAL REVOLUTION

The marginal revolution in economic theory that began in the 1870s is now considered by historians of economic thought as a paradigm shift (after Kuhn) or the replacement of a degenerating scientific research program (SRP) by a progressive SRP (after Lakatos).[31] It is also

30. See Milton Friedman, "The Methodology of Positive Economics" [1953], in *The Philosophy of Economics*, ed. Daniel M. Hausman (Cambridge: Cambridge University Press, 1984), 210–44.

31. See Mark Blaug, "Paradigms versus Research Programmes in the History of Economics," in *The Philosophy of Economics*, ed. Daniel M. Hausman (Cambridge: Cambridge University Press, 1984), 360–89. As in most theoretical shifts, neoclassical economics, or the marginal revolution, was not a sudden revolution. Blaug shows that

a shift from macroeconomics to microeconomics, the theory of the consumer and the firm. To the culturalist, it is most significant that it represents a turn from economic man as producer to economic man as consumer, from labor or pain to pleasure, and from the substantive to the formal. Crucial to the turn that economics took in the last quarter of the nineteenth century is the elimination of intersubjective comparisons from its "research programme." By denying that one subject's desires or needs could be compared with another's, that is, by necessitating a focus on the isolated individual, and by rejecting the labor theory of *value* in favor of the more circumspect theory of *price*, economics deemphasized the relations of production that had effectively provided its social base and jettisoned one of its key motors for self-criticism.[32]

In "The Emergence of Economics as a Science 1750–1870," Donald Winch describes the marginal revolution as follows:

[In their attacks on the classical labour theory of value, Stanley Jevons in England, Carl Menger in Austria, and Leon Walras in Switzerland] focussed attention on the subjective determinants which underlie the demand for goods, rather than the objective factors which determine the cost and supply of goods. The proper foundations for a new economics, they argued, lay in the quasi-psychological law of diminishing marginal utility—a law which posited a definite (if subjective) relationship between the quantities of goods possessed and the extra satisfaction to be derived from additional amounts of them. With such a law in his possession the economist was able to explain the market behaviour of buyers faced with an array of prices, their responses to changes in price, the gains to be made from exchange, and the

marginal utility was "in the air" throughout the nineteenth century in Europe and kept turning up afresh every ten years or so: Lloyd and Longfield, 1834; Dupuit, 1844; Gossen, 1854; Jennings, 1855; Jevons, 1862; Menger, 1871. See Blaug, *Economic Theory in Retrospect,* 299–308. Certainly Samuel Bailey provided a thorough analytic defense of value as relative in his 1825 critique of Ricardo, Malthus, and other proponents of labor, or other absolute, standards of value in his *Critical Dissertation on the Nature of Value* (1825; reprint, London: London School of Economics, 1931).

32. By focusing on the "hedonics" or calculus of utility at the margins, Jevons, Menger, and Walras claimed to revive the pre–political-economic theory of Hutchesonian and Benthamite utilitarianism. They claimed to be reverting to Bentham, but in fact Bentham had a much more substantive theory of utility (see chapters 2 and 7). In the preface to the second edition (1879) of the *Theory of Political Economy,* Jevons himself claimed that in promoting the labor theory of value, Ricardo and Mill had "shunted the car of Economic Science on to a wrong line," and he recommended jettisoning the name political economy in favor of economics *tout court,* having been pleased to see that Henry Dunning Macleod and Alfred Marshall had already done so. Stanley Jevons, *The Theory of Political Economy,* 3d ed. (London: Macmillan, 1888), 1.

optimal allocation of a given stock of resources among alternative uses. The classical approach to economics was dominated by
the problems of capital accumulation, population growth, and
diminishing returns in agriculture. The interest of the classical
theorists in the economics of allocation and value in exchange,
though it was profound and led them to make permanent contributions to our understanding of these questions, was largely subservient to their interest in economic growth and macro-
distribution. After the marginal revolution attention shifted away
from such grand speculations towards a narrower and more precise inquiry into the determination of relative prices. Economics
became a quasi mathematical discipline in which the important
questions were posed as scarcity or choice problems.[33]

The first thing one notices in turning from the political economists
to Jevons or Menger is the latter's relative simplicity. Smith and Ricardo struggle with the social complexities of three different kinds of
value (use, exchange, labor)—see especially *The Wealth of Nations,*
book 1, sections 4–7 and the tortuous chapter 20 in Ricardo's *Principles*—and Marx struggles to reveal by analytic technique the obfuscation of the production process that political economy allegedly
entailed (as in the nature of profit in the wages fund theory or the
"mysterious" nature of a commodity in *Capital*'s section on commodity fetishism). In contrast, for Jevons economics is a mathematical science whose full development depends only on the full development of
a perfect system of statistics, or price lists of all markets, showing the
precise manifestations of human will and choice stripped of epistemo-
logical, psychological, and social complexities.

For Jevons, value depends entirely on utility, and utility depends on

---

33. Donald Winch, "The Emergence of Economics as a Science 1750–1870," in *The
Fontana Economic History of Europe* (London: Collins, 1973), 564–65. In *Great Economists Before Keynes* (Cambridge: Cambridge University Press, 1986), Mark Blaug suc-
cinctly describes the contributions of the founding marginal theorists thus: Jevons's *Theory of Political Economy* (1871) provided half the field of microeconomics, the theory
of consumer behavior, but not the theory of the firm. Carl Menger's *Principles of Economics* (1871) expressed doubts about mathematical models in economics and emphasized disequilibrium and the subjective elements in economic activity, thus founding the
so-called Austrian School. Leon Walras's *Elements of Pure Economics* (1874) provided
a consistent emphasis on the concept of general, multimarket equilibrium. Unlike Jevons
and Menger, Walras is still read by economists, and his economic ideas were compared
to theoretical physics by Schumpeter. For the classic statement of economics as concerned with scarcity and choice, see Lionel Robbins, "The Nature and Significance of
Economic Science," in *The Philosophy of Economics,* ed. Daniel M. Hausman (Cambridge: Cambridge University Press, 1984), 113–40.

the quantity of a commodity in our possession. Economic science is a "hedonic calculus," a calculus of pleasure and pain; we measure feelings of pleasure and pain by studying our actual decisions, or consumption patterns. It is a maxim of Jevons's utility theory that intersubjective comparisons are impossible; as Jevons says, we cannot "compare the amount of feeling in one mind with that in another. . . . Every mind is thus inscrutable to every other mind, and no common denominator of feeling seems to be possible" (14). Here, as in comparable passages in Menger, are the origins of Vilfredo Pareto's theory of optimality (1906), the linchpin of modern—as opposed to "old" (see below)—welfare economics: since intersubjective comparisons of value are impossible, the criterion of optimality is met when no possible redistribution is such that at least one party gains utility (subjectively defined) and no one loses any. There is no common metric that allows comparison between individuals. If there are no grounds for assessing inequalities in utility, there can be no grounds—no *economic* grounds—for advocating redistribution, as Lionel Robbins argued against Pigou's welfare economics in the 1930s.[34]

So that there should be no misunderstanding, this is probably the place for a digression on welfare economics, which postdated the marginalists but which until the 1930s maintained something of the substantive values of the political economists. Not the least of these values was a substantive notion of utility. In the 1980s Robert Cooter and Peter Rappoport argued in the *Journal of Economic Literature* that the notion that utility could not be compared across individuals, a notion that began with the marginalists and became generally accepted with the "Ordinalists" of the 1930s, crucially changed the meaning of utility in economics.[35] The "Material Welfare School," which included most prominently Edwin Cannan, Alfred Marshall, Arthur Pigou, and John Bates Clark, is now called "old welfare economics" because it employed definite interpersonal comparisons of utility as if such comparisons were scientific, that is, measurable. To the early welfare economists, utility was measurable to the extent that it referred specifically to the comparative welfare of different people. Utility, that is, referred to needs, such as physical health. In *The Economics of Welfare* (1920), for example, Pigou argued that maximum welfare would result from maximum growth plus distribution downward, and he redistributed wealth from rich to poor through school meals, healthcare, and indus-

34. See Robert N. Proctor, *Value-Free Science? Purity and Power in Modern Knowledge* (Cambridge: Harvard University Press, 1991), 189–92.

35. Robert Cooter and Peter Rappoport, "Were the Ordinalists Wrong About Welfare Economics?" *JEL* 22 (June 1984): 507–30.

trial training. Although the ostensible reason for relieving poverty was its detrimental effect on industrial efficiency, Cooter and Rappoport point out that the unifying "goal of the welfare economists was to liberate the race from the wants of 'the brute and the savage' in order to permit people to develop their 'higher faculties'" (514)—a traditional goal of political economy. And Marshall claimed that such faculties could not be cultivated in conditions of material deprivation.

Beginning with Jevons and Menger, however, and triumphing with the Ordinalists, this notion of utility as need was conflated with desires or preferences that gave pleasure to consumers, and it was denied that the amount of pleasure subjectively experienced by individuals could be compared (although Pareto himself had wisely reserved the term *utility* for needs and used *ophelimity* for desires or preferences distinguishable from bodily needs [515]). For the welfare economists, banishing poverty depended on economic investigations and "imparted to them," in Marshall's terms, "their chief and highest interest" (519). The Ordinalists, on the other hand—Lionel Robbins, John Hicks, R. G. D. Allen, and the rest—were interested in price rather than welfare, and so, while using the term *utility* to include all human needs, desires, preferences, likings, whims, and fancies, moved economics into the positivist and ultimately behaviorist direction that followed from an emphasis on price. By the 1980s, Cooter and Rappoport concluded, cautiously, that "It is necessary to balance the gains in understanding markets which the ordinalist framework facilitated against the losses in understanding human welfare suffered by abandoning the material welfare framework" (528).

Jevons's work shows the beginnings of the occlusion of the material welfare framework. He describes his economics not as Smith had in *The Wealth of Nations,* as providing for the needs and desires of the people, but rather as "the mechanics of utility and self-interest" (21). Its inductive bases, from which the laws of supply and demand, value, and commerce can be deduced, are (1) that every person will choose the greater apparent good; (2) that although their total number increases with advances in civilization, individual human wants are more or less quickly satiated; and (3) that prolonged labor becomes more and more painful. The economist deals only with the most primitive means to maximize pleasure and minimize pain, and with wealth rather than welfare.

The calculus of utility aims at supplying the ordinary wants of man at the least cost of labour. Each labourer, in the absence of other motives, is supposed to devote his energy to the accumulation of wealth. A higher calculus of moral right and wrong would be needed to show how he may best employ that wealth for the good of others as well as himself [that is, welfare]. But when that higher calculus gives no prohibition, we need the lower calculus to gain us the utmost good in matters of moral indifference. There is no rule of morals to forbid our making two blades of grass grow instead of one, if, by the wise expenditure of labour, we can do so. And we may certainly say, with Francis Bacon, "while philosophers are disputing whether virtue or pleasure be the proper aim of life, do you provide yourself with the instruments of either." (27)

With such modest claims, Jevons lifts the veil of mystery from the customary lexicon of political economy. A commodity is any object, substance, action, or service that can afford pleasure or ward off pain. A utility is anything that an individual is found to desire and labor for; it is always utility *for someone,* the abstract quality whereby an object serves a purpose—any purpose, real or apparent, for good or ill—and becomes entitled to rank as a commodity. Economics must be founded on a full and accurate investigation of the conditions of utility, and to understand this element, we must examine the wants and desires of humankind, which for Jevons are "insatiable": "The necessaries of life are so few and simple, that a man is soon satisfied in regard to these, and desires to extend his range of enjoyment. His first object is to vary his food; but there soon arises the desire of variety and elegance in dress; and to this succeeds the desire to build, to ornament, and to furnish—tastes which, where they exist, are absolutely insatiable, and seem to increase with every improvement in civilisation" (40).

The concept of insatiability plus the Victorian idea of progress led to an important conception of a hierarchy of tastes that we shall return to repeatedly in aesthetics as well as economics: from T. E. Banfield, Jevons quotes "the first proposition of the theory of consumption": "that the satisfaction of every lower want in the scale creates a desire of a higher character. . . . The highest grade in the scale of wants, that of pleasure derived from the beauties of nature and art, is usually confined to men who are exempted from all lower privations" (42–43). This hierarchy of values is the key to the true theory of value (43), proving that utility is a *subjective* and not an objective property.

Also in 1871, Carl Menger was developing the subjective theory of utility that came to be identified with the Austrian school of economics.[36] In Menger, the formal equivalence of all goods that leads to the lack of distinction between labor and other commodities is even clearer than in Jevons. For Marx and Mill, who thought that labor had a special status as a commodity precisely for its ability to *contest* its status, and to a lesser extent for Smith and Ricardo, labor was not just one commodity or utility among others. Menger defines goods as things that can be placed in a causal connection with the satisfaction of human needs. All goods can be divided into the two classes: material goods and useful human actions. The causal connection between goods and the satisfaction of need may be direct (like bread) or indirect (like flour, baking utensils, or the baker's services). As a complementary indirect good (that is, a good that requires other goods to fulfill its function), labor can lose its goods-character: "When, in 1862, the American Civil War dried up Europe's most important source of cotton, thousands of other goods that were complementary to cotton lost their goods-character. I refer in particular to the labor services of English and continental cottonmill workers who then, for the greater part, became unemployed and were forced to ask public charity."[37] On the other hand, when a direct good (Menger uses the example of tobacco) ceases to be one (that is, when people give up smoking), all the indirect goods that processed it, including labor services, also lose their goods-character. This kind of structural, or formal, leveling of utility finds its culmination in late twentieth-century systems theory,[38] although it was evident in early Victorian writers on the manufacturing system such as Babbage and Ure, for whom labor was merely one type of "moveable capital" (see chapter 2). As in Babbage and Ure, in Menger social progress depends on the proliferation of indirect goods, "the increasing employment of goods of higher order upon the growing quantity of goods available for human consumption (goods of first order)" (73).

36. For a recent defense of subjectivism and its corollary, methodological individualism, see Ludwig M. Lachmann, "Methodological Individualism and the Market Economy," in *The Philosophy of Economics,* ed. Daniel M. Hausman (Cambridge: Cambridge University Press, 1984), 303–12.

37. Carl Menger, *Principles of Economics* (Glencoe, Ill.: Free Press, 1950), 62.

38. See J.-F. Lyotard's account of a systems-theoretic approach to social welfare, in which the efficient working of the system takes precedence over substantive need: "A request . . . gains nothing in legitimacy by virtue of being based on the hardship of an unmet need. Rights do not flow from hardship, but from the fact that the alleviation of hardship improves the system's performance. The needs of the most underprivileged should not be used as a system regulator as a matter of principle: since the means of satisfying them is already known, their actual satisfaction will not improve the system's performance, but only increase its expenditures." *The Postmodern Condition* (Minneapolis: University of Minnesota Press, 1984), 63.

By excluding history from their analyses, Menger and Jevons can give a static picture of the economy as a locus of scarcity. Since human wants are theoretically insatiable, humankind finds itself inevitably in conditions of scarcity. Given scarcity, self-interest dictates that each fights to secure her own requirements to the exclusion of others. "With this opposition of interest, it becomes necessary for society to protect the various individuals in the possession of goods . . . against all possible acts of force. In this way, then, we arrive at the economic origin of our present legal order, and especially of the so-called *protection of ownership*, the basis of property" (97). If property is founded naturally upon this psychological inevitability of scarcity, for Menger communism is founded "naturally" upon "non-economic relationships," that is, when the good in question provides a surplus for human wants.

> For men are communists whenever possible under existing natural conditions. In towns situated on rivers with more water than is wanted by the inhabitants for the satisfaction of their needs, everyone goes to the river to draw any desired quantity of water. In virgin forests, everyone fetches unhindered the quantity of timber he needs. And everyone admits as much light and air into his house as he thinks proper. This communism is as naturally founded upon a non-economic relationship as property is founded upon one that is economic. (100–101)

Given "economizing man's" insatiability of wants, however, it is unlikely that surpluses (of water, timber, or air) will last, and thus economizing men move ever further from the "natural" conditions of communism. Communism, or sharing of goods, is thus excluded by definition from the science of economics; or, put differently, communism is the natural arena of value, but scarcity necessitates competition, which necessitates price. As Fraser said, the new economic science was a "bourgeois" science in that it was most at home in the price economy.[39] The crucial point is one that had been made by Samuel Bailey in 1825 but was relatively ignored: that goods are economic or not, have *economic* value (now equal to price) or not, not according to their substantive properties but according to whether the demand for them exceeds their supply. Value, that is, was a concept like distance (Bailey's analogy), relative, always in reference to something else, not intrinsic or absolute.[40]

From this wholly consumption-driven perspective, labor has no dis-

39. Fraser, *Economic Thought and Language*, 44.
40. See Bailey, *Critical Dissertation*.

tinctive value except its exchange value, nor are there any objective distinctions between the values of different kinds of labor. For Jevons, it is the value of the produce, not the cost of the laborer's or laborer's family's subsistence, that determines his or her wages (163): "Industry is essentially prospective; not retrospective . . . the value of labour *is determined by the value of the produce, not the value of the produce by that of labour*" (164–65, emphasis in original).

Menger elaborates more fully his rejection of the labor theory of value:

> There is no necessary and direct connection between the value of a good and whether, or in what quantities, labour and other goods of higher order were applied to its production. . . . Whether a diamond was found accidentally or was obtained from a diamond pit with the employment of a thousand days of labor is completely irrelevant for its value. In general, no one in practical life asks for the history of the origin of a good in estimating its value, but considers solely the services that the good will render him and which he would have to forgo if he did not have it at his command. (147)

As I shall show in the aesthetic rejection of the values of the producer or creator in favor of the consumers of the artwork, this rejection of the labor theory of value was pervasive. And Menger's insistence that in practical life (he characteristically invokes "experience") no one cares about the investment of labor makes the care that pervades Smith, Mill, and Marx's political economy retrospectively prominent. Like the value of land, the value of labor, Menger says, is its utility in satisfying consumer needs, not the value of the producer's subsistence: "In Berlin, a seamstress working 15 hours a day cannot earn what she needs for her subsistence. Her income covers food, shelter, and firewood, but even with the most strenuous industry she cannot earn enough for clothing. . . . In reality, as we shall see, the *prices* of actual labor services are governed, like the prices of all other goods, by their *values*. . . . A laborer's standard of living is determined by his income, and not his income by his standard of living" (170–71, emphasis in original). Regarding the "morality" of raising wages to subsistence level, Menger says that this is a social rather than an economic issue, for revolutionaries rather than economists:

> The agitation of those who would like to see society allot a larger share of the available consumption goods to laborers than at present really constitutes, therefore, a demand for nothing else

than paying labor above its value. For . . . it requires that workers be paid not in accordance with the value of their services to society, but rather with a view to providing them with a more comfortable standard of living, and achieving a more equal distribution of consumption goods and of the burdens of life. A solution of the problem on this basis, however, would undoubtedly require a complete transformation of our social order. (174)

The cumulative effect of the theory is the diminishment of substantive value in all areas. To make no distinction between kinds of commodities—necessities and luxuries, labor and other commodities—in the service of mathematizing, or what Jevons calls "fluxional calculus," led in the twentieth century to theories of "choice." Proponents of economic choice defend its "democracy," claiming that intersubjective comparisons of value are not only "unscientific" (cannot be measured) but also "elitist," ranking "esoteric" moral concerns above individual self-interest, which each man or woman should judge for him- or herself (the assumption that "tastes are exogenous to the model"). In our own time, posing economic problems in terms of "choice" can obscure ethical and political questions involved in universal commodification: the marketing, for example, of education, air, blood, babies, sperm, or kidneys (see the introduction).

Just as Menger said that it would "require a complete transformation of our social order" to raise wages to subsistence level (that is, above labor's market price), he insists that such issues are not within the domain of economics. In addition to obliterating distinctions that for the political economists were substantive and normative, the neoclassical economists excluded welfare, as opposed to wealth, from the science of economics.[41] Education, drinking water, and virgin forests have no value, or economic character, until there is a shortage of them.

41. As the section above on the "old" welfare economics indicated, the exclusion of welfare from economics has, of course, been only intermittent. Marshall was partially concerned with welfare, as was Keynes, and beginning with Pigou in 1912 (*Wealth and Welfare*) and 1920 (*The Economics of Welfare*) there has been the field of "welfare economics," whose major preoccupation has been with the standard of living. It too foundered, with Pigou, when it maintained the subjectivist prohibition on interpersonal comparison, which characterizes the "new" welfare economics, or welfare economics as we know it today. The actual welfare of individuals or groups in any given society has been obscured by the methodological assumptions of the marginal revolution of evaluating pleasure, happiness, desire, and preference. For fuller clarification of these issues, see *The Standard of Living*, ed. Geoffrey Hawthorne (Cambridge: Cambridge University Press, 1987), especially the two essays by Amartya Sen, 1–38; and Neva R. Goodwin's Marshallian *Building Anew on Marshall's Principles*, vol. 1 of *Social Economics: An Alternative Theory* (New York: St. Martin's, 1991).

Wealth, on the other hand, is "the entire sum of goods at an economizing individual's command," *when* those goods are in short supply. "It is a relative measure of the degree of completeness with which an individual can satisfy his needs, never an absolute measure of welfare." From this it follows that "in a society of greatest welfare, no one would need wealth" (110). However aptly *wealthy* may characterize individuals who have large shares of scarce goods, Menger surprisingly foresees problems with the term *national wealth,* which, he admits, equals the sum of individual wealths but says nothing about a whole society's welfare.

Another consequence of defining economics as the science of choices among scarcity is a virtual shift of emphasis in the term *economic man.* Among Malthus and his followers, such as Thomas Chalmers, up to the middle of the nineteenth century, scarcity had figured largely in political economy, but this model of the science could be distinguished from that in Smith, Ricardo, and Mill, who, owing to colonial expansion, were much more optimistic about economic growth and supply creating demand.[42] Their economic man was the productive pursuer of gain. Jevons and Menger's "economizing" man, on the other hand, was a consumer choosing among scarce resources. Smith, Ricardo, and Mill's rational economic man, pursuing his self-interest, contributed to the wealth and, especially in Smith, Mill, and Marx, the progress of the world. After Jevons and Menger, rationality increasingly comes to mean simply an "insatiable" individual's ordering of preference among desirable goods, a purely formal definition.[43] With Jevons and Menger, the insatiable wants of economizing man became the defining feature of *modern* man, his insatiability distinguishing him from other times and other races less far along the evolutionary scale. Jevons concludes a discussion of whether agents prefer leisure or wealth:

It is evident that questions of this kind depend greatly upon the character of the race. Persons of an energetic disposition feel la-

42. For the two models of free trade, see Boyd Hilton, *The Age of Atonement: The Influence of Evangelicalism on Social and Economic Thought, 1795–1865* (Oxford: Clarendon, 1988), esp. 64–70. The current consensus on Malthus seems to be that he was more aware of demography and scarcity than of the increase in technological power that might alleviate it; hence his pessimism in *An Essay on the Principle of Population.* See "Malthus at 200: Minisymposium," in *History of Political Economy* 30, no. 2 (summer 1998): 302–56, esp. 305.

43. The neoclassicals were not the first economists to turn their attention to consumption. Jean-Baptiste Say, James Mill, and Ricardo in the first decades of the nineteenth century considered how "supply creates its own demand" and kept alive an interest in demand in contrast to the political-economic emphasis on supply.

bour less painfully than their fellow men, and, if they happen to be endowed with various and acute sensibilities, their desire of further acquisition never ceases. A man of lower race, a negro for instance, enjoys possession less, and loathes labour more; his exertions therefore soon stop. . . . The rich man in modern society is supplied apparently with all he can desire, and yet he often labours unceasingly for more. Bishop Berkeley has very well asked, "Whether the creating of wants be not the likeliest way to produce industry in a people? And whether, if our (Irish) peasants were accustomed to eat beef and wear shoes, they would not be more industrious?" (182)

The contrast that political economy had drawn between "civilized" and "barbaric," meaning "technologically advanced and with a division of labor" versus "technologically simple and with few occupations," had primarily expressed "civilization's" ambivalence about the industrial revolution. Thus Mill's concerns over increasing inequality, the lack of incentive in wage labor, and the unreflective pace of modern life and Smith's observation that, despite civilization's benefits to the few, "barbarism" was better for the great body of the people. With the marginal revolution, the critical force of the distinction was lost. Modern man would henceforth be known by the insatiability of his desires, and Others need only be inspired by envy to desire his desires, imitate his wants, to be on the road to his progress and his civilization. Conveniently, economic man's contribution to progress also provided Britain with new markets at a time when its own manufactured goods were "underconsumed" at home. Chapter 3 takes up this ethnicization of the global workforce and the universalism that accompanied it.

Finally, the marginalists shifted the analysis of economic phenomena from a methodology based on factors of production and class to one based on the individual. In *Theories of Production and Distribution 1776–1848* (1893), Edwin Cannan suggested that the Ricardian abstractions of landlords, laborers, and capitalists contributed to class warfare, and he praised the neoclassical economists for emphasizing the distribution of wealth among individual consumers.[44] In *The State in Relation to Labour* (1882), in the year he died, Jevons was at pains to rearticulate struggles between capital and labor as struggles between producers and consumers, between consumers as individuals, or between firms.[45] "All workmen are and must be competitors," that is,

44. See John Maloney, *Marshall, Orthodoxy and the Professionalisation of Economics* (Cambridge: Cambridge University Press, 1985), 206.
45. W. Stanley Jevons, *The State in Relation to Labour* (London: Macmillan, 1894).

one's pay rise causes another to pay more for a commodity; or "the real conflict is not between capital and labour but between producers and consumers" (101, implying of course that all of us are both, so there is no conflict); or "We ought not to look at such subjects from a class point of view, and in economics at any rate should regard all men as brothers" (107), that is, as consumers opposed to high prices. Whereas Jevons is opposed to class-based solidarity as exclusive of individual workers ("The Law of Industrial Conspiracy," 131–41), he does not object to professional trade unions in law or medicine. And, like Mill, he supports corporatism within competing firms: "The present doctrine is that the workman's interests are linked to those of other workmen, and the employer's interests to those of other employers. Eventually it will be seen that industrial divisions should be perpendicular, not horizontal. The workman's interests should be bound up with those of his employer, and should be pitted in fair competition against those of other workmen and employers" (149). Yet behind Jevons's attempt to reclassify social groups and classes as meritocratic individuals within competing firms is the specter of class warfare: "Our grandfathers and great grandfathers, not to speak of earlier ancestors, did their best to crush all societies of working men, and ignomineous was their failure[;] are we likely to succeed better when the working-class order has become immensely increased in numbers, in intelligence, organisation, wealth, and general resources?" (112–13). Although it always had some purchase within political economy, methodological individualism gained power as it was formulated as a solution to class conflict.

There is a view that the mathematizing of economics was a "scientific" response to the unequal distribution of wealth at a time when the rise of labor unions and the Labour Party challenged the social status quo; the corollary increase of abstraction duly shifted focus from actual workers and their environments to statistical variation in the labor market.[46] Although this seems plausible, the erosion of the social bases of political economy discussed in this section was overdetermined by multiple social conditions of the late nineteenth century. These included the expansion of technology and production that led to a "culture of abundance";[47] the professionalizing of economics as

46. This argument was proposed to the author in discussion with the economist Samuel Bowles. See also David Mitch, "Victorian Views of the Nature of Work and Its Influence on the Nature of the Worker," paper presented at the conference "Victorian Work," U.C. Santa Cruz, 4–7 August 1994. And see the discussion of "universalizing" in chapter 3.

47. Lawrence Birken, *Consuming Desire: Sexual Science and the Emergence of a Culture of Abundance, 1871–1914* (Ithaca: Cornell University Press, 1988).

an academic discipline heavily influenced by psychology and by the calculation of pleasure and pain;[48] and a merger of economic and anthropological theory at the height of British imperialism, which imported into economics racist and cultural ideologies from which political economy, with its insistence on the division of labor and advances in technology, had been relatively—but only relatively—distant.[49] These contributing factors are taken up in the chapters below, where it should be clear that the late Victorian consumer who was also a psychological, anthropological, and biological subject—a subject now of formal institutional knowledge—was a systematically different kind of being from the "deep" psychological subjects of Shakespeare's Renaissance or the desiring and consuming subjects of eighteenth-century commodity culture. The difference was in part a consequence of the development of psychological, anthropological, and biological knowledge.

ECONOMIC MAN AS AESTHETIC: WALTER PATER

Although one might distinguish between the transcendent critique of a Ruskin or a Morris and the immanent (or from-inside-the-whale) critique of a Pater or a Wilde, virtually all the aesthetes were only too conscious of their own implication within consumer, or commodity, culture, from Rossetti's ambivalent ruminations on the male client's responsibility for the prostitute in "Jenny," to Ruskin's revulsion after *The Stones of Venice* at Victorian Gothic architecture, to Morris's anguish at the price of The Firm's furniture and textiles, to Wilde's notorious self-advertisement. Recent critics of the fin de siècle have established more subtle conjunctions between late Victorian aesthetics and commodity culture via recent commodity theorists such as Jean Baudrillard and Guy Debord.[50] Here I want to show how Jevons, the math-

48. See Ian Small, *Conditions for Criticism* (Oxford: Oxford University Press, 1991), Birken (1988), and John Maloney, *Marshall, Orthodoxy and the Professionalisation of Economics* (Cambridge: Cambridge University Press, 1985).

49. On Victorian anthropological theories of stages of development, see George W. Stocking Jr., *Victorian Anthropology* (New York: Free, 1987) and *After Tylor: British Social Anthropology 1888–1951* (Madison: University of Wisconsin Press, 1995) and Henrika Kuklick, *The Savage Within: The Social History of British Anthropology, 1885–1945* (Cambridge: Cambridge University Press, 1991).

50. See Gagnier, *Idylls of the Marketplace: Oscar Wilde and the Victorian Public* (Stanford: Stanford University Press, 1986); Ian Small, *Conditions for Criticism: Authority, Knowledge, and Literature in the Late Nineteenth Century* (Oxford: Clarendon, 1991); Garry Leonard, "Women on the Market: Commodity Culture, 'Those Lovely Seaside Girls,' and 'Femininity' in Joyce's *Ulysses*," *Joyce Studies Annual* 2 (summer 1991): 27–68; Thomas Richards, *The Commodity Culture of Victorian England: Adver-*

ematical economist, and Pater, the donnish aesthete, converge in their promotion of subjectivism, individualism, consumption, and ultimately formalism. For though some economists and some cultural critics, particularly those concerned with subordinated economies and cultures, tried to maintain something of the substantive value of earlier political economists and novelists, there was a clear shift toward formalism that became central to modernism in both economics and aesthetics.

Pater begins the 1873 preface to *The Renaissance: Studies in Art and Poetry* with the denial of absolute value and the demand for quantification, "discriminating between what is more and less." (In his first chapter Jevons insists that economics is mathematical "simply because it deals with quantities . . . with things greater or less" [3].) If one were to substitute "value" for "beauty" and "economics" for "art and poetry," the text could read like Jevons's of two years earlier:

> Many attempts have been made by writers on art and poetry to define beauty in the abstract, to express it in the most general terms, to find some universal formula for it. . . . Such discussions help us very little to enjoy what has been well done in art or poetry, to discriminate between what is more and what is less excellent in them. . . . Beauty, like all other qualities presented to human experience, is relative; and the definition of it becomes unmeaning and useless in proportion to its abstractness. To define beauty, not in the most abstract but in the most concrete terms possible, to find, not its universal formula, but the formula which expresses most adequately this or that special manifestation of it, is the aim of the true student of aesthetics.[51]

In the same passage where he pronounced economics a quantifying science, Jevons also pronounced it a "calculus of pleasure and pain" within one individual subject. Rejecting Matthew Arnold's critical and objectivist aim "to see the object as in itself it really is," in the second paragraph of the preface Pater claims that the first step of aesthetic criticism is "to know one's own impression as it really is" (xix): "What is this song or picture, this engaging personality presented in life or in a book, to *me*? What effect does it really produce on me? Does it give

tising and Spectacle 1851–1914 (Stanford: Stanford University Press, 1990); Joel Kaplan and Sheila Stowell, *Theatre and Fashion* (Cambridge: Cambridge University Press, 1994); and Jonathan Freedman, *Professions of Taste: Henry James, British Aestheticism, and Commodity Culture* (Stanford: Stanford University Press, 1990).

51. Walter Pater, *The Renaissance: Studies in Art and Poetry*, ed. Donald Hill (Berkeley: University of California Press, 1980), xix.

me pleasure? and if so, what sort or degree of pleasure? . . . The aesthetic critic regards all the objects with which he has to do . . . as powers or forces producing pleasurable sensations, each of a more or less peculiar or unique kind" (xx). This science of pleasure, or aesthetics, "becomes complete in proportion as our susceptibility to these impressions [of pleasure] increases in depth and variety" (ibid.). Just as economic man chooses between scarce commodities, so aesthetic man discriminates between pleasures.

The conclusion to *The Renaissance* provides images of an external world in flux that some have associated with consumer society ("at first sight experience seems to bury us under a flood of external objects" [187]), and an inner life subjective to the point of solipsism. As in Jevons, there are no intersubjective comparisons: "Experience, already reduced to a group of impressions, is ringed round for each one of us by that thick wall of personality through which no real voice has ever pierced on its way to us. . . . Every one of those impressions is the impression of the individual in his isolation, each mind keeping as a solitary prisoner its own dream of a world" (188).

Yet as if in mockery of the wealth of impressions, the time for enjoyment is scarce: had we but world enough and *time*. In his *Essay on the Nature and Significance of Economic Science* (1935), commonly taken as a major triumph of neoclassical over welfare economics, Lionel Robbins described the centrality of time to modern economic theory thus: "Here we are, sentient creatures with bundles of desires and aspirations, with masses of instinctive tendencies all urging us in different ways to action. But the time in which these tendencies can be expressed is limited. The external world does not offer full opportunities for their complete achievement. Life is short. Nature is niggardly. . . . The disposition of [economic man's] time and his resources has a relationship to his system of wants. It has an economic aspect."[52] (In Becker's *Accounting for Tastes* [1998], in the chapter called "The Economic Way of Looking at Life," the economist reiterates that our most fundamental constraint is time, "which ensures that wants remain unsatisfied in rich countries as well as in poor ones" [140].) Pater ends the conclusion with mortal thoughts of how "on this short day of frost and sun" one must not "sleep before evening"; of "the splendour of our experience and of its awful brevity"; of how "theories or ideas or systems which require of us the sacrifice of any part of this experience in consideration of some interest into which we cannot enter" have "no real claim upon us" (189), concluding this litany of scarcity and self-

52. Hausman, *Philosophy of Economics*, 114.

interest by acknowledging that "we are all under sentence of death but with a sort of indefinite reprieve." Now one of the worldly philosophers, in Robert Heilbroner's phrase, indeed perhaps the most sensuous of his generation, Pater advises us to "get as many pulsations as possible into the given time" (190). In "Aesthetic Poetry" (1889), he defined the aesthetic economy of his contemporaries as "the desire of beauty quickened by the sense of death." [53]

Pater's 1889 essay "Style" suggests how scarcity amid abundance leads to a preoccupation with form in aesthetic matters, as it led to formalism in twentieth-century economics. Here Pater's return to *ascesis,* which for him means a "self-restraint, a skilful economy of means" that is central to *Marius the Epicurean* (1885) and his later work on the Greeks, calls up the discipline that would make modernists such as Pound write of stylistics after Flaubert as a "science." Pater begins with a rejection of the "false economy" of contemporary distinctions between verse and prose. [54] He defines all literary art as individualist, "the representation of fact as connected with soul, of a specific personality, in its preferences, its volition and power" (106). Thus literary art is *subjective,* involving choices (preferences) and desire (volition). Choice comes in the form of "ascesis," which is a formal property of works of art. Pater deplores "the narcotic force of [literary ornament] upon the negligent intelligence to which any *diversion,* literally, is welcome" (111) and makes masculine leanness (youth's asceticism) a characteristic to be prized: "Surplusage. [The artist] will dread that, as the runner on his muscles" (111). [55] Flaubert is Pater's type of the ascetic artist, or economizing aesthete, whose "idea of a natural economy" (choice) amid surplus (117) becomes the formal principle of literary modernism—the discriminating artist or critic's economy (Pound's *le mot juste*) that distinguished him from the "negligent" public that "welcomes" diversion, ornament, the "flood" of commodities of consumer society: "the one word for the one thing, the one thought, amid the

53. Walter Pater, "Aesthetic Poetry," in *Selected Writings of Walter Pater,* ed. Harold Bloom (New York: Signet, 1974), 198.

54. Water Pater, "Style," in *Selected Writings of Walter Pater,* ed. Harold Bloom (New York: Signet, 1974), 103–25, 103.

55. For impressive treatments of the masculinity, or gender implications, of Pater's science of style, see James Eli Adams, "Gentleman, Dandy, Priest: Manliness and Social Authority in Pater's Aestheticism," *ELH* 59 (1992): 441–66; "Pater's Muscular Aestheticism" in *Muscular Christianity: Reading and Writing the (Male) Social Body,* ed. Donald E. Hall (Cambridge: Cambridge University Press, 1994), 215–38; and Herbert Sussman's "Masculinity Transformed: Appropriation in Walter Pater's Early Writing," in *Victorian Masculinities: Manhood and Masculine Poetics in Early Victorian Literature and Art* (Cambridge: Cambridge University Press, 1995), 173–203.

multitude of words, terms that just might do: the problem of style was there!" (117). Flaubert's referent is not objective but subjective. The word is chosen not by reference to the external world but by Flaubert's introspection, the inventory of his subjective needs. Flaubert managed his economy, that is, by ranking his preferences: "The first condition of [style, "the word's adjustment to its meaning"] must be, of course, to know yourself, to have ascertained your own sense exactly" (118). Upon the discerning artist and the discerning critic "a flood of random sounds, colours, incidents, is ever penetrating from the world without" (ibid.). "The mind sensitive to 'form'" selects from these in conformity with that "other world it sees so steadily within," and "it is just there, just at those doubtful points" between external objects and inner needs and desires, "that the function of style, as tact or taste, intervenes" (ibid.). This is Flaubert's formal aesthetic, of taste or tact or choice.

Pater's Flaubert represents rational aesthetic man, who sounds much like rational economic man: "The style, the manner, would be the man [revealed preference], not in his unreasoned and really uncharacteristic caprices, involuntary or affected, but in absolutely sincere apprehension of what is most real to him [rational choice]" (121). The style is the man. In true behaviorist fashion, we know him by the choices he makes. Truth is Beauty; Beauty, Truth.

The flaw in the argument, however, is that Pater was ultimately not a behaviorist. His rich, ornamental, reverie-ridden prose was not an example of lean, masculine ascesis; nor did he finally believe, when you considered a "Leonardo," that what you saw was what you got (behaviorism), or even that what you got was what you wanted (revealed preference). While emphasizing the subjective and formal aspects of aesthetics at both levels of production and consumption, Pater, finally, was unwilling to perform Jevons's reduction. He perversely concludes the essay on style with the subordination of rational aesthetic man to a "greater," romantic aesthetic reminiscent of Marx or Ruskin. He compares good art to music in its formal excellence but then retracts in favor of substantive and ethical value. This value entails a shift from methodological individualism to concern for social welfare, the relation between individual interests and the interest of the community.[56]

Good art, but not necessarily great art; the distinction between great art and good art depending immediately, as regards litera-

<hr>

56. In "The Law of Progress and the Ironies of Individualism in the Nineteenth Century" I discuss this aspect of Pater's work, especially in *Marius the Epicurean*. See *New Literary History* 31 (spring 2000): 315–36, esp. 327–31.

ture at all events, not on its form, but on the matter. . . . It is on the quality of the matter it informs or controls, its compass, its variety, its alliance to great ends, or the depth of the note of revolt, or the largeness of hope in it, that the greatness of literary art depends, as *The Divine Comedy, Paradise Lost, Les Miserables, The English Bible,* are great art. Given the conditions I have tried to explain as constituting good art;—then, if it be devoted further to the increase of men's happiness, to the redemption of the oppressed, or the enlargement of our sympathies with each other, or to such presentment of new or old truth about ourselves and our relation to the world as may ennoble and fortify us in our sojourn here, . . . it will be also great art; if . . . it has something of the soul of humanity in it. (123)

As with Marshall, most subsequent readers of Pater retained his formalism and ignored his ethics. Yet "the soul of humanity" was greater than a partial (economic or aesthetic) man; even the ascetic aesthete Pater would not, like Jevons or Menger, entirely abandon it to the dustbin of history.

In the last chapter of Pater's exquisite novel *Marius the Epicurean,* the dying Marius takes a "final account" of the "economy" of his life, "with a jealous estimate of gain and loss," a "wistful calculation as to what things cost him" and of what "one might well exchange one's life for."[57] His is a life that consumes itself "from dying hour to dying hour" like "music, all-sufficing to the duly trained ear, even as it died out on the air. Yet having not used life as the means to some problematic end," Marius worries about the consequences of the pleasure principle: "Yet now . . . that the moment of taking final account was drawing very near, a consciousness of waste would come, with half-angry tears of self-pity, in his great weakness—a blind, outraged, angry feeling of wasted power" (264). Marius ultimately suppresses the feeling of waste, the feeling of an unproductive life, in memories of "all the persons he had loved in life—on his love for them . . . rather than on theirs for him" (266), and on the "new hope" of life everlasting, of a life not bound by scarcity, mortality, or economy of any kind, a "perpetual afterthought, which humanity henceforth would ever possess in reserve, against any wholly mechanical and disheartening theory of itself and its conditions" (265). Himself ambivalent to the end, the childless and imaginatively male-loving Pater can only figure such a timeless world in material terms, in terms of "practical" generation

57. Walter Pater, *Marius the Epicurean* (1885; reprint, New York: Dutton, 1968), 264, 261, 262.

that transcends scarcity and death: "Yes! through the survival of their children, happy parents are able to think calmly, and with a very practical affection, of a world in which they are to have no direct share; planting with a cheerful good-humour, the acorns they carry about with them, that their grandchildren may be shaded from the sun by the broad oak-trees of the future. That is nature's way of easing death to us" (265). Thus the economizing aesthete finally escapes from economy and the hedonic calculus by way of "natural" production ("broad oak-trees of the future") and reproduction. We shall see these tensions multiply in subsequent chapters.

This chapter has described the transition from a productivist to a consumerist ideology in economics and, more briefly, in aesthetics. It should be emphasized that though this transition was real and had lasting effects, it was not achieved immediately or without ambivalence, as in the cases of Marshall, the welfare economists, or Pater. Another author who has studied the economic transition from the 1870s to World War I, not in relation to aesthetics as here but in relation to sexology, especially psychoanalysis, is more sanguine than this chapter suggests concerning the possibilities of economic man as consumer. In *Consuming Desire* Lawrence Birken argues that in slowly abandoning the bourgeois system in which only property ownership, production, and labor bestowed individuality and citizenship in favor of a system of sovereign, desiring, perfectly competitive "ids," neoclassical theory extended the ideology of democracy further than it had been extended before.[58] With the abandonment of an ethic of work and need in favor of an ethic of pleasure and desire, late Victorian sexology saw an increasing ambivalence about gender that was centered in reproduction in favor of an all-desiring genderlessness. Although he frequently nods to the Foucauldian thesis that the discourses of sexology have been as repressive as liberating, Birken calls this society of individuals freely pursuing their desires "democratic" and "consumerist" interchangeably.

Although such an argument has its appeal after two decades of postmodern theory, we may conclude this chapter by expressing two reservations concerning it. First, the desire to consume or to express one's individuality through that desire is not the same thing as the power to consume. In *The Joyless Economy,* the economist Tibor Scitovsky pointed out that there were two kinds of power in consumer society:

---

58. Lawrence Birken, *Consuming Desire: Sexual Science and the Emergence of a Culture of Abundance, 1871–1914* (Ithaca: Cornell University Press, 1988).

individual wealth to consume what one desired ("the eccentric million-aire") and the power of the mass to fulfill its desires through its pressure for mass-production (or for many people to buy one thing).[59] Birken acknowledges that the consumer ideology he equates with democratization was an effective desire ("effective demand") for only a small elite; so whether desire deserves to be called democratic is a question at least as much of power as of desire. Second, mass power in consumption is certainly power, but it is not individualist. Such reservations make one uncomfortable with Birken's characterization of "consumer choice" as women's "active desire," or feminism (145), or with children's "sexualization" as consumers as their "democratization" and "claim to citizenship" (149). Other interpretations of the social values of the transition to consumption and its corollary commodification are explored in chapter 2.

59. Tibor Scitovsky, *The Joyless Economy: An Inquiry into Human Satisfaction and Consumer Dissatisfaction* (New York: Oxford University Press, 1976).

TWO

Is Market Society the *Fin* of History?

Market Utopias and Dystopias

from Babbage to Schreiner

In 1989, Irving Kristol's *The National Interest* devoted a volume to Francis Fukuyama's article "The End of History?" and commentary on it. Fukuyama, former analyst at the Rand Corporation and then deputy director of the United States State Department's policy planning staff, offered the "Hegelian" argument that with the "triumph of Western economic and political liberalism" we are witnessing "the end of history as such . . . the end point of mankind's ideological evolution and the universalization of Western liberal democracy as the final form of human government."[1] Citing the "spectacular abundance of advanced liberal economies and the infinitely diverse consumer culture made possible by them" (8), Fukuyama announced that political liberalism is following economic liberalism "with seeming inevitability" (10) and that class and race antagonisms are merely "historical legacies of premodern conditions," already on the way out. Only in his last paragraph, when describing the way that passions under market economies give way to interests, which are subsumed under bureaucratic rationality, does Fukuyama theatrically express a nostalgia for history as such: "The end of history will be a very sad time. The struggle for recognition, the willingness to risk one's life for a purely abstract goal, the worldwide ideological struggle that called forth daring, courage, imagination, and idealism, will be replaced by economic calculation, the endless solving of technical problems, environmental concerns, and the satisfaction of sophisticated consumer demands" (18).

On the other hand, the economist Samuel Bowles addressed a work-

An earlier version of this chapter appeared as "Is Market Society the *Fin* of History?" in *Cultural Politics at the Fin de Siècle*, ed. Sally Ledger and Scott McCracken (Cambridge: Cambridge University Press, 1995), 290–310.

1. Francis Fukuyama, "The End of History?" *The National Interest* (summer 1989): 3–35; quotation is on 3–4. The argument was developed in the author's *The End of History and the Last Man* (New York: Avon, 1992).

ing group in Moscow in 1991, when Russia was still enamored of markets, in terms that Muscovites today might recall with irony.[2] Warning against simplistic formulations of alternatives between command or market economies, Bowles invoked Smith, Mill, and Marx as examples of economists sensitive to the peculiarities of objects of exchange, for example, the natural limits to the supply of land and water or the unusual status of labor as a commodity embodied in human beings. Using Albert Hirschman's now-familiar terms of voice and exit,[3] Bowles argued that democratic values require the ability to process and communicate complex information and to make collective decisions and the capacity to feel empathy and solidarity with others, abilities and capacities of "voice" that were not fostered by the market, or economic, right of "exit."

In this chapter I shall recall some of the historical roots of Fukuyama's and Bowles's positions, which may be described, respectively, as the belief that the unconstrained development of markets and technology will provide the values most conducive to the social good and the belief that the values of the market are insufficient to produce the social good. In these historical perspectives on market society, models of human production and reproduction, or creativity, will be contrasted with hedonic models.

The most unreserved faith in the market to provide the social good goes back not to the early political economists, who typically understood the structural flaws of laissez-faire, but to the early technophiles just postdating the proverbial take-off period. In the ur-systems analyst Charles Babbage's *On the Economy of Machinery and Manufacture* (1832), the universe itself is one large system of potentially free markets, of the freedom "every man has, to use his capital, his labour, and his talents, in the manner most conducive to his interests."[4] Within this universal system, Britain's role is to export machinery and commodities. Babbage is confident that British industry will not be threatened by its competitors insofar as the success of British industry is predicated on the British system of government. He writes that "These great advantages cannot exist under less free governments. These circumstances . . . give such a decided superiority to our people, that no injurious rivalry, either in the construction of machinery or the manufac-

2. Samuel Bowles, "What Markets Can and Cannot Do," *Challenge* (July–August 1991): 11–16.

3. Albert Hirschman, *Exit, Voice, and Loyalty* (Cambridge: Harvard University Press, 1970).

4. Charles Babbage, *On the Economy of Machinery and Manufacture* (1832; reprint, New York: Kelley, 1963), 370.

ture of commodities, can reasonably be anticipated" (364). Babbage's view of progress is that British people will use time saved by machines in gratifying some other wants and that each new machine will add new luxuries that will then become socially necessary to our happiness (335). Within this technological advance, workers must be subjectively as flexible as the flow of commodities. Babbage asks whether machines should be made so perfect as to supplant workers suddenly or be slowly improved to force them out of employment gradually. He concludes that workers should be forced out immediately, so that they will have no choice but to retrain, and in addition recommends that workers in one family diversify their labor, so that parents and children will not be thrown out of work simultaneously and so plunge the entire family into destitution (336). Thus for Babbage the human population will be forced to progress at the rate of technology. Babbage does not anticipate Marx's view that one's labor might be relevant to one's sense of identity. Rather, he anticipates postmodern theory in that, for him, identity is as fluid and exchangeable as other commodities.

If Babbage is optimistic about the flexibility of human subjectivity adjusting itself to technology, Andrew Ure in *The Philosophy of Manufactures* (1835) thought that the human component of the manufacturing market should be subordinated to its function by any means necessary. Ure propounds "the great doctrine . . . that when capital enlists science in her service, the refractory hand of labour will always be taught docility," and he treats workers' failure to conform to the needs of production as infractions of natural law.[5] Of workers stopping when they need to, he writes, "Of the amount of the injury resulting from the violation of the rules of automatic labour, [the worker] can hardly ever be a proper judge; just as mankind at large can never fully estimate the evils consequent upon an infraction of God's moral law" (279).

In passages that contrast with Dickens's *Hard Times* (1854) or with autobiographical accounts of workers who were children in the textile industry, Ure describes how the factory system improves women and children:

> The children seemed to be always cheerful and alert, taking pleasure in the light play of their muscles,—enjoying the mobility natural to their age. The scene of industry, so far from exciting sad emotions in my mind, was always exhilarating. It was delightful to observe the nimbleness with which they pieced the broken ends. . . . As to exhaustion by the [ten-hour] day's work,

5. Andrew Ure, *The Philosophy of Manufactures* (1835; reprint, London: Frank Cass, 1967), 368.

they evinced no trace of it on emerging from the mill in the evening; for they immediately began to skip about any neighbouring play-ground, and to commence their little amusements with the same alacrity as boys issuing from a school. (301)

In a series of examples of "model" factories, Ure writes of the women who run the power looms, who are beautified by their work: "Their light labour and erect posture in tending the looms, and the habit which many of them have of exercising their arms and shoulders, as if with dumb-bells . . . opens their chest[s], and gives them generally a graceful carriage . . . and . . . not a little of the Grecian style of beauty" (350). He has pages on the health and beauty ("symmetry of form") of female spinners and of the stove-girls hanging calico print in temperatures exceeding 140°F: "Some are very fine-looking girls, and all appear to be in perfect health. They work barefooted, and have often leisure to sit. Mr. R. states that they are as healthy as any girls in the establishment, and that when any of them happen to catch cold, they are very soon cured by going into the stove again" (392–93). Ure presents a mechanistic universe in which the input of goods and services produces the desired outcome.

Most of the great political economists did not share Babbage's and Ure's unreserved faith that market values alone would result in desirable social outcomes. Although the rhetoric of supply-side economics since the 1980s has often invoked the Invisible Hand of *The Wealth of Nations,* in which Smith often seemed as sanguine as Ure about the orderliness of the market, the single most cited passage of Smith in the massive scholarly literature is that cited above, in which he contrasts the brutalizing effects of the division of labor, the source of national wealth, with the simple but pleasant equality of barbarous societies. Despite the manichaean functions that the term *civilization* accumulated in the course of the nineteenth century, it was a technical term in historical political economy meaning "characterized by technological superiority based on the division of labor." Although its corollary, *barbarism,* meant "having little or no industrial technology," it could also imply complex capabilities at the individual level, especially among the "masculine," "savage," or "aristocratic" virtues appreciated in the Scottish Enlightenment. Using *barbarism* to critique the brutality of "civilization," in the passage referred to Smith concluded that the elite few who do benefit from "civilization" may not contribute any benefits to society at large.[6]

Smith, of course, believed that the "moral sentiments" of empathy

6. Adam Smith, *Wealth of Nations* (New York: Modern Library, 1965), 734–36.

and sympathy were as innate to humankind as the political-economic virtues of self-interest and the desire for wealth.[7] Indeed, "sympathy" played the important role in early political economy of allowing interpersonal comparisons of utility—a possibility that economics after 1870, as we have seen, largely rejected. On balance, Smith believed that, unless government took steps to prevent it, under global market conditions the large mass of humankind might well acquire great material benefits on one hand, but, on the other, decline in its ability to exercise faculties and propensities such as reason, imagination, and sympathy, on which ethics—or the justification of our behavior toward one another—depended. Granting that Smith predated democracy as we know it, the compatibility of his views on the limits of the market to set democratic values with Bowles's comments to Muscovites in 1991 is noteworthy.

Smith was particularly concerned about the low status of liberal education in market society.[8] In general the political economists approved of government assistance to locally provided schools and in some cases what we would call today a uniform curriculum, including reading, writing, and mathematics. Yet these were usually justified in terms of social control rather than as direct investment in wealth creation.[9] Nassau Senior made an influential distinction between learning, or knowledge, and training, and claimed that greater economic value lay in training. As we saw in chapter 1, J. S. Mill himself argued that education under capitalism would tend to promote hedonistic and self-interested citizens and eventually drive out "moral sentiments" like sympathy and altruism.

Thus, while confident of economic progress, the early political economists typically expressed reservations about market society. The first problem was the division of labor itself, the source of the market's spectacular achievement. Perhaps the single greatest sociological—or, in nineteenth-century terms, anthropological—insight of political economy was that differences among people derived from the division of labor. Smith is clear about the superiority of nurture over nature in book 1 of *The Wealth of Nations:*

The difference . . . between a philosopher and a common street porter . . . seems to arise not so much from nature, as from habit,

7. Adam Smith, *Theory of Moral Sentiments* (London: George Bell, 1907).

8. Adam Smith, *Lectures on Jurisprudence 1762–66* (Oxford: Oxford University Press, 1977).

9. See Mark Blaug, "The Economics of Education in English Classical Political Economy: A Re-examination," in *Essays on Adam Smith*, ed. Andrew S. Skinner and Thomas Wilson (Oxford: Clarendon, 1975): 568–600.

custom, and education. When they came into the world, and for the first six or eight years of their existence, they were, perhaps, very much alike, and neither their parents nor playfellows could perceive any remarkable difference. About that age, or soon after, they come to be employed in very different occupations. The difference of talents comes then to be taken notice of, and widens by degrees, till at last the vanity of the philosopher is willing to acknowledge scarce any resemblance. But without the disposition to truck, barter, and exchange, every man must have procured to himself every necessary and conveniency of life which he wanted. All must have had the same duties to perform, and the same work to do, and there could have been no such difference of employment as could alone give occasion to any great difference of talents. (15–16)

Without the division of labor, "every man must have procured to himself every necessary and conveniency of life." But while liberating him from necessity, the division of labor constrains him to social inequality and worse, even making him, as Smith said in book 5, "as stupid and ignorant as it is possible for a human creature to become. . . . His dexterity at his own particular trade seems . . . to be acquired at the expence of his intellectual, social, and martial virtues. But in every improved and civilized society this is the state into which the labouring poor, that is, the great body of the people, must necessarily fall, unless government takes some pains to prevent it" (735). In barbarous societies, on the other hand, "every man does, or is capable of doing, almost every thing which any other man does, or is capable of doing. Every man has a considerable degree of knowledge, ingenuity, and invention" (735). By constant necessity the noble savage keeps the "intellectual, social, and martial virtues" alive at the individual level. Constructing barbarous society, Smith imagines a poor but prelapsarian society of equals; with market society he imagines wealth and inequality deriving from the division of labor. The neoclassical economists would imagine postlapsarian inequalities based on biology.

In that most political-economic of novels, Dickens's *Hard Times*, human character, like fictional characters, derives from the division of labor. The circus people differ systematically from the Gradgrinds, Bounderbys, and Bitzers, who represent political economy's ideas of economic men, maximizing their self-interest. The patriarchs of the ring, on the other hand, are cooperative, trusting, and not competitive among themselves. That is, competition is not in the circus people's nature per se but is introduced, as Marx thought competition was historically introduced, later in their relations with others. They are also, like Smith's noble savage, equally and broadly competent for all required tasks, and their labor is not drudgery: "The father of one of the families was in the habit of balancing the father of another of the families on the top of a great pole; the father of a third family often made a pyramid of both those fathers, with Master Kidderminster for the apex, and himself for the base; all the fathers could dance upon rolling casks, stand upon bottles, catch knives and balls, twirl hand-basins, ride upon anything, hump over everything, and stick at nothing."[10] The women are, predictably, mothers, that is, defined in relation to their physiological specialization, but they are not confined to the hearth. Rather, they are capable and uninhibited, by middle-class Victorian standards, and comparatively free: "All the mothers could (and did) dance, upon the slack wire and the tight rope, and perform rapid acts on barebacked steeds; none of them were at all particular in respect of showing their legs; and one of them, alone in a Greek chariot, drove six in hand into every town they came to" (77). Their characters are formed by their occupations, as if the sentiments they evoked during their performance had come to be lodged in their own breasts: "There was a remarkable gentleness and childishness about these people, a special inaptitude for any kind of sharp practice, and an untiring readiness to help and pity one another" (77). That is, their employment—public entertainment—cultivates the social emotions of sympathy and altruism, which Smith and Mill feared would be obliterated by market society. The aesthetic function or role is precisely to maintain social effects and relations that would atrophy without it. When Sissy Jupe is selected out of this sympathetic, artistic fellowship by Gradgrind, he tells her that her change of labor will be a change of life, the beginning of her "history": "I have explained to Miss Louisa . . . the miserable but natural end of your late career; and you are expressly to understand that the whole of that subject is past, and is not to be referred to any more. From this time you begin your history" (88). Just as history began, for political economy, with modern technology and the division of labor, so Sissy's history begins with her confinement in gendered domesticity.

Political economy recognized three geohistorical stages of development: the primitive tribe, loosely called "savagery"; the commune (in the city) and fiefdom (in the country), loosely called "barbarism"; and the market, loosely called "civilization," especially when based on technological superiority and a complex division of labor. In its ac-

10. Charles Dickens, *Hard Times* (London: Penguin, 1969), 77.

counts, the tribe had a chief and slaves and distributed the produce of hunting, fishing, and agriculture with little further division of labor. It was ruled by passion, or "the law of the strongest." In the commune and the fiefdom, property and women were slowly privatized and removed from public use. The lord of a feudal estate in the countryside commanded the labor of retainers and serfs through sentiment, land rights, and, when necessary, violence. In the last stage of ownership, capital and wage labor, each individual was bound by contract alone, rather than passion or sentiment, and motivated by rational self-interest. Since women's labor in the home was excluded from market services, women qua women tended to have no place in the theory of this final stage. As we shall see, they were typically analyzed as slaves from a lower stage of development.

The anthropologist Lewis H. Morgan's *Ancient Society*, based on his investigations of Iroquois Indians in New York State, was influential in considering gender as a world-historical division of labor.[11] Under savagery, "the childhood of mankind," there was a consanguine family (the gens) descended from a common ancestress. While maternal law lasted, there were also common ownership of property, sexual intercourse restricted only by the incest taboo, rule by custom rather than written law, little difference between the sexes, and relative peace. When the matriarchate was defeated by men, pairing families and private property were established, and paternal descent was ensured by monogamy. August Bebel, whose history of women in *Woman and Socialism* (1879) relied heavily on Morgan (as did Marx and Engels in *On the Origin of the Family, Private Property, and the State* [1884]), said that "the matriarchate implied communism and equality of all. The rise of the patriarchate implied the rule of private property and the subjugation and enslavement of women."[12]

In the early stages of industrial market society, the ideologies of the three stages of development—force, sentiment, and contract—and their corresponding modes of rule competed. So in Dickens's novel the historical abstractions of political economy are juxtaposed onto separate groups: slavery is represented by the traffic in women; the circus is a tribe of equal comradeship and capacity sharing the produce of their labor; and contract rules in the marketplace. In *The German Ideology* (1845–46) and *On the Origin of the Family*, Marx and Engels, among the few political economists to address gender, wrote of the

11. Lewis H. Morgan, *Ancient Society: Or Researches in the Lines of Human Progress from Savagery Through Barbarism to Civilization* (London: Henry Holt, 1877).

12. August Bebel, *Woman and Socialism* (1879; reprint, New York: Socialist Literature, 1910), 33.

"latent slavery in the family" and "the world-historic defeat of the female sex" that occurred with the gendered division of labor and removed women from the public sphere. In *Hard Times*, the home is a place of coercion and violence. This is Louisa Gradgrind's tragedy. Educated as a man, a rational and autonomous economic agent, she remains subject to the sexual division of labor and is therefore an economic dependent violently subjugated to the will of her providers. In her teens she is molested by the forty-seven-year-old Bounderby (64), to whom she is traded by her father and brother (131–34), and she is permanently damaged, in every sense of the word alienated from herself. Her slavery is the condition of the economic rationality of the men in her life: her father and brother, Bounderby, and Bitzer.

A story in some ways even sadder than Louisa's is that of her mother, Mrs. Gradgrind, a woman so alienated from all capacities or power, from a sense of herself as an autonomous being, that even in dying she cannot claim her *pain* as her own: "I think there's a pain somewhere in the room, but I couldn't positively say that I have got it" (224). The philosopher Roger Scruton has offered Mrs. Gradgrind as a negative example of the unity of consciousness that defines an individual's point of view, or what Kant called the transcendental unity of apperception.[13] Feeling women's and workers' alienation, the narrator, notoriously, seeks a solution not in women's or workers' emancipation from domestic and wage slavery but in sentiment, the form of rule associated with the communal life of the ancient city or manor, Sleary's "love beyond self-interest" (308) and Gradgrind's vow to heal the division not of labor but of "Head and Heart" (246). Throughout the nineteenth century, Sentimentalists—in the term's technical nineteenth-century sense of workers in the aesthetic media who believed in the social force of feeling and emotion—such as Dickens tried to believe that a society could alter social relations of conflict, alienation, or apathy without changing the division of labor.[14] Yet as Lou-

13. Roger Scruton, *Kant* (Oxford: Oxford University Press, 1982), 32.

14. Some critics have found the novel deficient in this regard. See Patrick Brantlinger, *The Spirit of Reform: British Literature and Politics 1832–1867* (Cambridge: Harvard University Press, 1977); John Holloway, "*Hard Times*: A History and a Criticism," in *Dickens and the Twentieth Century,* ed. John Gross and Gabriel Pearson (London: Routledge and Kegan Paul, 1962), 159–74; Humphrey House, *The Dickens World*, 2d ed. (London: Oxford University Press, 1960), 203–22; Ivanka Kovacevic, *Fact into Fiction: English Literature and the Industrial Scene, 1750–1850* (Leicester: Leicester University Press, 1975), 117. Also see Nicholas Coles's "The Politics of *Hard Times*: Dickens the Novelist Versus Dickens the Reformer," *Dickens Studies Annual* 15 (1986): 145–80; and Dickens's own essay "On Strike," from *Household Words* in the Norton edition of *Hard Times* (New York: Norton, 1990), 285–96. Feminist critics have recently

isa's education suggests, an education that did not aim to change the division of labor was an education that tended to perpetuate the status quo.

Hard Times is a Sentimental critique of political economy at the same time that all its imaginative categories—of character, class, space, and so on—are precisely taken from political economy. In that way it is very much a mid-Victorian text: the later literature had much more emphasis on biology, pleasure, and individuals rather than social groups, and on urban and leisure spaces rather than home and workspace. While upholding political economy's axiom regarding the source of human difference in the division of labor, Dickens continually attacks specific tenets of the science. Sissy sensibly but correctly critiques the idea of economic "growth" from the perspective of distribution: "I couldn't know whether it was a prosperous nation or not, and whether I was in a thriving state or not, unless I knew who had got the money" (97). The Dickensian narrator ironically points out that Coketown survives interference in the market, specifically, social legislation favorable to workers and the environment: "[Capitalists] were ruined, when they were required to send labouring children to school; they were ruined, when inspectors were appointed to look into their works; they were ruined when such inspectors considered it doubtful whether they were quite justified in chopping people up with their machinery; they were utterly undone, when it was hinted that perhaps they need not always make quite so much smoke" (145). He points out ironically that Coketown survives the ultimate threat from capital: a flow of capital overseas if the domestic workplace were regulated: "Whenever a Coketowner felt he was ill-used—that is to say, whenever he was not left entirely alone, and it was proposed to hold him accountable for the consequences of any of his acts—he was sure to come out with the awful menace, that he would 'sooner pitch his property into the Atlantic'" (145–46). The narrator calls the abstractions of political economy the "fictions of Coketown": a bourgeois meritocracy and the improvidence of workers (152–53); economic man's sole motivation in self-interest and sole bond with others in contract (303–4); and the authority of scientific law (see the delicious moment when Tom says he embezzled *because* he was a victim of statistics [300]). Yet Dickens's critical treatment of political economy's basic tenets shows the extent to which his conceptual categories were derived

been more tolerant of the contradictions they see in *Hard Times*. See Rosemarie Bodenheimer, *The Politics of Story in Victorian Social Fiction* (Ithaca: Cornell University Press, 1988), 189–206; and Catherine Gallagher, *The Industrial Reformation of English Fiction 1832–1867* (Chicago: University of Chicago Press, 1985), 147–86.

from the science, including the category of "private sphere" as distinct from public market behavior.

In *Hard Times,* both "private" spheres, the home and the market under laissez-faire, are violent and exploitative of women and workers. Although Dickens appeals to government to mollify the effects of the factory system, in *Hard Times,* as in the industrial market society of the 1850s, we witness the challenge to the political and ethical, or Sentimental, spheres posed by the economic, or market, sphere. The use of the public-private dualism to describe social, especially gender, relations is therefore inadequate. The home was private with respect to public market relations, but both home and market were at least in theory private with respect to the public sphere of government or the state. Indeed, *Hard Times* is exemplary in the challenges it poses to any simple dichotomy between public and private. The violence of both private spheres in the novel suggests the need for government interference in the home as well as the market and goes a long way in showing why the spheres have—contrary to convenient paradigms— been contested for the past two centuries.

One major tool of economic domination was, and is, political economy's, and now economics', claim to scientific status. With the reservations noted above, Smith characterized the market as a global system that functioned best when left alone. Through the elaboration of laws that were increasingly mechanistic, political economy had presented the market as a system impervious to human interference. By the 1850s, social relations seemed to assume the same mechanization, as if social relations functioned best when left alone, as if they were impervious to human will or agency. "Life at Stone Lodge," Dickens writes, "went monotonously round like a piece of machinery which discouraged human interference" (96), a description repeatedly invoked to describe the industrial system of Coketown. As in all fetishism, or the imputation of magical properties to the material of the everyday, the inanimate is animated. The counterpart of fetishism is reification, the deanimation of the living. As the market or industry appears to be an autopoetic, or a self-making, autonomous system, human relations are reduced to mechanism. In political-economic metonymy, workers like Stephen Blackpool are reduced to "hands" or to a mere "labour market," that is, to one commodity among others, like wheat or nails, and the Preston strike, the living source of the novel, is reduced by Dickens to demagoguery and caricatured in the person of Slackbridge. Marx related the effects of the division of labor to the mechanism of scientific law. As workers are reified as commodities, or labor markets (or people looking for love are reified as traders in the

sex market), the economic system is fetishized as a finely tuned machine, the global market that, economic science tells us, will tolerate
no interference.

Dickens gave *Hard Times* the subtitle *For These Times.* Trollope's
The Way We Live Now (1875) was meant to be similarly timely in
exposing "the commercial profligacy of the Age."[15] It shows the
spreading commodification of life in financial markets, art markets,
and marriage markets. Yet like *Hard Times* it begins with the subjection of women in the home. The hack writer Lady Carbury is abused
by her husband then sacrifices her own and her daughter's happiness
to her son Felix. (Like Tom, "the Whelp," in *Hard Times,* Felix is a
man defined by his desire to consume, who cannot be redeemed by the
unqualified and self-immolating love of women.) Women in Trollope's
novel "must obtain maintenance and position at the expense of suffering and servility."[16] The American Mrs. Hurtle was abused by her husband and nearly raped by a man in Oregon. For resisting, she is marked
for life as a "wildcat," ensuring that she will be abandoned by her
English suitor. Throughout, she expresses women's rage at female dependency and the subsumption of women's interests under men's. Marie Melmotte is commodified by Felix Carbury and Lord Nidderdale
and abandoned by both when her income becomes doubtful. Bored by
speculation in wives, Nidderdale ultimately recommends that finan-
cially eligible women literally be marketed in a newsletter. Lady Carbury calculates that "Love is like any other luxury. You have no right
to it unless you can afford it" (2:326). The one marriageable working-
class woman in the book, Ruby Ruggles, has no option but to marry
John Crumb, a man too simple for her ever to love, whose name reflects his status in the grain trade. Trollope thus anticipates Becker's
"marriage market" by one hundred years, with the difference that
Trollopean women were not partners in trade but the involuntary objects of trade.

If women are still in the slave stage, or prehistory, of political economy, and middle-class men pursue their economic interests not so
much by their industry as by their idleness (wife-hunting in drawing-
rooms and gambling at the Club), Trollope's financier, Melmotte, is
fetishized as the inexorable law of the market, subject to neither God
nor Caesar. He is "the very navel of the commercial enterprise of the
world" (1:331). His railroad will regenerate Mexico (1:391), and his

15. Anthony Trollope, *An Autobiography* (London: Williams and Norgate, 1946),
307.
16. Anthony Trollope, *The Way We Live Now,* ed. John Sutherland (Oxford:
World's Classics, 1991), 1:335.

ventures will relieve the population of old countries by opening up New Worlds (1:412). His myth represents the fortunes magically made on equity trading. Regarding his motivations, those of a money economy, as Thorstein Veblen said of businessmen in general, "The hedonistically presumed final purchase of consumable goods is habitually not contemplated in the pursuit of business enterprise. Business men habitually aspire to accumulate wealth in excess of the limits of practicable consumption, and the wealth so accumulated is not intended to be converted by a final transaction of purchase into consumable goods or sensations of consumption."[17] In other words, as Marx said in the famous M-C-M formula, under capitalism, money buys commodities, which then are sold for money. With no subjectivity to speak of, Melmotte *is* the market, and he operates without interference. He is also a fraud, his company for the construction of a Mexican-American railroad being entirely bogus, merely an excuse to float shares. In his *Autobiography* Trollope asked of the novel, "Can a world, retrograding from day to day in honesty, be considered to be in a State of progress?" (308). Yet while he condemned society for its profligacy and dishonesty,[18] he maintained a national *amour propre* that made him distance the financier as alien, first as a probable Jew, then as an Irish American. Political economy held that the disposition to truck, barter, and trade transformed world history. After Melmotte brings the world of London "more than ordinarily alive" (311), and his house serves as the nucleus of a network of global capital, the financier commits suicide and his family and associates return to the United States whence they came, with the barbarous Mrs. Hurtle.

The United States was "barbarous" in Trollope for two reasons: because people shot one another with guns, and because Americans made social distinctions based on money rather than on solid property and tradition. Indeed, it is the conservative nature and solidity of British property, represented by the prig Roger Carbury, and even the comparatively solid *debt* on property, that reveals by contrast the volatility of equity associated with Melmotte and America. Trollope banishes Hurtle, the Melmottes, and Fisker to the United States, thus returning English society to stable property relations in the country. Nor was Trollope alone; throughout the nineteenth century, Europeans viewed

17. Veblen, "The Limitations of Marginal Utility," in *The Philosophy of Economics,* ed. Daniel M. Hausman (Cambridge: Cambridge University Press, 1984), 184.

18. For the way that Trollope analyzes social relations in terms of individualistic honesty, see "Owning Up: Possessive Individualism in Trollope's *Autobiography* and *The Eustace Diamonds,*" in Andrew Miller, *Novels Behind Glass: Commodity Culture and Victorian Narrative* (Cambridge: Cambridge University Press, 1995), 159–88.

the United States as the most advanced market society: some thought it advanced to the point of decadence. Marx was fond of quoting a text called *Men and Manners in North America* by Thomas Hamilton (1833) to the effect that in the view of an American "the world is no more than a Stock Exchange, and he is convinced that he has no other destiny here below than to become richer than his neighbour. . . . Even the . . . relation between man and woman," Marx comments, "becomes an object of commerce. Woman is bartered away."[19] With his customary aversion to excess at the levels of production and reproduction, Mill called Americans mere "dollar-hunters and breeders of dollar-hunters."[20] By the mid-twentieth century, intellectual historians typically contrasted two conceptions of "progress." One they called the "American" idea, which concerned itself with growth in scientific knowledge, technology, and wealth, and the other they called "humanist" or "optimist," concerning itself with moral, social, or political change for the better.[21]

The previous quotation from Marx is from his early study of market values, "The Jewish Question" (1843), an attempt to analyze the social relations of commodification that define *Hard Times* and *The Way We Live Now.* Marx's use of the term *Jewish* to designate market relations—as when he described the United States as the most Jewish society—has embarrassed and outraged generations of Marxists and Jews, but it constitutes an illuminating case of reification. In the essay Marx defines Judaism as the private arena of property relations, the arena of need and private interest, which he also alternately calls "commerce," "huckstering," or "capitalism." He defines Christianity as the correlative ensconcement of abstract individualism (the value of the individual soul) in the political arena. Modern society (the way we live now) is therefore economic man maximizing his individual self-interest based on entrenched property relations and protected by the laws of the state: "Christianity is the sublime thought of Judaism; Judaism is the vulgar practical application of Christianity" (48). This means that the Christian state is the political support of the individual property rights of civil society. Christians are ideal abstractions of Jews.

Marx comes to this conclusion through a logic of equivalences. The basic elements of bourgeois civil society are individuals and the mate-

19. Karl Marx, "On the Jewish Question," in *The Marx-Engels Reader,* ed. Robert Tucker (New York: Norton, 1978), 49–51.

20. John Stuart Mill, *Principles of Political Economy* (London: Routledge, n.d.), 496.

21. Sidney Pollard, *The Idea of Progress* (London: Watts, 1968), 189–90; see chapter 3.

rial and cultural elements that form their life experience and situation. Since, according to the materialist, or political-economic, view, which relates political and legal institutions to the basic economic facts of life, political life is premised upon civil life, the (Christian) Rights of Man reflect the (Jewish) economic relations: the individual man (or soul) is considered sovereign. The rights of man include equality, liberty, security, and property, with security of property being "the supreme social concept of civil society" (43).

Thus property is the basis of human rights under capitalism—a theory that would later be elaborated as "possessive individualism." [22] Marx understands equality in bourgeois society as the state of being equally regarded as a self-sufficient monad; liberty as liberty in isolation, determined by the extent of one's means, or property; security as the assurance of egoism; and property as that which belongs wholly to oneself alone, pertains solely to one's self-interest. In the liberal state, political man, or abstract man with formal rights, simply preserves established property rights. For Marx, the "Jewish Question," the question of the specificity and autonomy of Jews, dissolved in the face of the total occupation of modern life by market relations. Christians and Jews are indistinguishable in market society, where social relations are dominated by contract rather than community. Marx, in short, was so blinded by market relations that he could not see the communities— of Jews and Christians—that were not coextensive with them.[23] Rather, he saw social atomism. Yet although critical of market society, Dickens, Trollope, and Marx saw it as an advance over slavery (for example, of women) and racial discrimination (for example, against Jews), and their criticisms remained within the terms of political economy.

While Dickens himself saw *Hard Times* as an attack on Benthamite utilitarianism from an aesthetic perspective, or the perspective of sense, emotion, and feeling, an equally powerful attack on political-economic notions of self-interest had been launched by two confessed Benthamites who set out to calculate pleasure and happiness. In 1825, William Thompson published under his name (probably for strategical reasons

22. See C. B. Macpherson, *The Political Theory of Possessive Individualism: Hobbes to Locke* (Oxford: Clarendon, 1992).

23. For scholarship on the history of the "Jewish Question," see Julius Carlebach, *Karl Marx and the Radical Critique of Judaism* (London: Routledge and Kegan Paul, 1978); Jonathan Frankel, *Prophecy and Politics: Socialism, Nationalism, and the Russian Jews* (Cambridge: Cambridge University Press, 1981); Arcadius Kahn, *Essays in Jewish Social and Economic History* (Chicago: University of Chicago Press, 1987); and (in Yiddish) A. Yuditsky, *Jewish Bourgeoisie and Jewish Proletariats in the First Half of the 18th Century* (Vilna, 1930).

related to reception) the views developed by Anna Wheeler and himself in the *Appeal of One Half the Human Race, Women, Against the Pretensions of the Other Half, Men, to Retain Them in Political, and Thence in Civil and Domestic Slavery; in Reply to a Paragraph of Mr. Mill's Celebrated "Article on Government."* Wheeler and Thompson objected to the clause in James Mill's popular essay in the *Encyclopedia Britannica Supplement* that dismissively subsumed women's interests under the male franchise: "One thing is pretty clear," Mill had written, "that all those individuals whose interests are indisputably included in those of other individuals may be struck off from political rights without inconvenience. In this light may be viewed all children up to a certain age, whose interests are involved in those of their parents. In this light also women may be regarded, the interest of almost all of whom is involved either in that of their fathers, or in that of their husbands." [24]

Mill's proposal to exclude women from the franchise "without inconvenience," Wheeler and Thompson claim, is the "inroad to barbarism under the guise of philosophy" (ix), that is, more in line with a stage of slavery or domination than with economic rationality. They reject Mill's thesis of identity of interest on the grounds that the happiness of any person cannot, methodologically speaking, be included in that of another. Whereas Mill had defined "the grand governing law of human nature" as the boundless "demand of power of all human beings over their fellow-creatures," Wheeler and Thompson, following Bentham, aver that "the first principle of human nature is the desire of happiness and the aversion to misery, without any wish, kindly or malignant, to others" (13). A simple calculation of the comparative pleasures of men and women indicates that men have more happiness than women. The authors write, "Happiness is the aggregate; of which pleasures are the items. Do wives enjoy as many pleasures of all sorts as their husbands, having the Guardianship of their volitions, do? This is the experimental touchstone to prove or disprove an identity of interest" (76). They list the privileges of men and privations of women, concluding that "one moral mass is to be saturated with liberty and enjoyment, the other with slavery, privation, and insult" (20). Moreover, the existing inequalities will be self-perpetuating, for men, saturated with happiness, will be decreasingly able to sympathize with the interests of women at all: granted the same pleasures and pursuits, fathers and sons will have "mutually sympathizing efforts"; yet "with [women's] blank of life and of active pursuit, how can the active father

24. Quoted in full on the title page of the *Appeal* (London: Longman, 1825).

sympathize?" (40). (This, ironically, is what happened to Mill's own son, John Stuart, who, while absorbed into his father's professional circles virtually from infancy, came to be painfully conscious that he could only conceive of his mother as a "drudge." As he wrote in his *Autobiography*, "With the very best intentions, my mother only knew how to pass her life in drudging for [her children]. Whatever she could do for them she did, and they liked her, because she was kind to them, but to make herself loved, looked up to, or even obeyed, required qualities which she unfortunately did not possess."[25] While acknowledging that his mother took pains for him, Mill despises her for not being able to sympathize with his and his father's pleasures. She was neither beautiful [to be loved] nor sublime [like his father, to be obeyed]. See the appendix, "Taste, or Sex and Class as Culture.")

Without sympathy, Thompson and Wheeler conclude, there can be no representation of interest. Political rights are desirable because they will afford the means of development of intelligence and benevolence, which are pleasurable in themselves; but communal childcare will liberate women even more than political rights, for it will equalize between women and men the concrete freedom to pursue other pleasures.

This is economic analysis, hedonic calculus, with a vengeance, but it is as grounded in sense, feeling, and emotion as Dickens's critique in *Hard Times*. Thus far Wheeler and Thompson have criticized the condition of women in civilized society: a state of slavery (see esp. 66–72). Two aspects of civilization, modern technology on one hand and the multiplication of higher-order pleasures on the other, will contribute to the decline of brute force, the only quality in which men are superior to women (183); and with the decline of domination, everyone's happiness will be increased: "As your bondage has chained down man to the ignorance and vices of despotism," the *Appeal* concludes its Address to Women, "so will your liberation reward him with knowledge, with freedom, and with happiness" (213). Thus in this case the Benthamite calculation of happiness, including interpersonal comparisons of utility, was directly opposed to political economy's narrow—androcentric—notions of rationality. On the gender question, the only "identity of interest" that Wheeler and Thompson are prepared to accept is the interest that both men and women have in women's equal status. This is not self-interest but the interest of the greatest happiness of the greatest number. Or rather it opposes enlightened self-interest to self-interest as understood by political economy.

25. John Stuart Mill, *Autobiography*, ed. Jack Stillinger (Boston: Houghton Mifflin, 1969), 33 n. See my fuller discussion of J. S. Mill's *Autobiography* in Regenia Gagnier,

This example from the Owenite socialists indicates how multifariously the early Victorians contested the values of market society. Although their kind of socialism was soon eclipsed by the "scientific socialism" of Marx and Engels, the Owenites had actually gone much further than Marx in envisioning the democratization of personal relations in the home, including household production and the potential for birth control—in the deepest sense economic issues that were ignored by both political economy (except the Malthusians) and its Marxist critics. Indeed, feminist economists are only now pursuing the insights of the Owenites of the 1830s, including their exposure of the nonidentity of interest within families.[26]

Subjectivities: A History of Self-Representation in Britain, 1832–1920 (Oxford: Oxford University Press, 1991), 249–57.

26. For example, the sociologist Paula England challenges the assumption in the "New Home Economics" school of neoclassical theory that altruism is the rule between family members. Just as Wheeler, Thompson, and, later, Mill's son John Stuart attacked the Sentimentalists on the grounds that their paternalism occluded real manipulations of power, even real brutality, in the Victorian family and the Victorian state, so England points out that men do not use the power they derive from earnings—even when (as is decreasingly the case) they are the proverbial breadwinners—entirely altruistically and that women's lesser earnings disadvantage them in daily interactions within marriage. To the extent that altruism does exist within the family, England asks whether this altruism implies an ability to empathize with others that might permit making at least rough interpersonal utility comparisons—a possibility that neoclassical economists deny. See Paula England, "The Separative Self: Androcentric Bias in Neoclassical Assumptions," in *Beyond Economic Man: Feminist Theory and Economics,* ed. Marianne A. Ferber and Julie A. Nelson (Chicago: University of Chicago Press, 1993), 37–53.

In another feminist critique of the New Home Economics, the economist Diana Strassmann reinvents Wheeler and Thompson's critique of identity of interest. She describes the neoclassical model of the family as "a story of a benevolent patriarch": "In this story, the patriarch makes choices in the best interests of the family. A patriarch is necessarily male, and as head of the prototypical family, has a wife and one or more children dependent upon him for providing for their needs. Although family members may have conflicting needs, the good provider dispassionately and rationally makes decisions which are in the best interests of the family. In particular, the patriarch participates in markets, making choices that link market values to his own assessment of family needs." The story is useful for economic theory, Strassmann continues, "because it allows the family to be treated as an individual agent. The metaphor of the invisible hand and its modern expression in general equilibrium theory rest critically on this assumption by linking decision-making with individual well-being, implicitly assuming that family decisions (made by the patriarch) give equal weight to the needs of all family members. By subsuming the needs of all family members into one utility function, the story of the benevolent patriarch provides an economic parallel to the historical invisibility of children and women in much of British and American law" (Diana Strassmann, "Not a Free Market: The Rhetoric of Disciplinary Authority in Economics," in Ferber and Nelson, *Beyond Economic Man,* 54–68; quotation is on 58.).

Like Wheeler, Thompson, and the younger Mill, Strassmann notes that widespread

Conceiving the root of social disunity to be in the political-economic philosophy of self-interest, the Owenites sought to achieve what they called a New Moral World of social and economic equality for all through Reason, the mind's ability to discern and promote the improvement of society. With Benthamite planning and calculation of happiness, they demanded both individual freedom and social equality. They rejected equally political economy's vision of the earthly paradise as the maximization of economic growth and the incipient romanticization of domestic slavery ("Angel in the House") that would flourish by mid-century. The Owenites planned communities of two thousand persons in which all property was in common; marriage, contraception, and divorce were available on demand; and childcare was socialized. One brief passage must serve to indicate the feminism, time-efficiency calculations, and planning of the early socialists. "In 1838," Barbara Taylor writes,

Robert Cooper, a Manchester Socialist, published a tract in which he described the labours of the New World in detail, beginning with housework which, he suggested, should be performed by children of eleven years or younger. The "production of wealth" would be the responsibility of those aged between twelve and twenty-one, while its 'preservation and distribution' would be performed by everyone aged twenty-two to twenty-five. The "formation of the character of the rising generation" would be the responsibility of those aged twenty-five to thirty-five; at thirty-five community residents would shoulder the burden of government, which they would carry until middle age. At forty-five, however, they would be freed for artistic or intellectual

---

wife and child abuse undermines the notion that family members necessarily behave altruistically, and she refers to substantial evidence of unequal food distribution within the family. Policy treating the family as one economic unit embodied in the patriarch has led to significant harm to women and children: "For example, the story of the benevolent patriarch functions as background to theories of income distribution, taxation, welfare, and economic development. . . . Amartya Sen calls attention to 'the grave tragedy of the disproportionate undernourishment of the female children in distress situations' and the 'unusual morbidity of women' in India and in poverty more generally. Sen attributes these phenomena to the selfish behavior of family patriarchs; he concludes that the failure of family decision makers to behave altruistically calls into question the reliability of much of the analyses in the discipline based upon this premise, including the traditional efficiency or optimality results related to the market mechanism. Indeed there is evidence that children fare better in poor countries if transfers are given to mothers rather than fathers." Ferber and Nelson, *Beyond Economic Man*, 58–59. See also the essay by Nancy Folbre in the same work: "Socialism, Feminist and Scientific," 94–110.

pursuits, tours of other communities, and so on. At each stage women would perform exactly the same tasks as men.[27]

Taylor documents the Owenite critiques not just of the family wage and coverture (the legal nonexistence of a married woman) but of bourgeois sexuality itself, citing "the latitudinarian traditions of plebeian sexual behavior" that were coming to an end by the 1840s, including pragmatic domestic arrangements, more openly pleasure-seeking than those among the bourgeoisie or the Methodists (chap. 6). Undermined by the economic forces that were transforming the working-class family, these more liberal sexual attitudes, codified by socialists, were also exposed to virulent antisocialist propaganda and their proponents to terrorism. One critic of "Women and the Social[ist] System" in *Fraser's Magazine* (June 1840) expressed his indignation in terms that confirmed Robert Owen's belief that male self-interest was at the root of existing matrimony: "A woman in common would be like a field in common, there would be no concentration of care upon any particular female; all those ties and obligations which unite parties in marriage would be dissolved. The effect of this would be a depreciation of women in society . . . not being appropriated, they would have no exchangeable price" (206). Another critic of an Owenite community in the 1830s described the integration of the sexes at dinner with Malthusian alarm: "On certain nights they held a Social Supper . . . and when they met, it was customary for a member to take the first seat that was unoccupied, and so on in rotation, the women sitting on one side of the table and the men on the other, no distinction made between married and single . . . the consequence was that a common intimacy arose between all parties, and . . . a number of illegitimate children were begotten" (218). The debate over sexual freedom versus women's vulnerability in cases of pregnancy showed, throughout the 1830s and 1840s, divisions among the socialists themselves, especially along gender lines. Whereas men tended to emphasize the "naturalness" of sex and promoted sexual libertarianism, female socialists spoke more of rational relationships based on equality and mutual esteem. For women, sex was a corollary of advanced social sentiment; for men, it was a passion to be endured. According to the Owenites' rational, progressive view, women's sexuality had evolved to a higher stage of development than men's, which was still to be suffered as biological instinct. As we shall see below, the New Women of the 1890s would reinvent these arguments.

27. Barbara Taylor, *Eve and the New Jerusalem* (New York: Pantheon, 1983), 52. Unless otherwise noted, the quotations from the Owenites below are from Taylor's study.

The Owenites believed that capitalism was a transitory, fragile form of socioeconomic organization that would be swept away in the tide of cooperative progress. A comparison of their view of progress with those found in two later influential feminist documents, August Bebel's *Woman and Socialism* and Olive Schreiner's *Woman and Labour,* will show how the notion of progress itself was biologized and therefore narrowed, and how narrower feminist notions of progress converged with those of fin de siècle economists.

The heir to the utopian socialists in Britain, at least in equally opposing both sex- and wage-slavery, was August Bebel in Germany, whose massive *Woman and Socialism,* written in prison in 1877, was revised in 1883 and renamed *Woman in the Past, Present, and Future.*[28] Like the utopians' socialism, Bebel's offered a progressive narrative of the *"Zukunftstaat"* (the society of the future) while providing an analysis of the legal, social, political, and domestic situations of women in nineteenth-century Europe ("civilization"). The first section, however, was redolent of contemporary anthropological and biological theory concerning the world history of women.

Bebel describes the contemporary situation ("Woman at the Present Day") in naturalistic terms, which is significant in light of the fin de siècle's tendency to essentialize what in the earlier political economists was constructed within the division of labor. Sex is healthy, and "sexual desire," "the impulse of race preservation," "the will to live," and "the desire for love" are used interchangeably, with a characteristically later Victorian vocabulary drawn from Tylorian anthropology. "Mercenary marriage," on the other hand, and "the matrimonial market" are abominations. Bebel is incensed by the forced parasitism of upper-class women, as Schreiner would be, and sees their economic dependency on men as preventing the development of their talents and capacities. Although he is convinced that bourgeois marriage and other forms of prostitution are a necessary social institution of bourgeois society (chap. 12), he is also optimistic that these conditions are coming to an end. Advances in domestic labor-saving technology from the 1880s might liberate women from the drudgery of housework, and working-class women entering the workforce would depress wages. Both circumstances would contribute to the erosion of marriage and the family. Bebel approvingly cites statistics indicating the decline in marriage and birth rates, the increase in divorce, and the predominance of females in the population (chap. 11, "The Chances of Matrimony").

28. Bebel, *Woman and Socialism; Woman in the Past, Present, and Future* (1883; reprint, London: Zwan, 1988).

He discusses "depravity, demoralization, degeneration," and increased disease and death among working-class children. Yet he concludes from the evidence that the disintegration of the working-class family means progress toward communal society, where children will be nurtured collectively.

If one factor hastening socialism is women's full participation in the workforce, another is the Marxist recipe for revolution: increasing economic inequality coupled with increasing political democracy. Bebel assumes that revolution rather than reason will bring about the socialization of the community (1883, 178–229) and in passing so distinguishes Marxist socialism not only from the Owenites' but also from Mill's: "Mill took the greatest pains to reform the bourgeois world and bring it to reason, naturally to no purpose, and thus he at last became a socialist, like every other logical person acquainted with the actual condition of things" (1883, 197 n). The final section of his book is on women in the Zukunftstaat, where it will be the equal duty of all to labor "without distinction of sex" (181) and which will "know no other consideration than the wellfare [sic] of its members" (188), that is, profit will not exist.

In the Zukunftstaat human faculties will be developed rather than repressed by the division of labor, and life will be more aesthetic than economic. (Bebel cites Schiller on "the reconciliation of the world" [211].) Yet if the division of labor in Bebel has ceased to be coerced, it has also gone quite a way toward being naturalized:

> After the community has educated the young up to a given age on the principles laid down, it can leave them to decide their further training for themselves. . . . Each will practise and carry out those occupations for which his capacities and tastes qualify him, in the company of those who have made the same choice as himself. There will be no musicians, actors, artists and scholars by profession, but *by spontaneous choice, by right of talent and genius*. . . . "Education," [Bebel quotes Wagner] "starting with the development of strength and of physical beauty, will assume an artistic character, from unimpeded love to the child and delight in its growing charms, and *every human being will become an artist in truth in one direction or another. The variety of natural tastes will lead to the development of the most manifold talents to an unprecedented extent.*" These words are entirely Socialistic in spirit. (219–21, emphasis in original)

"Each will practise and carry out those occupations for which his capacities and tastes qualify him, in the company of those who have made the same choice as himself": taste, choice, and a rigidifying of possibilities into determination by "right of talent and genius"—this specification of different *kinds* of people—had many advocates at the fin de siècle. It may be contrasted with the political-economic premise that differences between people derive from the division of labor. It has also gone quite a distance from Marx and Engels's postulated socialist as one who can "do one thing today and another tomorrow, to hunt in the morning, fish in the afternoon, rear cattle in the evening, criticise after dinner, just as [one has] a mind, without ever becoming hunter, fisherman, shepherd, or critic."[29] Later in the same section, Bebel also naturalizes a human "need of change" to be satisfied by the conquest of geographical space—by way of leisure. In the new society "everyone will be able to visit foreign lands and continents, and to join expeditions and colonizing settlements of all kinds in order to satisfy the innate, natural need of change" (223). Bebel's characterization of a restless, desiring human nature with natural tastes and capacities is much closer to the fin de siècle tourist or consumer than political economy's productive subject. As we shall see in the contrast with Schreiner and other New Women, it is also more characteristic of male social theorists than female at the fin de siècle.

We note Bebel's inclusion of colonization as one of the pleasures of the Zukunftstaat. In his chapter on internationality, Bebel provides a Smithian paean to global, but presumably socialist, markets, a "Universal Economy" that will bring not only wealth but peace to the world, an idea that runs from Smith through Morris ("The Society of the Future" or "How We Live and How We Might Live") to Wilde ("The Critic as Artist") and the Fabians. Without foreign commodities, Bebel goes so far as to say, "we could no longer exist":

> The ease with which personal intercourse can be kept up between far distant lands is a new and important link in the chain of communication. Emigration and colonization are other powerful factors. One nation learns from another, and each seeks to out-do the other in the competitive race. Alongside of the exchange of every kind of ware, an exchange of mental products is going on at the same time; millions find themselves obliged to learn foreign languages; and nothing is better adapted to remove unfounded antipathies than material advantages in union with comprehension of the language and mind of a foreign nation. (233–34)

29. Karl Marx and Friedrich Engels, "The German Ideology" [1846], in *The Marx-Engels Reader,* ed. Robert Tucker (New York: Norton, 1978), 160.

National interests are, in short, like wage labor, sex slavery, and capitalism, a lower stage of development (235–36). The vehicle of progress—moral and political as well as technological and economic— is the global market, although Bebel is noticeably less concerned than Smith or Mill about its effects on labor markets. Stronger than "national hatreds" are "material interests, the strongest that exist." Bebel concludes the book with an essay on overpopulation, arguing that although numbers are important when they are multiplying in poverty, that is, under the conditions of capitalism, "a higher stage of evolution" will not result in "a rabbit hutch." For the women of the future will want to enjoy their freedom and independence and maximize their material interests. Aesthetic society will therefore regulate its numbers: an argument that ran through political economy's own evolutionary narrative at least since J. S. Mill and is a premise of demography today.

Bebel's *Woman and Socialism* and "The Communist Manifesto" were the most popular socialist texts of the European fin de siècle, Bebel's reaching its zenith with the Russian revolution. Olive Schreiner's *Woman and Labour* (1911) is the culmination of the liberal feminist or women's movement's appeal to put women on the market equally with men, and its plan is noticeably more productivist than Bebel's.

The long opening chapter on female "parasitism," the term Schreiner uses for women she considers idle or nonproductive, begins with the observation that with "civilization's" division of labor men's work has increased but women's has diminished: modern mothers are increasingly incompetent to educate their children. Because educating children for modernity takes a long time and is therefore costly to the state, the modern view, according to Schreiner, condemns "excessive reckless child-bearing": "Even those among us who are child-bearers are required, in proportion as the class or race to which we belong stands high in the scale of civilization, to produce in most cases a limited number of offspring."[30] Writing from her native South Africa, Schreiner assumes the accelerated stages of social development of modernity, with men and whites holding the power of rapid advance, and with gulfs growing between social groups at different stages: "Between father and daughter, mother and son, brother and sister, husband and wife, may sometimes be found to intervene, not merely years but even centuries, of social evolution" (126). Within one society, different races and classes may be "in totally distinct stages of evolution. So wide is the hiatus between them that often the lowest form of sex at-

30. Olive Schreiner, *Woman and Labour* (Johannesburg: Cosmos, 1975), 25–26.

traction can hardly cross it" (112). Schreiner's claim might be interpreted as quixotic or naive unless one recalls the Owenite feminist approach to sexuality, now filtered through New Woman eugenics (see chapter 5), as a sentimental social bond rather than as a passion. For Schreiner also believed that equal education and access to labor would strengthen the "sexual" bonding of men and women (106).

Schreiner explicitly contrasts the opportunities of "civilised" women in industrial society with those of "primitive" women in South Africa. She shares the Tylorian appreciation of the so-called primitive, whom Schreiner admires for her ability to analyze her situation, her stoic virtues, and her eloquence:

When I was eighteen I had a conversation with a Black woman, still in her untouched primitive condition, a conversation which made a more profound impression on my mind than any, but one other incident connected with the position of woman, has ever done. She was a woman whom I cannot think of otherwise than as a person of genius. In language more eloquent and intense than I have ever heard from the lips of any other woman, she painted the condition of the women of her race: the labour of women, the anguish of woman as she grew older, as the limitations of her life closed in about her and her sufferings under the condition of polygamy and subjection. All these she painted with a passion and intensity I have not known equalled, yet, and this was the interesting point, when I went on to question her, seething with a deep and almost fierce bitterness against life and the unseen powers which had shaped woman and her conditions, there was not one word of bitterness against the individual man. Nor was there any will or intention to revolt. In fact there was only a stern and almost majestic attitude of acceptance of the inevitable; life and the conditions of her race being what they were. It was this conversation which first forced upon me a truth, which I have since come to regard as almost axiomatic, that, the women of no race or class will ever rise in revolt or attempt to bring about a revolutionary readjustment of their relation to their society, however intense their suffering and however clear their perception of it, while the welfare and persistence of their society requires their submission. Wherever there is a general attempt on the part of the women of any society to readjust their position in it, a close analysis will always show that the changed or changing conditions of that society have made woman's acquiescence no longer necessary or desirable. (2)

Schreiner's complex views on race were influenced by both progressive political economy (for example, J. A. Hobson) and late Victorian
anthropology. Often in her works touching on race, she treats black
Africans in political-economic terms, as a labor force, but just as frequently she treats them sentimentally or anthropologically, as primitive, closer to nature. Always in her writing, indigenous Africans are
discussed in relation to Boers, who are also perceived in racial terms—
as they generally were in Britain, especially in the events surrounding the Boer War—as survivalists, primitives, close to nature. If she
saw the Afrikaner-African struggle as evolution in action, the struggle
of the fittest to survive, so Schreiner also saw the hoped-for Boer-
British union as an evolution in which contact with the British would
eventually bring the Boers modern enlightenment. Schreiner insisted
that the evolutionary absorption of the Boers was better than the impo-
sition of capitalist imperialism.[31] Given her evolutionary frame, she
confines her views in *Woman and Labour* to "civilized" women of
modern Europe.

Yet if civilization allows for the possibility of freedom and equality
across genders, it has been temporarily arrested with the degeneration
of bourgeois woman, "the human female parasite—the most deadly
microbe which can make its appearance on the surface of any social
organism" (34; see comparable criticisms in Bebel, 1879, 125–26).
Schreiner describes the middle-class woman with contempt similar to
Bebel's: "Finely clad, tenderly housed, life became for her merely the
gratification of her own physical and sexual appetites, and the appetites of the male, through the stimulation of which she could maintain
herself. And as kept wife, kept mistress, or prostitute, she contributed
nothing to the active and sustaining labours of her society" (39).
Schreiner compares the middle-class woman's decadence with that
of Roman women, who "accept[ed] lust in the place of love, ease in
the place of exertion, and an unlimited consumption in the place of
production" (39), and she attributes Greek homosexuality to men not
finding equal partners among women (36). The condition for female

31. See Schreiner's *Closer Union* (London: Fifield, 1909) and her collected essays,
Thoughts on South Africa (Johannesburg: Africana Book Society, 1976). See also Joyce
Avrech Berkman, *The Healing Imagination of Olive Schreiner: Beyond South African
Colonialism* (Amherst: University of Massachusetts Press, 1989); Greta Jones, *Social
Darwinism and English Thought: The Interaction Between Biological and Social The-
ory* (Sussex: Harvester, 1980); Douglas A. Lorimer, *Color, Class and the Victorians*
(Leicester: Leicester University Press, 1978) and "Theoretical Racism in Late-Victorian
Anthropology, 1870–1900," *Victorian Studies* 31, no. 3 (spring 1988): 405–30; Paula M.
Krebs, "Olive Schreiner's Racialization of South Africa," *Victorian Studies* 40, no. 3
(spring 1997): 427–44.

parasitism is the subjugation of other classes and races: "The debilitating effect of wealth sets in at that point at which the supply of material necessaries and comforts, and of aesthetic enjoyments, clogs the individuality, causing it to rest satisfied in the mere passive possessions of the results of the *labour of others,* without feeling any necessity or desire for further productive activity of its own" (43, emphasis in original). Whereas Bebel is a socialist who is also an enthusiast for global markets and consumer choice, Schreiner is rigidly productivist, upholding productive members of society rather than enervated consumers living off the labor of others. The book begins and ends with what she calls modern woman's cry, "Give us labour and the training which fits us for labour! We demand this, not for ourselves alone, but for the human race!"

Putting labor at the center of her analysis made Schreiner sensitive to the particular demands of women's labor in childbirth and -rearing, which necessitated, she thought, a different attitude to social conflict. Women, she claims, have no moral superiority, indeed the present conditions of their existence foster irresponsibility, competitiveness with other women, and pettiness; yet their very labor as women bequeaths to them a rejection of war: "She knows the history of human flesh. She knows its cost and he does not" (76). As a sculptor could not use works of art to fortify the ramparts, women will not use men's bodies: "Men's bodies are our women's works of art" (76). Production, reproduction, and creativity merge in an aesthetic grounded in the feelings and emotions of a woman's laboring body:

> There is, perhaps, no woman, whether she has borne children, or is merely a potential child-bearer, who could not look upon a battlefield covered with slain and think: "So many mothers' sons! so many bodies brought into the world to lie there! so many months of weariness and pain while bones and muscles were shaped within; so many hours of anguish and struggle that breath might be; so many baby mouths drawing life at woman's breasts—all this, that men might lie with glazed eyeballs, and swollen bodies, and fixed, blue, unclosed mouths, and great limbs tossed! . . . No woman, who is a woman, says of a human body, "It is nothing!" (75)

Schreiner, and to a lesser extent Bebel (with his emphasis on sex, desire, impulse of race preservation, and so on), have produced a physiological ethic that is mirrored in the physiological aesthetics dominant by the fin de siècle (see especially chapters 4 and 5). Critical of a society of passive consumers living off the labor of others, Schreiner extended her productivist theories to the production of the future. Relying on the market more than on Reason, her expectations were noticeably lower than the Owenites'. Yet in comparison with the economists for whom self-interest is ruling ideology, economism is explanatory model, commodification is universal, and market society is the end of history, the dedication of *Woman and Labour* signifies a love beyond self-interest and a satisfaction with one's fate as a laborer in the production of something bigger than the self:

> I should like to say to the men and women of the generations which will come after us: "You will look back at us with astonishment! . . . You will marvel at the labour that ended in so little. But what you will never know is how it was, thinking of you and for you, that we struggled as we did and accomplished the little which we have done. It was in the thought of your larger realisation and a fuller life, that we found consolation for the futilities of our own." (9)

William Morris's *News from Nowhere* (1890) is the story of a Victorian time traveler who is transported to a socialist England in A.D. 2050. The romance chronicles William "Guest"'s journey to a feast in the country, which is promised to be the culmination of his experience in the New World. When he finally arrives at the feast, however, he suddenly becomes invisible to his new comrades: the culmination of his journey is his exit; he has prepared a future to which he will not have access. The "Guest" does not resent that he fails to reap the fruits of his labor and abstinence, that his time is scarce, that he has miscalculated the opportunity costs of his investment in the future. Rather, like Schreiner, he bows to the yoke of production, to the creation of a better world: "Go back and be the happier for having seen us," the self-absorbed young Utopians tell him, "for having added a little hope to your struggle. Go on living while you may, striving, with whatsoever pain and labour needs must be, to build up little by little the new day of fellowship, and rest, and happiness."[32] Tasteful, happy, and static, the young Utopians show no anxiety or responsibility for a future beyond their "epoch of rest."

It is possible that, in the affective contrast between the Utopians and the laboring productive Guest, Morris was questioning whether consumption and leisure tended toward passivity, whether the consumers of others' labor ever really feel responsibility for the future. Such

---

32. William Morris, *News from Nowhere* (London: Routledge and Kegan Paul, 1970), 182.

was certainly Schreiner's view at the end of the century when she attacked the female parasite who contributed nothing to the sustaining labors of her society. Yet the earlier socialists and feminists, such as Mill and the Owenites, and the later ones, such as McNally, also looked forward hopefully to a disposable—unproductive—time that would come at the end of the day or the end of history, a time for pleasures beyond the utilitarian modes of production. Perhaps Morris and the Owenites offered the better answer to whether markets were the end of history in insisting on our dual nature as producers and consumers, creatures who provided for the next generation and seized the pleasures of the day for themselves. Between twelve and twenty-one they would produce the wealth; from twenty-two to twenty-five they would preserve and distribute it; from twenty-five to thirty-five they would teach the young; from thirty-five they would shoulder the responsibility of government; and at forty-five they would be freed for artistic or intellectual pursuits, travel, or what they liked, at each stage women performing exactly the same tasks as men.

THREE

Modernity and Progress toward
Individualism in Economics and Aesthetics

A recent book on Oscar Wilde's critical writings develops the thesis
that the fin de siècle Decadence was quintessentially modern in that it
sought to contain within itself all the moods and forms of the past.[1]
This view of modernity as summing up in itself all prior modes of
thought and life is not a new one. In his essay on Leonardo da Vinci,
Walter Pater called it "*the* modern idea": "All the thoughts and experience of the world have etched and moulded" La Gioconda's face, "the
animalism of Greece, the lust of Rome, the reverie of the middle age
with its spiritual ambition and imaginative loves, the return of the Pa-
gan world, the sins of the Borgias . . . like the vampire, she has been
dead many times and learned the secrets of the grave; and has been a
diver in deep seas, and keeps their fallen day about her; and trafficked
for strange webs with Eastern merchants; and, as Leda, was the mother
of Helen of Troy, and as Saint Anne, the mother of Mary."[2] Pater concludes the famous passage with the modernity of the Darwinian idea
of evolution: "modern thought has conceived the idea of humanity as
wrought upon by, and summing up in itself, all modes of thought and
life."

An earlier version of this chapter appeared as "Modernity and Progress in Economics
and Aesthetics" in *Rethinking Victorian Culture*, ed. Juliet John and Alice Jenkins
(Hampshire: Macmillan, 2000), 222–38.

1. Lawrence Danson, *Wilde's Intentions: The Artist in His Criticism* (Oxford:
Clarendon, 1997). The Decadent critic who knows the many moods and modes of the
past is a "personality" whose power comes from the masks through which he fashions
and refashions himself (for reasons that will become clear below, in the nineteenth century it was generally "he"). This reference to the past, or what Danson calls Decadence's
"backwardness," challenges mid-Victorian notions of progress: hence its "modernity."
Similarly, the Decadent idea of personality as multiplicity and surface rather than soul
within challenges the earnest Victorian idea of the singular and autonomous individual:
hence *its* "modernity."

2. Walter Pater, *Selected Writings* (New York: Signet, 1974), 46–47.

Now whereas Danson, in his book on Wilde's critical writings, would stress (after the manner of Paul de Man)[3] modernity's obsession with the past in its "summing up" of all previous modes and moods, I have emphasized the summing up itself, or modernity's capacity to consume randomly all experience. Pater's stunning ahistoricism in the juxtapositions and appropriations of the Renaissance exemplifies the modern (Decadent) critic's capacity to consume the treasures of the past as contributing to his own "unique" "personality," revealed by his distinctive tastes, or even by his psychological dispositions. For the psychological summing up—the layering of prior experience in the psyche—is also figured in La Gioconda's image and is being formulated as modern at the fin de siècle. The paradox is that the critic, Man of Taste, or "personality" who objectifies and consumes the exotica of the world in the service of establishing his own taste or discrimination is doomed by his own publicity: the individual in the age of "personality" in mass culture becomes a stereotype, a representative of a class. Thus Pater becomes the "Aesthete" and his tastes "Aestheticism," Wilde becomes the homosexual or an "Oscar," Beardsley becomes "Beardsley," or the *Mona Lisa* becomes the standard representative of "masterpiece" in the age of mechanical reproduction.

The key elements of modernity, then, are, first, consumption—not only of time, as in the past, but also of space, as in Bebel's and Schreiner's globalism or Decadent exoticism and its correlative fetishism[4]— and, second, a kind of individual or self produced by this ability to consume time and space. Central to Pater's description of the modernity of the *Mona Lisa* is *desire*: her image "is expressive of what in the ways of a thousand years men had come to desire" (46). Like the vampire, she has consumed the world, "trafficked for strange webs with Eastern merchants," and we have come to desire her for her "beauty wrought out from within upon the flesh, the deposit, little cell by cell, of strange thoughts and fantastic reveries and exquisite passions" (46). "Lady Lisa," says Pater, "might stand as . . . the symbol of the modern idea" (47), for consumption is the essence of modernity. Elsewhere, in a poem comprised of economic figures—"fees," "price," "payment," "interest," "gain," "use," "riches," "store"—another great modernist used another image of woman's brain as watery bin ("Sargasso Sea") of modernity. Ezra Pound concluded "Portrait D'Une Femme" (1912): "No! there is nothing! In the whole and all, / Nothing that's quite your

3. Paul de Man, "Literary History and Literary Modernity," in *Blindness and Insight* (New York: Oxford University Press, 1971), 142–65.
   4. Anne McClintock calls the latter "commodity racism." See *Imperial Leather* (New York: Routledge, 1995).

own. / Yet this is you."[5] These truisms of Western economics and political economy, that consumption is the essence of modernity and that women have a special role in consumption, were most uncompromisingly formulated in W. W. Rostow's "stages of economic growth," whose final stage, the end of history, culminated in American-style "high mass consumption."[6]

Rostow's book begins with a graphic representation of the nations of the world in the take-off, maturity, and high mass-consumption trajectories that by 1960 dominated economic thought. Given the seeming inevitability of the trajectory to high mass consumption, Rostow concluded with the question, what next? In good neoclassical fashion, what he predicted for the United States in 1960 was the declining utility of wealth itself. As the consumption of durable goods slowed down, Americans seemed to want not more commodities or even more income, but, as Mill had feared, more babies. They preferred the extra baby to the extra unit of consumption. Would the rest of the world, the economist speculated, "follow the Americans and reimpose the strenuous life by raising the birth-rate?" Would other societies turn to war? Outer space? Huntin', fishin', or shootin' in the suburbs? While thus worrying that "man" may not find sufficient outlet for the expression of his "energies, talents, and instinct to reach for immortality," Rostow notes parenthetically that this worry will probably not be shared by women. It is unlikely, he says, "that women will recognize the reality of the problem; for the raising of children in a society where personal service is virtually gone is a quite ample human agenda, durable consumers' goods or no. The problem of [the end of history] is a man's problem, at least until the children have grown up" (91).

Such was the end of history in 1960—women still excluded from its march, busy with the children, while men wondered what to conquer next. This chapter will focus on the economic aspects of "civilized" modernity in the European or white discourse of comparative civilizations. Other works, most notably Edward Said's Orientalism (1978) and Culture and Imperialism (1994), have considered much more broadly the cultural relations between the West and its imagined Others. The narrower focus here on the economic components of that cultural imaginary is meant to highlight a figure relatively neglected in the broad strokes of postcolonial studies: the man of taste as individual consumer. For this figure has come to be the model of modern man as

5. Ezra Pound, Personae: The Collected Shorter Poems of Ezra Pound (New York: New Directions, 1971), 61.

6. W. W. Rostow, Stages of Economic Growth (Cambridge: Cambridge University Press, 1960).

such, as pervasive a "model of man" by the late twentieth century as the colonial apparatus was at the height of imperialism.

In a classic critique of precisely the linearity of Rostow's analysis, *The Modern World-System* (1974), the political economist Immanuel Wallerstein pointed out the difference between precapitalist xenophobia (hatred or fear of *external* Others) and the institutional racism of the global division of labor.[7] In Wallerstein's global economic system, the Anglo-European "core" demanded the surplus, while the nonwhite "periphery" supplied the labor. In what Wallerstein calls the "ethnicization of the world's workforce," racism "was the ideological justification for the hierarchization of the workforce and its highly unequal distribution of reward."[8] While racism served to control direct producers, Western universalism—the scientific search for truth or, in Wallerstein's view, the West's self-interested rationalization—served to direct the bourgeoisies of peripheral states through the exaltation of Progress. The complicitous notion of "meritocracy" preserved the idea that individual mobility was possible without threatening the hierarchical allocation of the workforce. Thus capitalist racism buttressed the global division of labor and unequal distribution of surplus; universalism supplied the idea that there was but one road to Progress (Rostow's); and the ideology of meritocratic individualism allowed for the exception that proved the rule of domination. Wallerstein's was an organic account of the wealth of nations, of the global economy as one system of interdependent parts. For him, a professional Africanist, the West's master narrative of scientific and technological advance that, with the help of racism, universalism, and meritocratic individualism, provided the siren song of modernity, masked the irrationality of endless wasteful accumulation at the Anglo-European core.

Wallerstein's work purported to describe the rise of global markets since the sixteenth century. Up to this point we have merely described the shifts that took place in the core toward the end of the nineteenth. Economic man and woman as producer and reproducer gave way to economic man and woman as consumer, which gave rise to competing politics of labor and desire. Economic theory began to shift its focus from the social relations of population growth, landlords, entrepre-

---

7. Immanuel Wallerstein, *The Modern World-System: Capitalist Agriculture and the Origins of the European World-Economy in the Sixteenth Century* (New York: Academic, 1974); *The Modern World-System II: Mercantilism and the Consolidation of the European World-Economy, 1600–1750* (New York: Academic, 1980). A condensed version of the arguments about race and universalism summarized here is in Wallerstein's *Historical Capitalism* (London: Verso, 1984), 78–85.

8. Wallerstein, *Historical Capitalism*, 78.

neurs, workers, and international trade to the individual's subjective demands for goods. The labor theory of value, which had seen the human body and human labor as the ultimate determinants of price, was abandoned in favor of consumer demand. Consumer choice ceased to be a moral category. Value ceased to be evaluative across persons: it became individual, subjective, or psychological.

Jevons, Menger, and the other early theorists of consumption claimed that as the basic needs of subsistence were satisfied, humankind's desire for variety in shelter, food, dress, and leisure grew limitlessly, and thus the idea of needs—which were finite and the focus of political economy—was displaced by the idea of tastes, which were theoretically infinite. *Modern* man would henceforth be known by the insatiability of his desires, and Others on the road to modernity needed only to be inspired by envy to desire his desires, to imitate his wants, to be on the road to his progress and his *civilization*. His nature, insatiability, was henceforth human nature itself. His mode, consumer society, was no longer one stage of human progress but its culmination and end.

This was the burden of the "comparative civilizations" histories of the period. And here we begin to see the displacement of ideas of *progress,* which implied moral and political progress as well as economic growth, by ideas of development, which implied only an inevitable trajectory toward high mass consumption. The man of taste was poised in relation to the savage; this juxtaposition represented the relation of Britain to external Others. Yet equally important within Britain was the man of taste in relation to the barbarian, generally an internal figure, as in Matthew Arnold's distinctions in *Culture and Anarchy* (1869) between "Barbarians, Philistines, and Populace."[9] Unlike the savage, who, owing to a lack of modern technology and division of labor, had not achieved the higher orders of civilization, the barbarian willfully resisted civilization. Generally representing a degenerate aristocracy, as in Arnold, the profligate barbarian did not exercise the discriminating self-restraint of the middle-class ("Philistine") man of taste but reverted to the type of the wasteful, indulgent lords of feudalism. The man of taste distinguished himself equally from the simple foreign savage and the degenerate domestic barbarian. We shall return to Arnold later in this chapter.

9. Matthew Arnold, Culture and Anarchy *with* Friendship's Garland *and Some Literary Essays,* vol. 5 of *The Complete Prose Works of Matthew Arnold,* ed. R. H. Super (Ann Arbor: University of Michigan Press, 1965).

Whereas the savage's identity was absorbed in the life of his community (as would be his Fascist avatar with characteristic "blood and soil" vitalism), and the decadent barbarian was consumed by his own selfish profligacy, the man of taste cultivated a disciplined individualism consistent with modern notions of progress. Paramount here was the idea that all real progress, that is, moral and political progress, was progress toward individualism. The Victorian search for a law of progress was most pronounced in Herbert Spencer's *Social Statics* (1851) and *Progress: Its Law and Cause* (1857). Our organs, faculties, powers, and capacities grow by use and diminish from disuse, and we may infer, according to Spencer, that they will continue to do so. "Thus the ultimate development of the ideal man is logically certain"; humanity must in the end become completely adapted to its conditions, and progress will be a matter of evolutionary development. In the quotation below—representing a pervasive ideology of evolutionary progress—moral restraint, active conscience, and educated habit form the "perfected" man of taste for the social state.

> Progress, therefore, is not an accident, but a necessity. Instead of civilization being artificial, it is a part of nature; all of a piece with the development of the embryo or the unfolding of a flower. . . . As surely as the tree becomes bulky when it stands alone, and slender if one of a group; as surely as the same creature assumes the different forms of cart-horse and race-horse, according as its habits demand strength or speed; as surely as a blacksmith's arm grows large, and the skin of a labourer's hand thick; as surely as the eye tends to become long-sighted in the sailor, and short-sighted in the student; as surely as the blind attain a more delicate sense of touch; as surely as a clerk acquires rapidity in writing and calculation; as surely as the musician learns to detect an error of a semi-tone amidst what seems to others a very babel of sounds; as surely as a passion grows by indulgence and diminishes when restrained; as surely as a disregarded conscience becomes inert, and one that is obeyed active; as surely as there is any efficacy in educational culture, or any meaning in such terms as habit, custom, practice; so surely must the human faculties be moulded into complete fitness for the social state; so surely must the things we call evil and immorality disappear; so surely must man become perfect.[10]

10. Herbert Spencer, "Progress: Its Law and Cause," in *Essays: Scientific, Political, and Speculative* (London: Williams and Norgate, 1883), 1:58.

This picture of perfect adaptation in Spencer becomes increasingly organic, so that the law of organic progress, consisting in the change from the homogeneous to the heterogeneous, unique, or individuated, is revealed as the law of all progress. All progress is progress toward individuation.

> The investigations of Wolff, Goethe, and von Baer, have established the truth that the series of changes gone through during the development of a seed into a tree, or an ovum into an animal, constitute an advance from homogeneity of structure to heterogeneity of structure. In its primary stage, every germ consists of a substance that is uniform throughout, both in texture and chemical composition. The first step is the appearance of a difference between two parts of this substance; or, as the phenomenon is called in physiological language, a differentiation. Each of these differentiated divisions presently begins itself to exhibit some contrast of parts: and by and by these secondary differentiations become as definite as the original one. (2–3)

Spencer conjectures that the scope of the process is literally universal, that all things participate in a grand division of labor that differentiates and individuates: "If the nebular hypothesis be true, the genesis of the solar system supplies one illustration of this law. . . . Whether it be in the development of the earth, in the development of life upon its surface, in the development of society, of government, of manufactures, of commerce, of language, literature, science, art, this same evolution of the simple into the complex, through successive differentiations, holds throughout" (3–4). His examples of increasing complexity include the global market, languages, human physiology, and transnational types—the European is more heterogeneous or individual than the Australian, the Anglo-American the most heterogeneous or individual, and therefore the most advanced, of all. (Later I shall address the nonnational bias of such claims: civilization is European or white, not national.) Spencer's explanation of this universal transformation of the homogeneous into the heterogeneous is the history of multiple effects from singular causes: "Every active force produces more than one change—every cause produces more than one effect. . . . From the law . . . it is an inevitable corollary that during the past there has been an ever-growing complication of things" (32–33).

From the early political economists, we have moved from a homogeneous human nature, in which variation is caused by the division of labor and accidents of location, to, with Spencer, heterogeneous populations, the most elite of which were increasingly differentiated and complex. From the historical causes of variation or heterogeneity in specific populations, we have moved to the laws of variation or heterogeneity. Under the influence of Darwinian biology and armchair anthropology, Spencer had biologized the division of labor, making differences between people evolutionary, or organically purposive.[11] The logic of his system with respect to what he called the "higher races" was toward increasing individualism, voluntary cooperation, and mutual aid in a division of labor and markets.

With respect to the lowest races, as he called them in *Descriptive Sociology*, the logic of his system converged with evangelical conceptions, in which, for example, savages and barbarians acted on impulse for immediate gratification, whereas civilized man's instincts were modified by reason.[12] Thus, unlike the savage or the barbarian, modern economic man's instinctive aversion to labor was offset by his desire for wealth, or, in his sexual economy, his instinct for immediate gratification was offset by the sublimation of his sexual appetite ("saving" rather than "spending"). This cultural evolutionary variation of biological determinism, in which what was biologically hereditary could itself be the result of cultural processes, was mutually reinforcing with political economy's notions of restraint, abstinence, or saving (Marx famously called attention to political economy's paradoxical status at that time as both the science of wealth and "the science of renunciation").[13]

The philosopher of biology Michael Ruse has argued persuasively that nineteenth-century notions of evolutionary progress were inextricable from nineteenth-century notions of Progress, or regular social improvement.[14] And Spencer, Ruse rightly says, has no rivals when it

11. The economic historian David Mitch has discussed how under the influence of Francis Galton's eugenics, and utilizing the principle of noncompeting groups, economics similarly moved from definitions of homogeneous workers to inherently diverse species of workers. Mitch sees this as increasing elitism. See "Victorian Views of the Nature of Work and Its Influence on the Nature of the Worker" (paper presented at the University of California, Santa Cruz, August 1994).

For a detailed history of biologism in Victorian theories of progress, see George Stocking Jr., *Victorian Anthropology* (New York: Free Press, 1987) and *After Tylor* (Madison: University of Wisconsin Press, 1995); and see Peter J. Bowler, *Evolution: The History of an Idea* (Berkeley: University of California Press, 1989), 288.

12. Herbert Spencer, *Descriptive Sociology* (London: Williams and Norgate, 1873).

13. Karl Marx, *Economic and Philosophical Manuscripts of 1844*, in *The Marx-Engels Reader*, ed. Robert Tucker (New York: Norton, 1978), 95–96. See also Stocking, *Victorian Anthropology*, 234–35, and James Eli Adams, *Dandies and Desert Saints: Styles of Victorian Masculinity* (Ithaca: Cornell University Press, 1995).

14. Michael Ruse, *Monad to Man: The Concept of Progress in Evolutionary Biology* (Cambridge: Harvard University Press, 1996).

comes to open, flagrant connection of social Progress with evolutionary (biological) progress (187). Ruse concludes that social Progress fu-
eled Spencer's theories of evolutionary progress; the latter were not deduced from the biological phenomena (191). Yet the force of Ruse's
research, which spans conceptions of progress in evolutionary biology
from the eighteenth century to the present, is that Spencer's bedrock of
social Progress was, and still is, consistently the popular basis of biological theories of progress. A belief in social Progress comes first, and
then people look to scientific theories to prop it up.

Central to this long-lived popular view is the division of labor that
leads to increasing specialization, differentiation, and individuation.
Ruse subscribes to Marx's thesis that Darwin's genius had been to
transfer the insights of political economy, which had at its heart a faith
in Progress through the division of labor, to the biological world: a
world of hard, slow physical groping gradually, though often unsuccessfully, toward a better state (Ruse, 169).

Nowhere is Spencer's biologization of Progress clearer than in *The
Social Organism* (1860), and nowhere, as Spencer says, is the "economic" model more "essential."[15] He sums up the evidence that justi-
fies, in detail, the comparison of societies to living organisms:

> That they gradually increase in mass; that they become little by
> little more complex; that, at the same time their parts grow more
> mutually dependent; and that they continue to live and grow as
> wholes, while successive generations of their units appear and
> disappear; are broad peculiarities which bodies politic display, in
> common with all living bodies; and in which they and living bod-
> ies differ from everything else. And on carrying out the compari-
> son in detail, we find that these major analogies involve many
> minor analogies, far closer than might have been expected. (432)

Thus Spencer writes of *profit:* "It is manifest that what in commercial
affairs we call profit answers to the excess of nutrition over waste in a
living body" (414). Of *commodities:* "We have come upon the analogy
which exists between the blood of a living body and the circulating
mass of commodities in the body politic" (415). Of *distribution* (after
a discussion of the railroads): "In living bodies, the local and variable
currents disappear when there grow up great centres of circulation. . . .
When in social bodies, there arise great centres of commercial activity,
producing and exchanging large quantities of commodities, the rapid
and continuous streams drawn in and emitted by these centres, subdue

15. In Spencer, *Essays,* 390.

all minor and local circulations" (421). Of *industrial arrangements:* "Having noticed some of the leading analogies between the development of industrial arrangements and that of the alimentary apparatus . . . we have to compare the appliances by a which a society, as a whole, is regulated, with those by which the movements of an individual creature are regulated" (423). Of *government:* "The analogy between the evolution of governmental structures in societies, and the evolution of governmental structures in living bodies, are [*sic*] more strikingly displayed during the formation of nations by the coalescence of small communities—a process already shown to be, in several respects, parallel to the development of those creatures that primarily consist of many like segments" (425).

Such analogies between the socioeconomic and the biological lead Spencer to cry no rivers over the tragedies that befall "simple" societies in the course of Progress: "Simple communities, like simple creatures, have so little mutual dependence of parts, that subdivision or mutilation causes but little inconvenience" (397; see the same language— "without inconvenience"—that James Mill had used when denying women the franchise; the biological analogy facilitates the denial of others' rights). Or, "The classes engaged in agriculture and laborious occupations in general are much less susceptible, intellectually and emotionally, than the rest; and especially less so than the classes of highest mental culture" (400). As Ruse says, in Spencer, according to the law that every active force produces more than one change and every cause produces more than one effect, phenomena explode or ripple outward and thus homogeneity necessarily evolves into heterogeneity (Ruse 186), assuming an increasing division of labor. The opposite of Progress, of course, was degeneration, which was defined in biology (for example, by E. Ray Lankester) as "a loss of organisation making the descendent far simpler or lower in structure than its ancestor" (cited in Ruse, 224). Lankester and others feared that Europeans might degenerate owing to too much leisure or, conversely, too little need to apply themselves to tasks in the division of labor.

In the nineteenth century, the ideas of both biological and social progress were inextricably linked with the idea of civilization. This has been summarized by the geographer Peter Taylor.

> Social science evolved at the same time that Europe finally confirmed its dominium over the rest of the world. This gave rise to the obvious question: why was this small part of the world able to defeat all rivals and impose its will on the Americas, Africa, and Asia? . . . [A]nswers to [this question] were found not at the

scale of the state but in terms of civilizations. It was Europe as "Western" or "modern" civilization that had outgunned and outproduced all-comers, not Britain or France or Germany despite the sizes of their individual empires. The domination was a collective European enterprise, not a particular state enterprise. This concern with how Europe did it coincided with the major intellectual transition associated with Charles Darwin. . . . Evolutionary theory was popular in early social science because it provided scientific legitimation to the assumption of progress that culminated in the self-evident superiority of contemporary European society. Hence sociologists and anthropologists could produce their famous stage theories of social evolution ending in industrial civilization. Historians could identify paths of progress to modern civilization and the many cul-de-sacs of civilizations not blessed with the secret of progress. . . . Geographers joined in with their theories of geographical determinism to show that Europe and European-settler regions had the necessary climate to stimulate ever higher levels of civilizations, leaving other less fortunate civilizations "immobile." [16]

Taylor calls these studies "comparative civilization" studies. They included the global evolutionary comparisons of armchair anthropologists and historians working with newly generated statistical data, though they had roots in the universal histories of the Enlightenment. [17] Their function was to interpret the past and indicate improvement, to evaluate difference and propose that peoples could be ranked along a common course (the evolving Family of Man), and to supply an optimistic vision of human destiny and a faith in the ameliorative power of change. In them, the idea of European or white "civilization" implies civil society, private property, the social order, and, most important for the culturalist, refinement or taste at the individual level. The "civilized man," or Spencer's individual, is their apex, though he had a history in the discourse of civilizations that put him in dialectical relation with savage or barbarian Others who were lacking in taste or discrimination. [18]

16. P. J. Taylor, "Embedded Statism and the Social Sciences: Opening Up to New Spaces," *Environment and Planning A* 28, no. 11 (1996): 1917–28.

17. See especially Stocking, *After Tylor.*

18. For distinctions among savagery, barbarism, and civilization, see Lewis H. Morgan, *Ancient Society* (London: Henry Holt, 1877); Stocking, *After Tylor.* For an analytic account of the terms, see R. G. Collingwood, *The New Leviathan: Or Man, Society, Civilisation, and Barbarism,* rev. ed. (Oxford: Clarendon, 1992). For the most influential

Consider the world-historical formulations of comparative civilizations:

Shall all nations someday approach the state of civilization attained by the most enlightened, the freest, the most emancipated from prejudices of present-day peoples, such as the French, for example, and the Anglo-Americans? Shall not the vast interval which separates these peoples from the bondage of nations subservient to kings, from the barbarism of the African tribes and the ignorance of savages, gradually disappear? Do there exist on the globe countries whose inhabitants nature has condemned never to enjoy liberty, never to exercise their reason? Condorcet, *An Historical Picture of the Progress of the Human Mind* (1795).[19]

Condorcet's answer to the final rhetorical question was a resounding "No." In Hegel's *Philosophy of History,* the progressive disciplining through self-consciousness of "uncontrolled natural will" confers modern freedom, or freedom under constraint, producing the self-regulating modern Western individual:

The history of the world travels from east to west, for Europe is absolutely the end of history, Asia the beginning. . . . [F]or although the earth forms a sphere, history performs no circle around it, but has on the contrary, a determinate east, viz., Asia. Here rises the outward physical sun, and in the west it sinks down: here [in the West] . . . rises the sun of self-consciousness, which diffuses a nobler brilliance. The history of the world is the discipline of the uncontrolled natural will, bringing it into obedience to a universal principle and conferring subjective freedom. The east knew and to the present day knows only that *one* is free; the Greek and Roman world, that *some* are free; the German world knows that *all* are free. Hegel, *Philosophy of History* (1837).[20]

---

of recent theories of civilizing, see Norbert Elias, *The Civilising Process,* 2 vols. (Oxford: Oxford University Press, 1978 and 1982).

19. Excerpt in *The Idea of Progress: A Collection of Readings,* ed. J. Teggart, with an introduction by George H. Hildebrand (Berkeley: University of California Press, 1949), 336. For theories of progress, see also Sidney Pollard, *The Idea of Progress* (London: Watts, 1968); Charles Van Doren, *The Idea of Progress* (New York: Praeger, 1967); W. R. Inge, *The Idea of Progress* (Oxford: Romanes Lecture, 1920).

20. In Teggart, *Idea of Progress,* 405–6.

In Comte, who strongly influenced the Mills, who in turn strongly influenced policy in the colonies, the disciplined, self-regulating elite are specifically white, or European. Comte anticipates applying the knowledge acquired from the civilized elite to "the advantages of the inferior":

[It is only] the selectest part, the vanguard of the human race, that we have to study; the greater part of the white race, or the European nations,—even restricting ourselves, at least in regard to modern times, to the nations of Western Europe. . . . In short, we are here concerned only with social phenomena which have influenced, more or less, the gradual disclosure of the connected phases that have brought up mankind to its existing state. When we have learned what to look for from the elite of humanity, we shall know how the superior portion should intervene for the advantage of the inferior. Comte, *Positive Philosophy* (1830–42).[21]

Comte ultimately believed in political laissez-faire, perhaps only underestimating the degree of interference in other cultures "the maintenance of general peace" or "the natural extension of industrial relations" would entail: "It is not our business to suppose that each race or nation must imitate in all particulars the mode of progression of those who have gone before. Except for the maintenance of general peace, or the natural extension of industrial relations, Western Europe must avoid any large political intervention in the East; and there is as much to be done at home as can occupy all the faculties of the most advanced portion of the human race" (in Teggart, 396). Such assumptions as these pervade economic thought of the nineteenth century and are inextricable from notions of economic man as producer and, later, as consumer, culminating in the European man of taste.

This idea of civilized man as the progressively disciplined elite—as in "that's damned civilized of you" (notice how it is parallel with the American "that's damned white of you")—everywhere pervades late Victorian aesthetics of taste. And here the common speech of "civilization" is even more significant than the grand theories just cited.[22] From Disraeli's *Tancred* (1847, the secret of which is a white queen of Ara-

---

21. Ibid., 393.
22. For the importance of attention to popular discourse and local usages, see Paul Keating, "Cultural Values and Entrepreneurial Action: The Case of the Irish Republic," in *Culture in History: Production, Consumption, and Values in Historical Perspective,* ed. Joseph Melling and Jonathan Barry (Exeter: University of Exeter Press, 1992), 92–108.

bia) to Haggard's *She* (1887, the secret of which is a white queen of Africa), the empire of literature was tantamount to the literature of empire in its obsession with comparative civilizations and appropriation of popular evolutionary models. By the end of the nineteenth century, however, the narratives of progress were less likely to terminate in Reason or Freedom in their Hegelian or Kantian senses than in (1) the sublime and *irrational* images of degeneration, devolution, or fear of engulfment in the late Victorian Gothic or in (2) economic rationality and the individual's freedom to maximize self-interest. And we should note that in the course of the nineteenth century, the idea of "interest" was increasingly dissociated from the social good, the social body, or even sociology and used more in relation to individual psychology. (See the discussion of Smith and Arnold below.) As psychological models were replacing the sociological by the fin de siècle in both aesthetics and economics, deep, disturbed Unreason, on one hand, or economic rationality and instrumental reason, on the other, were replacing Reason as the mind's divine capacity to improve its own condition and that of others (the Owenite usage discussed above). The psychological aesthetics and psychological fiction of the fin de siècle calculated pleasure and pain in the pursuit of happiness as self-interest (which was very different from Bentham's utilitarian pursuit of happiness or Smith's Invisible Hand). Their economics were formalized in Richard Jenning's physiological psychology, which underlay Jevons's marginal utility theory, and in Francis Ysidro Edgeworth's *Mathematical Psychics* (1881).

One of the few late-Victorian economists who defended making interpersonal comparisons of utility, Edgeworth argued, against Mill, that in calculating the amount of utility economically possible in a given society we had to weigh "the comfort of a limited number" against "numbers with limited comfort." He opted for the comfort of a limited number on the principle that the capacity for pleasure evolves. Thus men have more capacity for pleasure than women, and Europeans have more capacity for pleasure than non-Europeans, so the greatest happiness, mathematically speaking, will be achieved by allocating it not to the greatest number (with their relatively low capacities) but to the most highly evolved. As Edgeworth says, "In the general advance, the most advanced should advance most."[23] "In fact," he writes in a mixed Darwinian metaphor, "the happiness of some of the lower classes may be sacrificed to that of the higher classes. . . . Contemplating the combined movements we seem to see the vast composite

23. F. Y. Edgeworth, *Mathematical Psychics* (London: C. Kegan Paul, 1881), 68.

flexible organism, the play and the work of whose members are continually readjusted, by degrees advancing up the line of evolution; the
parts about the front advancing most, the members of the other extremity more slowly moving on and largely dying off" (ibid., 71). In
this decadent image of a rough beast whose front parts advance while
its hindmost parts die, we see how the calculations of taste implied a
global and a gender politics.

The aesthetics were formalized in Pater's aesthetics as the precise
calculations of pleasure received by the critic from the work (the Decadent critic with which this chapter began, consuming the culture of the
world); Wilde's economies of desire in *Salomé* or *The Picture of Dorian Gray;* Vernon Lee's calculations of bodily pleasures derived from
art in "psychological aesthetics"; the aesthetico-psychological science
of stylistic analysis; and all the literature concerned with taste that
distinguished some social groups (women, Celts, Africans, working
people) from others.[24] Today the critique and cultural studies of comparative civilizations abound, whether the simianization of the Celt or
the African, the feminization of the gay male, or the eroticization of
the working or "productive" woman.[25] I have stressed how much these
historical practices of "Othering" revealed by our contemporary cultural critique evolved in contradistinction to taste and the individual
civilized man as consumer, with his self-consciousness, self-command,
autonomy, and capacity to discriminate.

"Comparative civilizational studies" ironically terminated in the
first half of the twentieth century, with the fragmentation of Europe
into warring states during the two world wars and the consequent de-
facement of Europe's civilized image. Ideas of civilization and progress
were replaced, under North American hegemony, by the language of
nation-states and of development. Peter Taylor describes the differences between the progress of civilizations, which was a putative
achievement and included moral and political progress, and the development—note the preferred biological term—of nations, which was
an economic inevitability:

First, theories of development are fundamentally state centric in
nature: whereas civilisations might "progress," it is states that
"develop." Second, the USA becomes the exemplar state. For in-

24. See Regenia Gagnier, "A Critique of Practical Aesthetics," in *Aesthetics and Ideology,* ed. George Levine (New Brunswick: Rutgers University Press, 1994), 264–82.
25. This literature is growing at a rate beyond comprehensibility, but one might begin with Edward Said, *Culture and Imperialism* (1994), McClintock, *Imperial Leather,*
Robert J. C. Young, *Colonial Desire* (London: Routledge, 1995), and Kelly Hurley, *The
Gothic Body* (Cambridge: Cambridge University Press, 1996).

stance, in the most famous of all development models, states are allocated to different stages but the highest level, the "stage of high mass consumption," hardly disguises the contemporary United States. . . . Third, unlike progress and civilizations, development and states define a world in which beneficial social change is available to all. The development message was a simple one: follow the required policy prescriptions and you too can be like us—developed, which meant affluent, which meant the United States. ("Embedded Statism," 1922)

Clearly the major drift that has taken place between nineteenth-century progress and twentieth-century development is that the ethical and political implications of progress and their accompanying exclusiveness and hierarchy are replaced by the global production of goods as commodities for mass consumption. As Disraeli presciently said quite early on, "the European who talks of progress mistakes comfort for civilisation."[26] Although there are still liberals who like to believe that the advantages of civilization in the form of the Good Life follow from economic development as we have known it, the second half of the twentieth century has produced a growing body of critical work on development as a discourse about economic transformation, specifically the integration of less developed states into the global market or, in fully depoliticized terms, the "war on poverty."[27] Indeed, Achebe's awesome charge against the fin de siècle novel *Heart of Darkness*—that Conrad was "a thoroughgoing racist" in that he supplied no alternative frame of reference for Africa than as setting and backdrop for Europe—could be applied to the development story.[28] "Can nobody see the preposterous and perverse arrogance in thus reducing Africa to the role of props for the breakup of one petty European mind?" Achebe asked, as an economist might ask whether that great and diverse continent is more than a debit line in the ledgers of the World Bank. Unlike civilization, development is not the culmination of Reason in the world (with the flash images from Hegel, Comte, and Co.) but economic fiddling with competing *interests* and an increasingly impenetrable discursive preoccupation with the development apparatus itself. This is the transition that Francis Fukuyama ambiva-

26. Benjamin Disraeli, *Tancred* (London: Peter Davies, 1927), 233. Also quoted in Inge, *Idea of Progress*, 29.

27. See James Ferguson, *The Anti-Politics Machine: "Development," Depoliticization, and Bureaucratic Power in Lesotho* (Minneapolis: University of Minnesota Press, 1994), 3–21.

28. Chinua Achebe, "An Image of Africa: Racism in Conrad's *Heart of Darkness*," in *Heart of Darkness* (New York: Norton, 1988), 251–62.

lently heralded as the end of history with its mighty rivalries and spectacular pageantry in economic cost-benefit analyses.[29]

In sum, the man of taste was also the modern, civilized man, and both notions were inextricable from political and economic notions of progress and civilization. He was conceived in dialectical relation not only with women but also with both the internal British barbarian, or the upper-class descendent of feudalism, and internal and external savages, who did not share his complexity or his self-command. Similarly, the end of taste in aesthetic relativism is also the principle that "tastes are exogenous" in neoclassical economics, and both are inextricable from economic individualism, social individuation, and twentieth-century ideas of development as having the aim of high mass consumption.

Recent work suggests that by the mid-nineteenth century earlier forms of sympathy and toleration had begun to contract as biological, psychological, or anthropological forms of explanation extended their domains. Using theories of race, Cora Kaplan sees pre-1850 recognition of likeness or universalism turning to intolerance of difference: economies of sympathy gave way to economies of instinctive repulsion between races just at the moment when races were technically emancipated to intermingle as equals.[30] The sociological explanation is the uncertainty of roles after mid-century: how would the growing presence of freed slaves, wage laborers, factory girls, and so forth affect traditional social relations? One contributing factor suggested by this chapter is the increased emphasis on individuation in the second half of the century. The fear of difference that Kaplan notes was in part fed by the perception of just how different—differentiated—people would become from one another as a result of the division of labor and multiplication of tastes that were essential to modernity. Spencer's idea that all progress was progress toward individualism instilled at the broadest cultural levels fears of anomie, isolation, and egoism that had gone well beyond Smith's idea of "self-interest" leading to the social good.[31]

It was precisely this fear of "selfish" individualism—as opposed to Smith's more benign, mechanistic "self-interestedness" mutually bene-

---

29. Francis Fukuyama, *The End of History and the Last Man* (New York: Avon, 1992). See chapter 2 above.

30. Cora Kaplan, "The Toyseller" (lecture presented at the University of Exeter, 17 May 1999). See also Kaplan's "Black Figures/English Landscape," *Victorian Literature and Culture* 27, no. 2 (1999): 501–5.

31. On the distinction between Smithian self-interest and mid-Victorian fears of selfishness, see Donald Winch, *Riches and Poverty: An Intellectual History of Political Economy in Britain 1750–1834* (Cambridge: Cambridge University Press, 1996), 390.

fiting all—that led to Matthew Arnold's *Friendship's Garland* (1866–71) and the more important *Culture and Anarchy* (1869), which offered aesthetics, or "Culture," as a solution to anomie, anarchy, and class conflict. (*Culture and Anarchy* was subtitled *An Essay in Political and Social Criticism.*) Elsewhere I have written about the roots of Arnold's literary method in contemporary practices of mass media, journalism, and advertising.[32] What has quite rightly been called Arnold's Platonism, dialectics, transcendentalism, or Idealism, may also be seen as mass society's competitive oppositions: best self versus ordinary self, sweetness versus light, Hellenism versus Hebraism, and so forth.[33] Arnold's problem in proposing the cultured individual as a solution to the egoism of mass anarchy was similar to the problem of the individual in mass society that began this chapter. The "inwardness" that Arnold thought essential to counteract the "machinery" and "fanaticism" of modernity, when presented in the rhetorical terms of mass market (commodified) society, was reduced to caricatures of "Culture"—like recent do-it-yourself lists of Great Books representing faded ideas of cultural capital. Yet Arnold's fears that the cultivation of the individual under mass market conditions could turn to competitive selfishness and social anomie remain some of the most prescient political and social criticism of modernity. At stake was the future of individualism itself: the bourgeois individual regulating herself for the social good or the self-interested, self-maximizing individual of "hedonic" consumer society.

"Perfection, as culture conceives it," wrote Arnold in *Culture and Anarchy,* "is not possible while the individual remains isolated. The individual is required . . . to carry others along with him. . . . [This is] at variance with our strong individualism and materialistic civilization" (94–95). In the chapter called "Doing as One Likes," Arnold first introduces the idea of anarchy: "The central idea of English life and politics is *the assertion of personal liberty* . . . but as feudalism dies out . . . we are in danger of drifting toward anarchy" (117, emphasis in original). At this point, Arnold introduces the state, "to control individual wills in the name of an interest wider than that of individuals" (117). Freedom without what Arnold calls right reason equals anarchy. And Arnold knows that for the British, as for Hegel, freedom is at present available only to those at the forefront of Progress: "It never was any part of our creed that the great right . . . of an Irishman, or,

32. Regenia Gagnier, *Idylls of the Marketplace: Oscar Wilde and the Victorian Public* (Stanford: Stanford University Press, 1986), esp. 27–29.

33. For criticism on Arnold's Idealism see Super's "Critical and Explanatory Notes" in Arnold's *Culture and Anarchy,* esp. 415–17.

indeed, of anybody on earth except an Englishman, is to do as he likes; and we can have no scruple at all about abridging, if necessary, a non-Englishman's assertion of personal liberty" (121).

Arnold's "principle" of the relation of the individual and the social group to the state is developed in this section—"Doing as One Likes"—and the next, on class conflict, "Barbarians, Philistines, and Populace"; for class egoism is as destructive to culture as individual egoism. Arnold's "principle" must distinguish the self-regulating bourgeois subsuming her desires to the right reason of the state from the self-interest-maximizing individual or class of political economy:

> Now, if culture, which simply means trying to perfect oneself and one's mind as part of oneself, brings light, and light shows us that there is nothing so very blessed in merely doing as one likes, that the really blessed thing is to like what right reason ordains . . . [w]e have got a much wanted principle, a principle of authority, to counteract the tendency to anarchy.
>
> But how to organise this authority? . . . How to get your *State,* summing up the right reason of the community? (123–24)

As the individual's warring passions must be harmonized by the regulating will, so the state's social groups must harmonize according to their "best selves" for the good of the whole. Like many Victorian social critics, Arnold admired the Germans for their commitment to duty, unity, and the state as against Anglo-American individualism (161 and passim). Yet owing to the peculiarities of the British class system he figures his state as an individual whose different capacities had to be harmonized. Thus a "hard middle class" that tended toward machinery (work and money) and fanaticism ("the one thing needful") needed the complementary aesthetic virtues of the aristocracy— "beautiful" ease, serenity, and politeness and their more "sublime" "high spirits, defiant courage, and pride of resistance" (125–34). For its part, the aristocracy needed the complement of ideas, lest its serenity degenerate, as it had under current conditions, to futility and sterility. Similarly, the idea of "country" or nation was a *sentiment* that needed a state's complementary "working power" (ibid.). The role of supporters of culture is to "hinder the unchecked predominance of that class-life which is the affirmation of our ordinary self and seasonably disconcert mankind in their worship of machinery" (146). If we want individual freedom, Arnold concludes, meaning enlightened self-interest rather than selfishness, "the State must act for many years to come" (162). Thus Arnold's efforts were continuously to elevate self-interest above the selfishness associated with competitive individualism.

In *Friendship's Garland*, in which Arnold used Europeans, especially Germans, to criticize British individualism, he also used America to represent the democratic spirit of the age, the *Geist* behind which Britain lagged. The Americans showed "a feeling for ideas, a vivacity and play of mind, which our middle class has not, and which comes to the Americans, probably from their democratic life with its ardent hope, its forward stride, its gaze fixed on the future" (30). Arminius, Arnold's European mouthpiece in *Friendship's Garland* (and an ancient Teutonic hero beloved in *Volk* mythology), warns the British that the Americans "have got the lead" in equality and democracy as well as trade: "After 1815, we believed in you as nowadays we are coming to believe in America . . . unless you change, unless your middle class grows more intelligent, you will tell upon the world less and less, and end by being a second Holland" (27).[34]

Yet in just three years' time, when Arnold wrote the last addition to *Culture and Anarchy,* the preface, he had come to fear democracy as much as selfishness. America's spirit of democracy had degenerated to massification. America now represented "that chosen home of newspapers and politics . . . without a general intelligence" (243), only "partiality of interestedness," not the "totality" of vision that culture now had to stand in for (252). "The best which has been thought and said in the world"—the hierarchical, evaluative idea of culture and aesthetics that Arnold's name has come to evoke—was explicitly introduced in the preface to oppose the "fanaticism" of religious sects. Under conditions of mass education, Arnold has been taken as representative of narrow and elite notions of culture; yet *Culture and Anarchy* is an extended polemic against the selfish interestedness of individuals, classes, and religions.

The consummate man of taste and spokesperson for the highest aesthetic life, Oscar Wilde drew heavily on Arnold in "The Soul of Man Under Socialism" (1891) when he proposed a welfare and industrial state as precondition of a "New Individualism" characterized by Christlike inwardness and claimed that the pen of contemporary journalism was "mightier than the paving-stone and can be made as offen-

---

34. See Immanuel Wallerstein on Dutch investment in British wars: "this symbiotic arrangement between a formerly hegemonic power and the new rising star provided graceful retirement income for the one and a crucial push forward against the rival for the other. The pattern was repeated later in the period from 1873 to 1945, with Great Britain playing the Dutch role and the US in the English role." Wallerstein, *Modern World-System II,* 281.

sive as the brickbat."[35] I shall conclude this chapter, however, not with
Wilde's most sustained polemic about individualism but with two
works by Wilde that explore, tragically, the pleasures of "doing as one
likes" and that will return us to the consuming image of the *Mona Lisa*
with which it began. *The Portrait of Mr. W. H.,* "The Soul of Man
Under Socialism," "The Critic as Artist," "Pen, Pencil, and Poison,"
and much of his criticism testify to Wilde's interest in taste, distinction,
style, subjectivism, and individualism. Like the connoisseur Des Esseintes consuming the exotica of the world outside the West, Wilde
was tempted by the revelation of personality through choice, preference, and leisure or idleness (as opposed to work or productivity).
Chapter 11 of *The Picture of Dorian Gray* (1891) is a textbook psychology of fin de siècle economic man. Chapter 10 concludes with Dorian's discovery of a fascinating book, a story of an insatiable young
Parisian "who spent his life trying to realize . . . all the passions and
modes of thought that belonged to every century except his own."[36]
For years, we are told in chapter 11, Dorian could not free himself
from its power of suggestion: "The more he knew, the more he desired
to know. He had mad hungers that grew more ravenous as he fed
them" (142). He cultivates "a new Hedonism" that, à la Pater, "was
never to accept any theory or system that involved the sacrifice of any
mode of passionate experience" (13). Scarcity is again assured by mortality: one must "concentrate oneself upon the moments of a life that
is itself but a moment" (144). For years, Dorian "searches for sensations that would be at once new and delightful" (145). His conspicuous consumption, variously referred to as "collecting" and "accumulating," like Des Esseintes's, includes the products of "all parts of the
world" (147): perfumes, music, embroideries, tapestries, ecclesiastical
vestments, and finally up to the highest order of pleasure, not the crude
material goods themselves but rather "the wonderful stories" of the
goods, or the rarefied, distinctive pleasure of literature itself.

Yet while the desire for escalating orders of goods is itself insatiable,
each good reaches its point of diminishing marginal utility: "Yet, after
some time, [Dorian] wearied of them [all]" (147), and he experiences
"that terrible *taedium vitae* that comes on those to whom life denies
nothing" (157). In the midst of this cycle of excess and ennui, Dorian
finds himself in a society that prefers form to substance. The narrator

35. See my discussion of "The Soul of Man" in *Idylls of the Marketplace,* 29–34.
36. Oscar Wilde, *The Picture of Dorian Gray and Selected Stories* (New York: Signet, 1962), 138.

describes market society as society of the spectacle, of style or form over substance: "Civilized society is never very ready to believe anything to the detriment of those who are both rich and fascinating," says the narrator. "It feels instinctively that manners are of more importance than morals, and, in its opinion, the highest respectability is of much less value than the possession of a good chef" (154). The very lack of substance, for those who can afford the multiplication of pleasure, is liberating. "Form" or "insincerity" is "merely a method by which we can multiply our personalities . . . man was a being with myriad lives and myriad sensations, a complex multiform creature" (155). The chapter, a critique of the morality of excess, reaches a climax with a fantastic crescendo of insatiables: "Pietro Riario . . . whose beauty was equalled only by his debauchery . . . who gilded a boy that he might serve at the feast as Ganymede; . . . Ezzelin, whose melancholy could be cured only by the spectacle of death, and who had a passion for red blood as other men have for red wine . . . Giambattista Cibo . . . into whose torpid veins the blood of three lads was infused" (157–58), and so forth until the famous concluding sentence, "There were moments when [Dorian] looked on evil simply as a mode through which he could realize his conception of the beautiful."

The consequence of Dorian's insatiability, escalation of wants, and formal equivalencing of all desires in the cultivation of his personality is, of course, his portrait, where the shame of his consumption—his accumulated personality—is permanently, absolutely, recorded. At this price, he is given a beauty without limit, the scarcest commodity in a mortal world, that is his sole source of value to others, who commodify and consume him in turn. Pater had written that Mona Lisa's "experience of the world" and "imaginative loves" had "been to her but as the sound of lyres and flutes," and lived only in the delicacy with which it had "moulded the changing lineaments, and tinged the eyelids and the hands" (46–47). Dorian's portrait tells an altogether uglier story, indicating Wilde's substantial moralization of Pater.

Wilde's *Salomé* (1894) is perhaps the most dramatic representation we have of the world of neoclassical economics, a thought-experiment on the limits of desire, the assertion of personal preference over social values and of subjective isolation over social life. From the first lines of the play the characters are isolated within their subjective desires, without common standards or values. The Young Syrian cannot hear the Page; the Pharisees and Sadducees contest among themselves the existence of angels; the Nubian and the Cappadocian, the existence of gods; the Cappadocian thinks it a terrible crime to strangle a king, yet

the soldier finds kings to be "like other folk . . . having but one neck."[37]
Herodias's Page and the Young Syrian are lost in their respective love
lyrics, while their interlocutors the soldiers are concerned only with
Herod. Tigellinus finds the Stoics ridiculous. The Jews do not agree
among themselves. The Syrian and Herod are obsessed with Salomé,
Salomé with Iokanaan. Salomé and Iokanaan are simply the most mor-
bidly self-absorbed in their respective desires, with Iokanaan desiring
all to seek out the Son of Man and Salomé desiring the prophet's body,
his hair, and his mouth.

Nothing has value for its own sake, but all is made or marred by
the degree of desire it evokes from highly individuated personalities.
Salomé rejects Herod's wine, his fruits, and his offer to sit at the throne,
for she is not thirsty, hungry, or tired. He offers her jewels and "great
treasures above all price" (425) in exchange for the head she desires,
but she has a surfeit of these. Herod himself is currently experiencing
the diminishing marginal utility of his wife Herodias, and he therefore
desires the more novel pleasures of her daughter the Princess of Judea.
Moreover, the desires on display in the play are, as they say in economics, transitive and complete. As Salomé says, "I am athirst for thy
beauty; I am hungry for thy body; and neither wine nor apples can
appease my desire. . . . Neither the floods nor the great waters can
quench my passion" (428). As the kingdom (Arnold's state) crumbles,
Herod retires to contemplate himself in mirrors, and the soldiers advance to kill her, Salomé's only response is to ask, "But what matter?
What matter? I have kissed thy mouth" (429).

Critics of neoclassical economics frequently point out that the satisfaction of preferences does not equal the maximization of utility or the
maximization of welfare. Neoclassical economics is concerned with
the individual consumer getting the goods, not distributing them rationally or even using them. Salomé gets Iokanaan in the long run, but
only in the form of a dead head with bloody lips, and the kingdom is
destroyed in the process.

I shall get fairly technical for a moment and suggest that *Salomé*
illustrates the formal theory of rational choice. The play epitomizes the
Decadence, that is, presents the world that rational choice theorists
take to be the real world. The theory of rational choice gives agents
the aim of maximally satisfying their preferences. Agents are assumed
to be able to order comprehensively all states of affairs open to them
according to their preferences and then to choose the states of affairs

37. Oscar Wilde, *Salomé,* in *The Portable Oscar Wilde,* ed. Richard Aldington and
Stanley Weintraub (New York: Penguin, 1981), 396.

that they most prefer. Critics of the theory have claimed that there is no unified interpretation of what "preferences" are such that it is always rational to satisfy them.[38] In *Salomé,* for instance, preferences include (a) dispositions or habits to choose one thing over another (for example, the preferences of the Jews, the Nazarenes, and the soldiers), (b) desires ranked by their strength or intensity (Salomé's), (c) informed desires (Herodias's, her Page's), (d) desires of a higher order (Iokanaan's), (e) judgments of the relative worth of options (Herod's), (f) bare "likings" ranked by intensity (for fruit or wine or jewels), (g) whims, impulses, or yens, similarly ranked (a nonbiblical view of Salomé's caprice with regard to Iokanaan's head).

As mentioned above, the formal theory of rational choice demands that agents' preferences be ranked in a complete transitive ordering, for example, Salomé's overriding preference for Iokanaan's head. Indeed, one critic of choice theory has concluded that transitivity and completeness requirements are unconditionally valid only for fanatics and monomaniacs who value only one thing—Arnold's "one thing needful."[39]

Formal rational choice theory also maintains a "Sunk-Cost Rule" and a principle that "tastes are exogenous." The former says that it is irrational to consider sunk costs in choosing among future plans, thus working against the values of commitment and tradition and endorsing the perspective of speculators, opportunists, and casual lovers. Herodias has left her husband for the novel pleasures of Herod, and Herod, when the play opens, is bored with Herodias and eyeing Salomé. In the second case, of exogenous tastes, choice theory never questions the content of preferences or tastes, nor indicates with respect to maximization when "enough" can be "too much," nor does it sufficiently draw attention to tradeoffs when trading. Unlike in the biblical texts (Matt. 14:6–12, Mark 6:18–29), in which Salomé is instructed by her mother and has no evident desires of her own, in Wilde's play Salomé's, the Young Syrian's, Herod's, the Jews', and the Nazarenes' tastes are given as overdeterminedly individual. It is a world without critique, or self-critique, or even dialogue. It is the world of neoclassical economics, but it is, in fact, a very un-Wildean world.

It is an un-Wildean world because in the majority of his works Wilde is critical not just of the status quo ante but also of the construc-

38. See Elizabeth Anderson, "Some Problems in the Normative Theory of Rational Choice with Consequences for Empirical Research" (University of Michigan, Ann Arbor, 1990); and Neva R. Goodwin, *Building Anew on Marshall's Principles,* vol. 1 of *Social Economics: An Alternative Theory* (New York: St. Martin's, 1991).

39. Anderson, "Rational Choice," 9.

tion of taste or preference, including the constraints on the formation of taste and preference. He is also self-critical to the point of paradox, and dialogical rather than monological.[40] Although Wilde was tempted by the individualism, subjectivism, anarchy, even the consumerism central to fin de siècle aesthetics and economics, he, like Pater, never entirely abandoned his commitment to the more substantive values of the earlier Victorians.

Both classical and neoclassical Victorian economists equally shared the *Buddenbrooks* model (after Thomas Mann's novel of that name—the novel most cited by economic theorists from 1902, when it was published, to 1980). In *Buddenbrooks,* the first generation sought money; the second, born to money, sought civic position; the third, born to comfort and status, sought the life of music. Victorian economists, that is, believed that with maturity, society would increasingly develop appreciation of the *highest* order of goods, what Jevons called "the pleasure derived from the beauties of nature and art" (*Theory of Political Economy,* 43), and that the man of taste would evolve correspondingly. Then came the 1980s, when many economists abandoned the notion of declining marginal utility of income: there was no amount of wealth that sufficed for the comfort of Edgeworth's "limited number," and that limited number displayed its insatiability, its highly evolved capacity for pleasure, but not in the sense that the Victorians meant. Modern consumers no longer subscribed to the hierarchy of goods as they pursued markets in everything from music to education to babies to blood, opting for individualism over evolution or progress. We shall return in the last two chapters to the 1980s.

40. See Gagnier, *Idylls of the Marketplace;* Gagnier, "Critique of Practical Aesthetics."

FOUR

Production, Reproduction, and Pleasure in Victorian Aesthetics

From the time of Kant until the end of the nineteenth century, there were at least three aesthetics that coexisted and sometimes converged and that are strikingly revealed in a novel by Thomas Hardy. Even naive readers typically sense something "Aesthetic" about *Jude the Obscure*. It was published in 1895, toward the sunset of late-Victorian Aestheticism, and it includes a number of tropes familiar to that declining genre: a Romantic longing for the Beautiful, a Ruskinian appreciation of creativity and the conditions of creation, and themes of taste and discrimination, each representing a distinct, if permeable, aesthetic tradition. Ostensibly the story of a working-class autodidact who attempts unsuccessfully to make the proverbial "better life" for himself and his family, it is also the proverbial struggle between spirit and flesh: Jude's youthful attraction to his carnal first wife has disastrous consequences for his subsequent union with a soulmate and equal, the delicate and intellectual "New Woman" Sue Bridehead. First Sue's body and then her spirit are tortuously subjugated to Victorian marriage laws. This chapter will refer to *Jude* to illustrate the three strands of aesthetics that have been obscured in recent literary and aesthetic theory and that knowledge of the economic models of the period renders salient: the ethical (having to do with self-regulation), the political economic (having to do with models of production and reproduction), and the biological or physiological (having to do with taste,

Earlier versions of this chapter appeared as "Production, Reproduction, and Pleasure in Victorian Aesthetics and Economics" in *Victorian Sexual Dissidence*, ed. Richard Dellamora (Chicago: University of Chicago Press, 1999), 127–46 (© 1999 by The University of Chicago. All rights reserved); as "Productive Bodies, Pleasured Bodies: On Victorian Aesthetics" in *Women and British Aestheticism*, ed. Talia Schaffer and Kathy Psomiades (Charlottesville: University Press of Virginia, 1999), 270–89; and as "Productive, Reproductive, and Consuming Bodies in Victorian Aesthetic Models" in *Body Matters: Feminism, Textuality, Corporeality*, ed. Avril Horner and Angela Keane (Manchester: Manchester University Press, 2000), 43–57.

pleasure, and consumption). I am especially eager to analyze this history of aesthetics just now, when the perception of aesthetics' social utility is at a low point and its history of contestation reduced to "*the* Aesthetic*.*" Before turning to the history, however, it is instructive to consider some of these recent treatments of aesthetics.

Currently, the most popular account of aesthetics holds that it has functioned as a mode of social control and self-regulation since the early days of bourgeois society. This interpretation, of art as ideology, has been strongly emphasized in recent treatments of the novel as a genre and has been the concern of structuralist, poststructuralist, and Foucauldian students of power, control, and self-regulation.[1] In the second account, "the Aesthetic" has been the site of individualist, passionate revolt. This follows the tendency of emancipatory or utopian aesthetics, which certain kinds of Marxists often trace from Schiller through Marx, to Marcuse, to the aesthetics of marginal groups today.[2] A third account I call the narrow view of art for art's sake, the view that art and literature comprise a disinterested realm of beauty that provides an escape from the vicissitudes of modernity; that is, only art can make one free, for society never will.

Very ambitious critics, such as Terry Eagleton in *The Ideology of the Aesthetic,* combine the first and second, ideological and utopian, accounts to produce a duality of "the Aesthetic."[3] The argument for the duality of the aesthetic goes like this: The aesthetic has been a site of state power since the rise of modernity, whose social organization depends less on external constraints and visible exercises of authority than on an ideological model of self-regulating and self-determining subjectivity. Modern society cultivated a new form of human subjectivity that inscribed the law in itself rather than in an external authority. Instead of relying on the coercive powers of absolutism, bourgeois so-

1. See aesthetic applications of Foucault's *Discipline and Punish* such as Nancy Armstrong's *Desire and Domestic Fiction* (New York: Oxford University Press, 1987), John Bender's *Imagining the Penitentiary* (Chicago: University of Chicago Press, 1987), and D. A. Miller's *The Novel and the Police* (Berkeley: University of California Press, 1988).

2. I have discussed emancipatory aesthetics and the third account—art for art's sake—in "A Critique of Practical Aesthetics," in *Aesthetics and Ideology,* ed. George Levine (New Brunswick: Rutgers University Press, 1994), 264–83. See also my introduction to *Critical Essays on Oscar Wilde* (New York: G. K. Hall, 1991), 1–19, and my entry on value theory in *The Johns Hopkins Guide to Literary Theory and Criticism,* ed. Michael Groden and Martin Kreiswirth (Baltimore, 1994), 719–23.

3. See Terry Eagleton, *The Ideology of the Aesthetic* (Oxford: Basil Blackwell, 1990), although with "*the* Aesthetic" Eagleton is not referring to the limited sense of taste as discrimination of the beautiful but rather to the whole domain of artistic creation and reception.

ciety relocated the power of the state within the subject herself, within the region of perception, sensation, sensuous material life (sometimes called "sensibility"). Like the modern notion of the aesthetic artifact, the modern bourgeois subject was "autonomous," that is, self-regulating.

On the other hand—and here is the duality—the state was now in danger of the subject's subjective revolt, which it had authorized even while it sought to control it. A new kind of subject—individualist, sensuous, passionate, deriving the law from itself—posed a potential challenge to the status quo. When art or literature is something more than cultural capital, this challenge is more apparent in works of art and literature than in works of philosophy per se, which deal more exclusively with the cognitive.

Although Eagleton went to great lengths to balance both current views of art and culture as domination and as emancipation, others have reduced "the" aesthetic to its hegemonic role, as if to emphasize not only *one* aesthetic but also *one* ideology.[4] An original attempt, first, to take the history of aesthetics out of "the tradition of great minds speaking with one another" through the medium of "pure philosophical reflection"—to which even Eagleton, for all his historical materialism, has succumbed—and, second, to avoid the reification of one monolithic ideology toward which all art and culture are supposed to tend, is Martha Woodmansee's *The Author, Art, and the Market* (1994).[5] Woodmansee proposes a new history of aesthetics that situates classic philosophical statements such as Kant's *Critique of Judgement* (1790) within the historical societies that produced them. Thus she has little direct "interpretation" of Kant's text but comments on it

4. In *Outside Literature,* for example, Tony Bennett rejects all philosophical aesthetics as insufficiently historical and materialist, claiming that the tradition has always posited a "universalized valuing subject." See Tony Bennett, *Outside Literature* (New York: Routledge, 1990), 117–92. He concludes in full neo-Foucauldian declamatory style that aesthetics "is part of a technology of person formation whose effects are assessed as positive and productive in serving as a means of normalising the attributes of extended populations as a part of the more general procedures and apparatuses of government through which, in Foucault's conception, the attributes of modern citizenries have been shaped into being" (181).

On the other hand, Geoffrey Galt Harpham responded to Eagleton's balancing act with the judgment that "the aesthetic" was precisely "theoretical confusion"—the undecidability "between object and subject, freedom and the repressive law, critical and uncritical passages, grievous and necessary misreadings, even art and ideology." See "Aesthetics and the Fundamentals of Modernity," in *Aesthetics and Ideology,* ed. George Levine (New Brunswick: Rutgers University Press, 1994), 135.

5. Martha Woodmansee, *The Author, Art, and the Market: Rereading the History of Aesthetics* (New York: Columbia University Press, 1994), 7.

obliquely, through the larger debates on culture that coincided with its birth.

The story that Woodmansee tells is how the *Aufklärer* (enlighteners) responded to what they perceived as demotic literature by proclaiming art to be autonomous and how they responded to booksellers before "intellectual property" was conceivable and protected by copyright by reconceiving (the) work as the private property of genius and posterity rather than common property in the promotion of learning. In this reconfiguration, Schiller's "art of the ideal" evolves precisely in contrast with—to combat—a more populist "emancipatory and egalitarian" program for poetry for the masses (ch. 3); "art literature" was distinguished from "women's literature" (ch. 5); and Wordsworth's successive editions of the *Lyrical Ballads* show his efforts to distinguish himself from popular poets and to distinguish a social body called the people (who have classics) from the public (who are contemptibly attracted to ephemera) (ch. 6). In her concluding chapter Woodmansee recounts how Coleridge, enlisting Kant in his service, reacted to popular associationist writers who argued against any "standard of taste" in favor of diverse custom, and there is little doubt that for Woodmansee the defeat of the associationists' "resounding affirmation of diversity" (136) was significant in the history of aesthetics. Like Schiller before him, Coleridge decreed that one's "associations" of art were as irrelevant to it *as art* as was anything else "separate" from it: people, he said, who think that a taste for Milton and a taste of mutton are commensurable should be disqualified from talking about art.

Woodmansee concludes that "Coleridge seeks to discredit the practice that from Joseph Addison to Francis Jeffrey had seemed both natural and rational of treating all of our pleasures as *continuous* in the sense at least that, whether they derive from the palate or the intellect, we deem their effect—their satisfaction of our desires and needs—a relevant consideration in deciding their value" (139). By suppressing individual associations, indeed by surrendering our *selves* to the work, Coleridge affirms the possibility of universally valid judgments and of opening ourselves to the guidance of the artist. Woodmansee sees this as the eradication of the empirical recipient so prominent in the associationist model in favor of a recipient who, as Coleridge wrote, would "judge in the same spirit in which the artist produced, or ought to have produced." In our contemporary criticism, she points out, we term this construct "a *competent*, an *implied*, sometimes an *ideal* recipient" (140). The 1814 and 1842 copyright laws legitimated, according to Woodmansee, this elevation of the writer above the public. Woodmansee does not discuss Bentham, but obviously the associationists' commitment to diversity of taste owed much to Benthamite utilitarianism, which in maximizing pleasure did not want to distinguish between "pushpin and poetry" (Coleridge's mutton and Milton).[6]

Woodmansee's historical work clarifies the debate in some fruitful ways. She has persuasively argued that authors were pursuing their self-interest—and at the crudest economic level of monetary gain—in establishing the autonomy of the artist and the work from the public. On the other hand, two centuries later and in a country (the United States) that really does *not* distinguish between a taste for pushpin or poetry, McDonald's or Milton—when and where, as economists say, tastes really are exogenous or above disputation—one is not entirely persuaded that the associationists' "resounding affirmation of diversity" is as liberating as we might have thought, or Kantian universalism as repressive as current theory likes to make out. Kantian universalism, at least, never intended to privilege the artist in the way Coleridge had. It obliterated individual self-interest in favor of the social good, and thus was not entirely alien to Coleridge's notions of "geniality," but Kant's system of the relations between the Good, the True, and the Beautiful cannot be reduced to Coleridge's brief for genius.

An interesting intermediate position between Woodmansee's desublimation of philosophical aesthetics and the deracination of much of that tradition heretofore is Linda Dowling's *Vulgarization of Art*.[7] Dowling sees Ruskin, Morris, and Wilde as attempting to mediate between a universal aesthetic (*To Kalon* and *sensus communis*) and popular access to art and culture. In Dowling's view, Ruskin's accessible theory of mimesis was defeated by Whistler's professional artist, and art came to exacerbate class divisions rather than heal them. In Morris's case, his extraordinarily visceral response to Beauty led him, also, to believe in its universality: his alleged response to good craftsmanship was a warmth in his tummy (Dowling 52, 111 n. 2). Furthermore, his own temperament, his "ability to merge himself into the social totality without suffering either anxiety or loss of identity," provided him with an "innate socialism" conducive to what Dowling calls "aesthetic democracy," or a belief in the universal accessibility of aesthetic experience.

Dowling sees Wilde's much-remarked-on fraternization across classes as a case of his most fundamental belief in a *sensus communis*, a belief that by the end of the century could not help but come in

6. See chapter 2.
7. Linda Dowling, *The Vulgarization of Art: The Victorians and Aesthetic Democracy* (Charlottesville: University Press of Virginia, 1996).

conflict with "a liberalism that had at long last grasped the pointlessness of trying to claim for itself any grounding in transcendent values" or "any source of legitimation other than that provided by popular opinion" (98–99). Thus Dowling brilliantly accounts for the pathos of Wilde in court by his deep belief in aesthetic democracy, taking seriously his defense of sex with lower-class boys: "I make no social distinctions"; "I didn't care twopence what they were. . . . I have a passion to civilize the community" (100).

After the fin de siècle, according to Dowling, the ideal of aesthetic democracy died away to be replaced by either the subjectivism of Whistler's expressivist painting, which, paradoxically, could only be interpreted by a specialist (47), the hedonism denounced by Arnold under the name of "doing as one liked" (98), or the decadent yearning for cultural salvation whose manifestation is the mere salvaging of cultural bits (68). The subjectivism, hedonism, and consumerism of these late-Victorian aesthetics are the themes of this book.

Although I share Dowling's appreciation of aesthetic democracy as envisioned by Ruskin, Morris, and Wilde, in this chapter I shall focus on the way that these different aesthetic tendencies correspond to economic models.[8] Both disciplines matured with industrial market soci-

---

8. In a recent article the British Wilde scholar and cultural theorist Ian Small labeled a school of critics distinctively "American." See Small, "The Economies of Taste: Literary Markets and Literary Value in the Late Nineteenth Century," *ELT* 39, no. 1 (1996): 7–18. In contradistinction to the British tendency to emphasize production and producers, these critics had brought to the fore the institutions of the marketplace, the commodification of culture and artists, consumerism, and the psychology of desire for the goods and services of modernity. Small used my work in *Idylls of the Marketplace* and more recently on the histories of economics and aesthetics, but he might have used any number of recent works on commodification, largely but not exclusively from the United States: Andrew Miller's *Novels Behind Glass,* Anne McClintock's work on commodity racism, or Rita Felski's on feminine modernity as the erotics and aesthetics of the commodity; Kathy Psomiades's work on how the duality of femininity permitted Aestheticism to both acknowledge and repress art's status as commodity; and Laurel Brake's work on the periodicals market. Writing on Wilde, Richard Dellamora has recently used Bataille to talk about "nonproductive expenditure." In *The Ruling Passion,* Christopher Lane has focused on exchange as a motive for empire, which would be nothing new except that he means exchange of sexual desire among men rather than goods. Talia Schaffer has shown how the respective commodifications of "interior design" versus "home decoration" in the fin de siècle were gendered. See Regenia Gagnier, *Idylls of the Marketplace: Oscar Wilde and the Victorian Public* (Stanford: Stanford University Press, 1986); Andrew H. Miller, *Novels Behind Glass: Commodity Culture and Victorian Narrative* (Cambridge: Cambridge University Press, 1995); Anne McClintock, *Imperial Leather: Race, Gender, and Sexuality in the Colonial Contest* (New York: Routledge, 1995); Rita Felski, *The Gender of Modernity* (Cambridge: Harvard University Press, 1995); Kathy Alexis Psomiades, *Beauty's Body: Femininity and Representation in British Aesthetics* (Stanford: Stanford University Press, 1997); Laurel Brake, *Subjugated*

ety, economics to provide for the needs and desires of the people (or "public"), aesthetics to express their needs and desires.[9] Hardy's novel, about the needs and desires of a working man and woman, illustrates popular conceptions of both aesthetics and economics at the fin de siècle.

The so-called Decadents themselves expressed a range of emotions about modern market society, as I suggested by the quotations in the introduction. As early as 1863, Baudelaire had reacted, via his figure of the dandy, against a bourgeois ethos of productivity and domestic reproduction, rejecting virility itself: "the more a man cultivates the arts, the less often he gets an erection."[10] Attacking the socialist-feminist George Sand, he wrote, "Only the brute gets really good erections. Fucking is the lyricism of the masses." He went on to explore the more voyeuristic pleasures of the *flaneur*. The dandy Barbey gave Huysmans the choice between renunciation of worldly goods and total, self-destructive consumption: after *A Rebours* he could only choose between "the foot of the cross or the muzzle of a pistol." *A*

Knowledges: Journalism, Gender, and Literature in the Nineteenth Century (London: Macmillan, 1994); Richard Dellamora, "Wildean Economics" (paper presented at the City University of New York Graduate Center, May 1995); Christopher Lane, *The Ruling Passion: British Colonial Allegory and the Paradox of Homosexual Desire* (Durham: Duke, 1995); Talia Schaffer, *The Forgotten Female Aesthetes: Literary Culture in Late-Victorian England* (Charlottesville and London: University Press of Virginia, 2000).

It is not surprising that this emphasis on markets, commodification, and consumption is more prominent in U.S. scholarship than in British. As we have seen, as early as the 1840s John Stuart Mill, Marx, and other observers of the spirit of capitalism anticipated that the United States would go further than Europe in the unrestrained pursuit of markets, and it is a commonplace of political economy that U.S. consumer capitalism had advanced on British industrial capitalism by the end of the nineteenth century. Small is also right to point out that there has been a shift in emphasis in U.S. scholarship away from an aesthetics of production to an aesthetics of consumption. Once dominated by figures of industrial revolution, Victorian studies in the United States have been increasingly dominated by figures of speculation, finance, circulation, exchange, and desire in all its modern forms. This drift has entailed a new focus on the late Victorian period and the way that commodity theory has converged with other key themes of the fin de siècle such as gender, sexuality, and empire.

9. Peter de Bolla's *The Discourse of the Sublime: Readings in History, Aesthetics, and the Subject* (Oxford: Blackwell, 1989) addresses parallel developments in aesthetics and economics. De Bolla, however, is less interested in the institutions of the aesthetics and economics and their historical development than in a particular rhetoric of excess in the discourse surrounding the aesthetic sublime and the national debt. His book provides deconstructive close readings of this discourse and then links it to transformation in the human subject during the period of the Seven Years' War (1756–1763).

10. See Charles Baudelaire, *The Painter of Modern Life and Other Essays*, trans. and ed. Jonathan Mayne (London: Phaidon, 1966), 28–29, and *My Heart Laid Bare and Other Prose Writings* (London: Soho, 1986), 175–210, 213.

Rebours itself proclaimed a weariness of both production and reproduction—Des Esseintes gave himself "a funeral banquet in memory
of [his own] virility" and set himself to decadent and "effeminate"
consumption of the exotica of the world.[11] George Moore's hero Mike
Fletcher treated women like cigarettes, consuming and disposing of
them in an insatiable search for stimulation:

> More than ever did he seek women, urged by a nervous erithism
> which he could not explain or control. Married women and
> young girls came to him from drawing-rooms, actresses from the-
> atres, shopgirls from the streets, and though seemingly all were
> as unimportant and accidental as the cigarettes he smoked, each
> was a drop in the ocean of the immense ennui accumulating in
> his soul.[12]

Oscar Wilde's description of a cigarette also described the perfect commodity: cigarettes, Wilde said, were the perfect type of the perfect pleasure, because they left one unsatisfied.[13] The fin de siècle's basic stances
toward the economy—boredom with production but love of comfort,
insatiable desire for new sensation, and fear of falling behind the competition—culminated in Max Beerbohm's publication of his *Complete
Works* at the age of twenty-four. "I shall write no more," he wrote in
the preface of 1896, "Already I feel myself to be a trifle outmoded. I
belong to the Beardsley period. Younger men, with months of activity
before them . . . have pressed forward since then. *Cedo junioribus*."[14]
Beerbohm satirized the duality of aestheticizing/commodifying one's
life in *Zuleika Dobson*, in the double images of dandy and female
superstar. Real women, like Mrs. (Mary Eliza) Haweis in her *Beautiful Houses* (1881), on the other hand, were packaging the world in
moments of taste and connoisseurship and commodifying them for suburban effects. Indeed, in political economy it is the comfort of the suburban home, comfort increasingly—or illusorily—accessible to common folks, that won for consumption its status as the essence of
modernity.[15]

Previous chapters have provided many more examples of the late

11. *Against Nature* (Harmondsworth: Penguin, 1982), 27.
12. George Moore, *Mike Fletcher* (1889; reprint, New York: Garland, 1977), 261.
13. Oscar Wilde, *The Picture of Dorian Gray,* in *The Portable Oscar Wilde,* ed.
Richard Aldington and Stanley Weintraub (New York: Penguin, 1981), 228.
14. Max Beerbohm, *Complete Works* (London: John Lane, 1896).
15. See, e.g., Peter J. Taylor, "What's Modern About the Modern World-System?
Introducing Ordinary Modernity Through World Hegemony," *Review of International
Political Economy* 3, no. 2 (summer 1996): 260–86.

Victorian awareness of a shift from production to consumption. Here I shall situate these basic stances toward the economy—the love of comfort, the fear of falling behind the competition, and the insatiable desire for new sensation—in relation to some broad anthropological models in the history of aesthetics and cultural critique. These models include conceptions of people as producers or creators; of people as consumers, or creatures of taste and pleasure; of work as alienable or creative; and of works and markets as autonomous or heteronomous. The history of aesthetics consists of a diverse and often overlapping group of claims made for art and culture, each with particular motivations and specific audiences in a web of social relations. Ethical aesthetics arose with industrialism and was concerned with the creation of self-regulating subjects and autonomous works; the aesthetics of production was concerned with producers or creators of work and the conditions of creativity and production; the aesthetics of taste or consumption, often with a physiological base, became dominant by the fin de siècle, largely through the dominance of psychology as a discipline in academic institutions; and the aesthetics of evaluation, as we have seen in Matthew Arnold, was historically linked with the idea of national cultures and races (remembering the range of meanings these terms encompassed in nineteenth-century Britain).

These aesthetics had a number of points of contact or overlap, but they were often promoted with very different motivations. Mill, like Kant before him, was concerned with the moral good and the creation of the liberal, ethical individual who could be relied on to subjugate individual desires to the social good. The self-styled "political economists of art" (Ruskin's phrase), Ruskin and Morris, wanted to provide the conditions for producers whose work would be emotionally, intellectually, and sensuously fulfilling and whose societies would be judged by their success in cultivating creators and creativity.

Aesthetics of taste, deriving from Hume and Burke and merging with associationist psychology after mid-century, distinguished between objects of beauty and then distinguished between those who could and could not distinguish, often claiming that such capacities correlated to physiological or social stages of development. In aesthetics of evaluation, like Arnold's, in which the point was to measure one object against another by standards of "truth" or "seriousness," the "tact" that was thus demonstrated in one's ability to discriminate was less a matter of physiology than of status, for Arnoldian evaluation was in the service of locating individuals in relation to class, class in relation to nation or culture, and nation or culture in relation to globe or "civilization." Yet physiology remained in the association of Arnold's ideas of culture with racial types, as in his idea of the Celts.[16] Indeed it has been pointed out that, with the best will in the world to enhance the status of the Celts, Arnold only succeeded in effeminizing them as a race in relation to Germanic peoples. Like the Beautiful, they inspired love but not fear or admiration.[17]

Thus some aesthetics were concerned with the human as liberal, ethical individual and others with the human as creator fulfilling her role as producer of the world. Some aesthetics were concerned with the object produced or created and others with the consumers of objects and their mode of apprehension. Another way I have put this is that some were concerned with productive bodies, whose work could be creative or alienated, while others were concerned with pleasured bodies, whose tastes established their identities. All of these models were inflected by gender typologies and gendered divisions of labor. Granting overlap among these groups—for example, bodies that took pleasure in their labor—much confusion has nonetheless resulted from reifying something called "the Aesthetic" and something monolithic called "value"; these reifications have only recently begun to be rectified, primarily through feminist, gay, and postcolonial analytics.[18] The point is to see the tensions between competing aesthetic models and even within one model.

ETHICAL AESTHETICS AND THE DISCIPLINED BODY

In Kant, the moral good consists in acting autonomously, as one ought, rather than heteronomously, or from desire, emotion, or self-interest. This freedom to act autonomously can only be achieved by reason, but it can be prefigured by feeling, the feeling of freedom from desire or self-interest that we get when we perceive the beautiful object. When we perceive the beautiful object—which in Kant is typically a natural object theoretically accessible to all, rather than a work of art, which, Kant says, may give rise to an element of ego or possessiveness—the disjunction between our perception and our concept creates an excess, a free play of imagination, that prefigures moral freedom, or freedom

16. See Robert Young, *Colonial Desire: Hybridity in Theory, Culture and Race* (London: Routledge, 1995), 55–89.

17. "If any piece of scholarship illustrates how far the road to hell can be paved with good intentions," writes Vincent Pecora, "Arnold's *On the Study of Celtic Literature* (1867) is it." See Vincent P. Pecora, "Arnoldian Ethnology," *Victorian Studies: Special Issue: Victorian Ethnographies* (spring 1998): 355–79, esp. 365.

18. See Steven Connor, *Theory and Cultural Value* (Oxford: Blackwell, 1992) for an extended treatment of value in current theory.

from desire and self-interest. (I have no desire to possess the sunset, for there is enough of it for all; but I share with all the wonder of beholding it.) The free play prefigures the reconciliation between individual and social life that the moral good entails, that is, to act according to duty rather than according to desire or self-interest, or to act in such a way that one's actions embody a universal principle for action.[19] In Kant's *Anthropology*, making a man of taste falls short of making a morally good man, but the effort he makes in society to please others prepares him for morality.[20] This taste for freedom is thus, notoriously, a form of discipline, a freedom from the selfish desires.

A Kantian judgment of taste is neither simply subjective, relating to the consumer, nor objective, relating to the object. It begins with the harmonious workings of the faculties when a perceiver is confronted with certain objects. At first this aesthetic feeling is subjective and phenomenal. In the disinterested pleasure that comes to me without the element of desire or self-interest, I do not transcend the phenomenal sphere (see "Analytic of Aesthetic Judgment"). But Kant insisted, in line with the logic of his entire system, that judgments of taste were also objective. When we say that the beautiful object ought to please others also, we bring in rational and objective elements. Recognizing something in us that is common to the species, and something in each member of the species that is not owned but is universal property, we are freed from our former confinedness and limitations (see "Dialectic of Aesthetic Judgment"). Many people, of course, who are persuaded by Kant's phenomenology of aesthetic feeling—the "free play" of imagination synthesizing perception and concept—are not persuaded by his rationalizing or universalizing of it to make it a symbol of the moral good, or freedom.[21]

Without Kant's metaphysic, John Stuart Mill's aesthetic also functioned as a discipline. In his two major essays on poetry of 1833, Mill distinguishes poetry from mere eloquence by its discipline and autonomy: poetry is overheard, whereas eloquence is heard; unconscious of listeners, whereas eloquence is directed toward an audience; an end in itself, whereas eloquence is a means to an end; thoughts tinged by feel-

19. Immanuel Kant, *Critique of Judgment*, trans. Werner S. Pluhar (Indianapolis: Hackett, 1987).

20. Immanuel Kant, *Anthropology from a Pragmatic Point of View*, trans. Mary J. Gregor (The Hague: Martinus Nijhoff, 1974), 111–12.

21. See, for example, Pierre Bourdieu, *Distinction: A Critique of the Judgment of Taste* (Cambridge: Harvard University Press, 1988); Stanley Fish, *Doing What Comes Naturally* (Durham: Duke University Press, 1989); and Barbara Herrnstein Smith, *Contingencies of Value: Alternative Perspectives for Critical Theory* (Cambridge: Harvard University Press, 1988).

ing, whereas in eloquence feelings pour themselves out to other minds; feeling unconscious of being watched, whereas eloquence is found in "attitudinizers" showing themselves off before spectators.[22] For Mill, the French—social, vain, and dependent on others—are eloquent but not poetic, subject to law or external constraint but not self-disciplined. The autonomous, disciplined lover of poetry is also distinguished from primitive peoples (or vulgar people in advanced societies), who prefer stories (or novels), as those who prefer "a state of sensibility" are distinguished from those drawn to "mere outward circumstance." Obviously Mill's lover of poetry, even in these early essays, prefigures his lover of liberty in *On Liberty* of 1859, who acts freely without inhibiting the freedom of others. Because the poet is a disciplined, ethical exemplar, poetry is disciplined feeling, and the lover of poetry is the autonomous, self-disciplined feeler. The poem embodies the process that will educate the hearers or readers how to be autonomous (rational, self-reflective) themselves.[23] For Mill, aesthetics partakes of rational self-reflection in the service of progressive individuals.

As in the Kantian aesthetic, the essays on poetry clearly partook of Mill's general response to democratizing social processes. They were published in 1833, a year after the First Reform Bill, when the pressing concern of idealistic reformers was how to instruct (some would say "subjugate") the masses in responsible citizenship. Now this figure of Kant's moral agent or Mill's reader is an autonomous, self-regulating male, not driven, like Economic Man, by passion or self-interest. To this extent, the ethical aesthetic is a liberal aesthetic and carries with it the masculine appurtenances of liberal autonomy. It should be noted that there is a rich cultural history of masculine autonomy associated with this repudiation of rhetoric, from the Scottish Enlightenment's stoic, masculine virtues to Mill's national distinctions between poetry (English) and rhetoric (French) to Pater's ascetic stylist and Wilde's repudiation of rhetoric in *De Profundis* (see chapter 5).

In fiction, Hardy's *Jude* provides an ethical aesthetic and disciplined bodies. The novel as a whole may be seen, as H. M. Daleski has argued, as Jude and Sue's attempt to carve out an ethics, an autonomy, of will in the face of necessity. Daleski interprets what might pass as

22. John Stuart Mill, "What Is Poetry?" and "The Two Kinds of Poetry," in *The Collected Works of John Stuart Mill*, ed. John M. Robson (Toronto: University of Toronto Press, 1963–91), 1:341–53, 354–65.

23. For a detailed analysis of Mill's aesthetic and of its compatibility with Mill's larger views in *On Liberty*, see Kenneth Brewer, "Lost in a Book: Aesthetic Absorption 1820–1880," Ph.D. diss., English Department, Stanford University, 1998, ch. 3, "The Absorption of John Stuart Mill," 41–57.

Sue's cruel virginity as, rather, an attempt at autonomy, or "self-containment."[24] Sue says, regarding her ascesis, that "I never yielded myself to any lover. . . . I have remained as I began," and the constant references to her epicene nature, her "curious unconsciousness of gender," indicate a technology of the self, if an eccentric one, opposed to her social role as a woman.[25] Jude's history as the autodidact, subjecting himself to study under conditions of severe deprivation, is similar. He studies the Bible and classical languages as if individual talent, self-discipline, and merit could surmount social barriers, as if through severe ascesis he could make himself. With their final chastisement, his and Sue's wills are broken and every attempt at their self-creation has been defeated—Jude's for education and for meaningful labor, Sue's for female independence, and their collective dream of unity.

We see a recent treatment of aesthetics as ethics inscribed in the senses or emotions in the final years of Michel Foucault, from his last interviews, in which he spoke of social practices amounting to ascesis, or self-discipline,[26] to the posthumously published *The Use of Pleasure* (1984) and *The Care of the Self* (1984), volumes 2 and 3 of the *History of Sexuality*. Kant's ethics derived from the systematic relations between the good, the true, and the beautiful; Mill's and Foucault's, respectively, from education and a system of institutional practices; but they share an idea of the aesthetic creation of an ethical being.[27] This notion of aesthetics as ethics, of self-regulation in a disciplined society, has been the dominant one among Foucauldians and New Historicists, who have focused on bourgeois forms of hegemony such as the high Victorian novel, but its assumptions of constraint, self-restraint, and internal regulation render it inadequate to analyze the hedonics of modern consumer culture. (More on these hedonics below.) It has been argued that Foucault's "aesthetics of the self" ought to be interpreted

24. H. M. Daleski, *Thomas Hardy and the Paradoxes of Love* (Columbia: University of Missouri Press, 1997).

25. Thomas Hardy, *Jude the Obscure* (London: Macmillan, 1974), 169. All further references to *Jude* will be in the text.

26. Michel Foucault, "On the Genealogy of Ethics," in *The Foucault Reader*, ed. Paul Rabinow (Pantheon: New York, 1984), 340–73.

27. Two critics strongly influenced by Foucault have emphasized this aesthetic-as-ethic: Tony Bennett, *Outside Literature*, and Ian Hunter, who sees aesthetics as "the instruments and objects of a special practice of the self, deployed for essentially ethical purposes. They are the phenomena whose systematically polarized structure is symptomatic of their systemic use as reflexive instruments of self-problematization and self-modification." See "Cultural Studies and Aesthetics," in *Cultural Studies*, ed. Lawrence Grossberg et al. (New York: Routledge, 1992), 356. In *Outside Literature* Tony Bennett makes much use of Hunter's book on the teaching of literature in the schools (*Culture and Government*) in Bennett's attack on philosophical aesthetics.

not as a technology of the self but as an alternative to it, as a way that sexual practices or "pleasures" might enable other selves and new relationships to emerge.[28] Yet whether the "care of the self" or the "use of pleasure" inclines toward the subjection or liberation of the subject, Foucault's emphasis remains the ethico-aesthetic production of the self, whose freedom and autonomy (but not of course its sexual desires) seem characteristic of a liberal tradition that some have found to be both idealist and masculine in its freedom and self-control.

THE POLITICAL ECONOMY OF ART AND THE PRODUCTIVE BODY

The movement that Ruskin called the political economy of art focused not on the spectator or the consumer but on the producer of the work and the conditions of production: this was Ruskin's aesthetic, Morris's after him, and, of course, Marx's and generations of Marxists' (although Marxist aesthetics has typically included a critique of ideology with its critique of production). Contrary to an aesthetics located in the object (Plato's) or in the perceiver (Kant or Burke's), the political economists of art (Ruskin's phrase)[29] began with the very body of the artist and ended with a theory of creative production. In *Jude the Obscure*, the builder reads the buildings at Christminster (that is, Oxford) as Ruskin "reads" (his own term) the cathedrals at San Marcos or Amiens:[30] "less as an artist-critic of their forms than as an artizan and comrade of the dead handicraftsmen whose muscles had actually executed those forms" (103). These muscles, of course, have been aestheticized and eroticized, along with their feminine counterpart, the reproductive woman, as part of a productivist ethics for a century and a half; if the model was broadly heterosexual it was also rooted in the body and its labor as firmly as Kant's or Mill's ethico-aesthetic was rooted in reason and the mind. One must not underestimate the extent to which the political economists of art were concerned with ethics and reception ("reading"). Ruskin is considered the founder of "moral consumption," or the appeal to consumers' social responsibility, and he had affinities with physiological aesthetics in his precise calculations

28. See Dellamora, "Wildean Economics" and *Postmodern Apocalypse* (Philadelphia: University of Pennsylvania Press, 1995), 1–16.

29. See John Ruskin, *The Political Economy of Art*, in *Unto This Last and Other Essays* (London: Dent, 1932), 1–106.

30. See John Ruskin, "The Nature of Gothic," in a later edition of *Unto This Last and Other Writings*, ed. Clive Wilmer (London: Penguin, 1985) and *The Bible of Amiens*, in *On Reading Ruskin*, trans. and ed. Jean Autret et al. (New Haven: Yale University Press, 1987).

of aesthetic impact on the body, especially on the eye (see the role of "seeing" throughout his work). In fact, one economist who took his work very seriously indeed, J. A. Hobson, wrote not only *John Ruskin, Social Reformer* (1903) but also *The Physiology of Industry* (1899).[31] Yet despite these concerns and affinities, a theory of creative labor motivated the political economists of art; their object was the relation of production and reproduction and the possibilities for human creativity within them.

We should pause here, in an age of consumer demand, to remark how seriously the nineteenth century, from a wide range of perspectives, took the labor theory of value, from Ricardo to Marx, Mill, and Ruskin, to Hardy at the fin de siècle. The theory said that the cost of a commodity was the value of the labor power it took to produce it, plus the value of the laborer's wear and tear in production, plus the value of the laborer's family's subsistence—or, as Marx said, the value of labor power was "the necessaries by means of which the muscles, nerves, bones, and brains of existing laborers are reproduced and new laborers are begotten."[32] Making labor the center of his own economic theory, Hobson thought Ruskin's main contribution was his reckoning of wealth as the balance of utility to the consumer against the cost to the laborer. Much of the outrage in novels such as *Jude*, written well after the theory had been discredited as a theory of price, is directed toward a society that literally undervalues its producers. And Hardy's terms are, like *labor*, those of political economy: production, reproduction, and the body whose labor was its defining feature. They are also specifically Malthusian in the body's reproductive capacity. From the beginning Jude is conscious of himself, of his "unnecessary life" (36), as part of Malthus's "surplus population," and his children die "because we are too menny" (356). Correspondingly, Sue's gendered, reproductive labors are what she seeks, hopelessly, to avoid in pursuit of a (bodiless) aesthetic partnership. And reproductive, like productive, labors are, again, embedded in thick social and material relations (see, for example, how bodies are typically marked by gender, race, and class relations).

The impulse to historicize art, to read in art the history of social relations, goes back, of course, to Hegel, a student of political econ-

---

31. For Ruskin's economic theory of consumption, see esp. ch. 4, "Ruskin's Constructive Political Economy" (70–99), and 147–50 in John Tyree Fain, *Ruskin and the Economists* (Nashville: Vanderbilt University Press, 1956). See also J. A. Hobson, *The Physiology of Industry* (London: Murray, 1889) and *John Ruskin: Social Reformer* (Boston: Estes, 1898).

32. Karl Marx, *Capital* (New York: International Publishers, 1967), 572.

omy. Kant's examples in the third *Critique* of the Sublime and the Beautiful are drawn from nature, for example, sublime cataracts and mountains or the beautiful song of a bird. Hegel, on the other hand, made representation central to his aesthetics, deriving the aesthetic impulse from the fact that it was human nature to, as he said, represent ourselves to ourselves. Thus art is an index of its time, its producers, and their conditions of production.[33] At the end of the nineteenth century, in his magisterial *History of Aesthetic* (1892), Bernard Bosanquet saw the culmination of this tradition of philosophical aesthetics in the materialism of Ruskin and Morris. Insofar as the worker was free in his producing activity, so far would he produce the work of creative humanity. (Or, as Ruskin sums up his own social philosophy, "life without industry is guilt, and industry without art is brutality.")[34] The dissolution of romantic art into excessive internality and subjectivity predicted by Hegel would presage the birth of Morris's unalienated worker, whose "art [was] the expression of pleasure in labor," where "pleasure," again, indicates that labor can be creative and fulfilling rather than alienated "toil and trouble."[35] Unlike the monumentally abstract eighteenth-century science of aesthetics, for the Victorians aesthetics was the realm of daily life and its "sense data," or sensuous experience, its pains and pleasures. Bosanquet, for example, was particularly interested in Morris's production in the applied arts of furniture-making, tapestries, textiles, and carpets.

Such practical aesthetics involving a critique of daily life—what Dowling calls "aesthetic democracy"—defines the political economists of art. Consider Ruskin's contrasting of the "Two Boyhoods" from the fifth volume (1860) of his defense of Turner, *Modern Painters.* (I note only in passing the practical nature of *Modern Painters:* a defense of

33. G. W. F. Hegel, *Introductory Lectures on Aesthetics,* trans. Bernard Bosanquet, ed. Michael Inwood (Penguin, 1993). Contra Kant, Hegel ranked natural beauty low in relation to art. Plants and animals were more beautiful, because closer to the Idea, than inanimate natural objects, but what we see of them is their outward coverings, not the soul within, for that is concealed by the visible feathers, scales, fur, and the like that cover them. In the *Philosophy of History,* Hegel opposed human creativity to natural beauty, which was the "prose of the world": "in nature there happens 'nothing new under the sun,' and the multiform play of its phenomena so far induces a feeling of *ennui.*" See Hegel, *Philosophy of History,* in *The Idea of Progress: A Collection of Readings,* ed. Frederick Teggart (Berkeley: University of California Press, 1949), 400.

34. Cited in Fain, *Ruskin and the Economists,* 25; John Ruskin, *Works,* ed. E. T. Cook and Alexander Wedderburn, 39 vols. (London: George Allen, 1903–1912), 20:93.

35. Bernard Bosanquet, *History of Aesthetic* (London: George Allen and Unwin, 1892), 441–71. The definition of art as "the expression by man of his pleasure in labour" is Morris's in "The Art of the People" [1879], in *Collected Works of William Morris,* 23 vols., ed. May Morris (London: Longman and Green, 1914), 22:42.

the work of a contemporary.) In "Two Boyhoods" Ruskin contrasts the Venice of Giorgione (1477–1510) with the England of Turner (1775–1851). He begins with a(n idealized) description of social order and physical beauty, the (romanticized) Venice of the quattrocento, whose beauty is premised on its justice:

> A wonderful piece of world. Rather, itself a world. It lay along the face of the waters, no larger, as its captains saw it from their masts at evening, than a bar of sunset that could not pass away; but for its power, it must have seemed to them as if they were sailing in the expanse of heaven, and this a great planet, whose orient edge widened through ether. A world from which all ignoble care and petty thoughts were banished, with all the common and poor elements of life. . . . Such was Giorgione's school.[36]

He then turns to Turner's school, Covent Garden, and makes the essential Ruskinian aesthetic statement, reducing aesthetics to a material base: "With such circumstances round him in youth, let us note what necessary effects followed upon the boy['s art]." Turner's impoverished childhood resulted in his "notable endurance of dirt . . . and all the soilings and stains of every common labour"; an "understanding of and regard for the poor . . . and of the poor in direct relations with the rich"; and a discreditable and discredited religion, "not to be either obeyed, or combated, by an ignorant, yet clear-sighted youth, only to be scorned" (146–50). Turner saw beauty neither in the works nor the souls of humankind, nor in God, but, by contrast, in the solitude of nature. In the Yorkshire hills, he found

> Freedom at last. Dead-wall, dark railing, fenced field, gated garden, all passed away like the dream of a prisoner. . . . Those pale, poverty-struck, or cruel faces;—that multitudinous, marred humanity—are not the only things God has made. Here is something He has made which no one has marred. Pride of purple rocks, and river pools of blue, and tender wilderness of glittering trees, and misty lights of evening on immeasurable hills. (150)

Yet Turner is not an escapist nature painter, nor does Ruskin praise him for his representations of the green and pleasant land. The typical Turner painting was a wash of light—the beauty of the physical earth—now exposing the piteous failures of humankind. Ruskin attri-

---

36. John Ruskin, "Two Boyhoods," in *Unto This Last and Other Writings* (1985 ed.), 144–45.

butes these failures first to the European drive for conquest and domination.

The European death of the nineteenth century was of another range and power [than that depicted by Salvator or Dürer]; more terrible a thousand-fold in its merely physical grasp and grief; more terrible, incalculably, in its mystery and shame. What were the robber's casual pang, or the range of the flying skirmish, compared to the work of the axe, and the sword, and the famine, which was done during [Turner's] youth on all the hills and plains of the Christian earth, from Moscow to Gibraltar? He was eighteen years old when Napoleon came down on Arcola. Look on the map of Europe and count the blood-stains on it, between Arcola and Waterloo. (152)

In his condemnation of empire, Ruskin alludes to Turner's projected epic poem on the decline and fall of naval powers and to Turner's own verses accompanying his "Slavers Throwing Overboard the Dead and Dying—Typhoon Coming On" (1840). In the painting and verses, Turner extends his censure of the slave trade to the global market in general.

After slavery and empire, Ruskin turns to "the English practice" of exploitation, as embodied in the domestic casualties of the industrial revolution: "The life trampled out in the slime of the street, crushed to dust amidst the roaring of the wheel, tossed countlessly away into howling winter wind along five hundred leagues of rock-fanged shore. Or, worst of all, rotted down to forgotten graves through years of ignorant patience . . . infirm, imperfect yearning, as of motherless infants starving at the dawn" (152). This was what Turner painted—nature casting its blinding light on human misery of human making: "Light over all the world. Full shone now its awful globe, one pallid charnel-house,—a ball strewn bright with human ashes, glaring in poised sway beneath the sun, all blinding-white with death from pole to pole—death, not of myriads of poor bodies only, but of will, and mercy, and conscience; death, not once inflicted on the flesh, but daily fastening on the spirit" (153).

One can find the same rich sympathy regarding human need, human suffering, and human memory in Morris's utopian novel *News from Nowhere* (1890), in which the virtues of an economically just, sexually liberated, and ecologically preserved utopia pale, for generations of readers, before the psychological splendor of the one character from the pre-utopian past—a character with memory—William Guest. An old man, one of the few in utopia conscious of the miserable temporal-ity of the body, Guest's bafflement and pain in the new world order characteristically remain Morris's (and most readers') imaginative center. If, according to the customary dialectic of utopian fiction, the idyllic nature of the utopia throws into relief the deficiencies of the present that the author is criticizing, William Guest's complex relation to memory (the hell that Victorian society was) and desire (the vision of what it could be) cannot help but make the callow young utopians look thin. Even Pater, generally taken to be an apolitical writer, introduced Morris's and pre-Raphaelite poetry in general as "the desire of beauty quickened by the sense of death."[37] The essay, "Aesthetic Poetry," which Pater withheld from publication until 1889, formed the basis of his aesthetic manifesto, "The Conclusion" to *Studies in the History of the Renaissance* (1873) and its notorious materialism.

In his critical writing, Morris differed from Ruskin in that he found the class system—today called "functionally interdependent juxtapositions"—more detrimental to society than poverty: "I went to Iceland and I learned one lesson there, thoroughly I hope, that the most grinding poverty is a trifling evil compared with the inequality of classes,"[38] a notion that put him fundamentally at odds with the political economists, who, with the exception of Mill, equated growth with production rather than distribution of wealth. In "Art Under Plutocracy," a lecture Morris delivered in 1883 (Ruskin chaired the session), he denied the autonomy of art, claiming first that "art should be a help and solace to the daily life of all men" (57), and he extended art's arena "beyond those matters which are consciously works of art . . . to the aspect of all the externals of our life" (58). In "How We Live and How We Might Live" (1884), Morris says that after competition between nations, firms, and classes has ceased (that is, under socialism), humankind will be free to determine its genuine needs. He anticipates the first demand to be for the body: the demand for good health, for the "vast proportion of people in civilization scarcely even know what it means" (148). This good health extends to liberatory sensuous experience: "To rejoice in satisfying the due bodily appetites of a human animal without fear of degradation or sense of wrong-doing . . . I claim it in the teeth of those terrible doctrines of asceticism, which, born of the despair of the oppressed and degraded, have been for so many ages used as instruments for the continuance of that oppression and degradation" (148). The second demand is for education: "Opportunity, that

37. Walter Pater, *Selected Writings of Walter Pater*, ed. Harold Bloom (New York: Signet, 1974), 195.

38. William Morris, *Political Writings of William Morris*, ed. A. L. Morton (New York: International, 1973), 17.

is, to have my share of whatever knowledge there is in the world according to my capacity or bent of mind, historical or scientific; and also to have my share of skill of hand which is about in the world, either in the industrial handicrafts or in the fine arts. . . . I claim to be taught, if I can be taught, more than one craft to exercise for the benefit of the community" (150). Morris then claims the right to reject certain kinds of work, those Ruskin had called "destructive" (for example, war) and "nugatory" (for example, jewel-cutting): "I won't submit to be dressed up in red and marched off to shoot at my French or German or Arab friend in a quarrel that I don't understand; I will rebel sooner than do that. Nor will I submit to waste my time and energies in making some trifling toy which I know only a fool can desire; I will rebel sooner than do that" (151–52). With the advent of useful and freely chosen labor, "Then would come the time for the new birth of art, so much talked of, so long deferred; people could not help showing their mirth and pleasure in their work, and would be always wishing to express it in a tangible and more or less enduring form, and the workshop would once more be a school of art, whose influence no one could escape from" (153). Morris concludes with the demand that "the mutual surroundings of my life should be pleasant, generous, and beautiful" (153), blaming urban squalor, overcrowding, disease, and industrial pollution not, as in political economy, on natural scarcity and human overpopulation, but rather on exploitation and the desire for profit.

In the tradition of great aesthetes who were also great social critics, Wilde's contribution to a political economy of art has lived longer than Ruskin's and Morris's, appearing most often, though not exclusively, today as toleration of thought and "lifestyle." Just as in aestheticism artwork was autonomous—it had to be true to its own organic development, to the laws of its own form—so Wilde insisted in *The Portrait of Mr. W. H.,* "The Soul of Man Under Socialism," "The Critic as Artist," and elsewhere that human individuals had unique temperaments and tastes that should be allowed to flourish according to the laws of their own being; and his fictional work, both novel and short stories, typically consisted of thought experiments on the social limits of this aesthetic autonomy. Yet unlike later proponents of the life-as-art thesis, such as Foucault in his last years, who wanted "to live life with the freedom of art," Wilde was sufficiently like his teachers Ruskin and Morris to insist on initial distributive justice as a precondition of genuine individual development and social utility.[39] That is, he refused to

39. For a comparative discussion of Foucault's and Wilde's aestheticism, see my *Critical Essays on Oscar Wilde,* 8–9.

entertain the idea of an opposition—often endorsed by political economists—between liberty and equality.

Several years ago I contrasted Wilde's socially oriented aestheticism
with the properly decadent aestheticism of Huysmans's Des Esseintes
in *A Rebours* (1884). I said that if Des Esseintes was solitary, neurotic,
reactive against the bourgeoisie he despised, formally monologic, and
concerned with perversion, Wilde was public, erotic, active, formally
dialogic, and concerned with the inversion of middle-class language
and life.[40] Des Esseintes buried himself in a fortress, made a fortress of
himself against others, and consumed the exotica of the world outside
the West. In "The Decay of Lying" (1891), Wilde debunked both the
connoisseur's practice of accumulation and the ethnographer's of objectification, saying, "the actual people who live in Japan are not unlike
the general run of English people; that is to say, they are extremely
commonplace, and have nothing curious or extraordinary about them.
In fact the whole of Japan is a pure invention."[41] The goal of the political economists of art was not to objectify others as art but to provide
the conditions that would allow oneself and others to live with the
freedom of art.

PHYSIOLOGICAL AESTHETICS AND THE PLEASURED BODY

Contrasted to this was biological or physiological aesthetics, which,
through its position of authority in the academy, rapidly gained dominance over the applied aesthetics of Ruskin and Morris, and in which
the cultivation of a distinctive "taste" in the consumption of art replaced concern for its producers. The roots went back to Hume and
Burke, who had analyzed the psychological bases of taste. According
to Hume, the structure of the mind made some objects naturally inclined to give pleasure or to inspire fear. In *Philosophy of the Beautiful*
(1895) William Knight estimated that Burke's influential essay of 1756
had reduced aesthetics to the lowest empirical level, identifying the
beautiful with the source of pleasant sensations.[42] In Burkean sensa-
tionism, the experience of an elite group of Anglo-Irish takes on the
appearance of universalism; the irrational feelings associated with the
sublime are given equal place with the sociable feelings associated with
the beautiful; and enlightenment or reason is subordinated to mechanism. Burke's very constrained subject—increasingly the subject of

40. Gagnier, *Idylls of the Marketplace,* 5.
41. Oscar Wilde, *The Artist as Critic: Critical Writings of Oscar Wilde,* ed. Richard
Ellmann (Chicago: University of Chicago Press, 1982), 315–16.
42. William Knight, *Philosophy of the Beautiful* (London: Murray, 1895).

political conservatism—is chained to physiology and driven by self-preservation and, to a lesser extent, benevolence. "We submit to what we admire, but we love what submits to us," Burke famously said of our respective reactions to the sublime and the beautiful (see chapter 1).[43] We respond naturally to the beautiful in the form of the small, the smooth, the curvilinear, the delicate, and the bright. We admire the sublime in the form of the vast, the rugged, the jagged, the solid and massive, and the dark. Erasmus Darwin perceived the associative basis of the beautiful when he named it a characteristic of beauty to be an object of love. We love the smooth, the soft, and the warm because we were once nourished thence. His grandson Charles later theorized the sense of beauty in relation to sexual selection. Many have remarked on the gender implications of Burke's theory.[44] Here I shall explore physiological aesthetics in relation to pleasure and consumption.

Since Hume, biological aesthetics had included custom with physiology in conditioning our response to the beautiful.[45] In the course of the nineteenth century biological aesthetics merged with established associationist psychology, which gained legitimacy as an academic discipline under Herbert Spencer and Alexander Bain in the century's second half. As it came to dominate economics, psychology, and sociology, it also came to dominate aesthetics, shifting the study from its German roots in ethics or reason and Victorian roots in production to that of reception, consumption, or individual pleasure. For our purposes, the empiricist tradition in aesthetics of Hume and Burke, which is typically opposed to Kantian reason, is significant for its grounding precisely in sense, in the pleasures of consumption. Bain banished everything but pleasure from aesthetics. Popularizing Bain, in *Physiological Aesthetics* (1877) Grant Allen defined the beautiful as that which afforded the maximum of stimulation with the minimum of fatigue or waste, in processes not directly connected with life-serving functions.

43. Edmund Burke, *A Philosophical Enquiry into the Origin of Our Ideas of the Sublime and the Beautiful*, ed. James T. Boulton (Notre Dame: University of Notre Dame Press, 1986), 113.

44. See, e.g., de Bolla, *Discourse of the Sublime*, 56–58; Terry Eagleton, "Aesthetics and Politics in Edmund Burke," in *Irish Literature and Culture*, ed. Michael Keneally (Gerards Cross: Colin Smythe, 1992), 25–34; Barbara Charlesworth Gelpi, "'Verses with a Good Deal About Sucking': Percy Bysshe Shelley and Christina Rossetti," in *Influence and Resistance in 19C English Poetry*, ed. G. Kim Blank and Margot K. Louis (New York: St. Martin's, 1993), 150–65; Mary Poovey, "Aesthetics and Political Economy in the Eighteenth Century: The Place of Gender in the Social Constitution of Knowledge" in *Aesthetics and Ideology*, ed. George Levine (New Brunswick: Rutgers University Press, 1994), 79–105.

45. David Hume, "Of the Standard of Taste," in *Essays Moral, Political, and Literary*, ed. Eugene F. Miller (Indianapolis: Liberty, 1963), 226–52.

Allen wrote, "The aesthetic pleasure is the subjective concomitant of the normal amount of activity, not directly connected with life-serving functions, in the peripheral end-organs of the cerebro-spinal nervous system."[46] Although taste had its source in the brain's hardware, whole societies could cultivate it, with Lamarckian consequences. Conditions of leisure give rise to two classes of impulse: play and aesthetic pleasure. In play we exercise our limbs and muscles; in aesthetic pleasure we exercise our eyes and ears—the organs of higher sense as opposed to the more functional senses of taste and smell. In this aesthetic, whose proponents included Spencer as well as Bain, the highest quality or quantity of human pleasure was to be derived from art.[47]

Contrary to the expressed goals of social justice and egalitarianism among the political economists of art, the experiencers of this pleasure fall into predictable hierarchies, and here is where aesthetics most heavily draws upon a lexicon of civilization and barbarism, or stages of development. With painstaking discussions of the physical origins of aesthetic feelings, Allen ultimately argued that existing likes and dislikes in aesthetic matters were the result of natural selection. Thence it was but a short step to distinguish between stages of aesthetic development, and Aesthetic Man, like Economic Man, was distinguished from others lower in the scale of civilization (whom Allen, following Spencer, Bain, and other associationists, interpret, after Burke, as "children" or "savages"). "Bad taste," writes Allen, "is the concomitant of a coarse and indiscriminate nervous organization, an untrained attention, a low emotional nature, and an imperfect intelligence; while good taste is the progressive product of progressing fineness and discrimination in the nerves, educated attention, high and noble emotional constitution, and increasing intellectual faculties" (48). "The common mind," as he put it, "translated the outward impression too rapidly into the reality which it symbolized, interpreting the sensations instead of observing them" (51). Rather than immediately translating the impression into its "real" analogue, on the other hand, the aesthetic mind "dwelled rather upon the actual impression received in all the minuteness of its slightest detail" (51). This, of course, meant that persons of taste dwelt upon the representation and their subjective response to it, rather than upon any referent it might have in the external

46. Grant Allen, *Physiological Aesthetics* (London: Henry S. King, 1877), 34.

47. See Herbert Spencer, "Use and Beauty" (1852), in *Essays: Scientific, Political, and Speculative* (London: Williams, 1883), 1:433–38; Alexander Bain, *The Emotions and the Will* (New York: Appleton, 1888), esp. ch. 14, "The Aesthetic Emotions," 225–63.

world. It is this preoccupation with the formal aspects of works that parallels the formalist economics of neoclassicalism. (The aesthete Pater, we have seen, emphasized this subjective and formalist response in his aesthetic.) Today, institutionalists such as Pierre Bourdieu have shown how the tendencies to dwell in the referent or in the representation are distinctive marks of social class.[48]

Allen did allow that taste could be educated by the exercise of attention and the growth of new intellectual and emotional associations, and he hoped that it would be a force for progress. The stages of aesthetic development predictably find their telos in a universal culture (the end of history) that will have outgrown the selfish interests of Economic Man as well as the merely sensuous pleasures of the beautiful: "The older appeals to the monopolist senses, to the selfish feelings, to the narrower sympathies of class, and race, and nationality, and creed, are yielding place, we may hope, at least in our poetry and possibly even in our imitative arts, to the nobler sentiments of all-embracing humanitarianism" (215). So long, he said, as it remained merely a means for the gratification of the senses, art could only claim to rank as the most exquisite and self-sustaining among the selfish enjoyments. When it rose, however, to be the handmaid of knowledge and ethical purpose (the True and the Good), it would "worthily take its place beside the grandest products of human development, Science and Right, having as its object to enrich and beautify our lives by tuning us unconsciously into harmony with whatever is noblest in nature or in man" (ibid.). Although this Kantian aspiration is consistent with Spencer's progressive theory of the development of taste, it was uncharacteristic of *Physiological Aesthetics,* which overwhelmingly described art as "a means for the gratification of the senses."

In Allen's influential article "The New Hedonism," the author of *Physiological Aesthetics* and by then publicist of the New Woman specifically contrasted the New Hedonism, or the philosophy of pleasure and pain, with the Old Asceticism, which he associated with the work ethic and self-restraint, specifically targeting the productivist tradition represented by Carlyle.[49] "Self-development," he proclaimed, "is greater than self-sacrifice" (382). Yet although Allen's interest is in pleasure, feeling, and sensation, these are inextricably linked with sexual reproduction, and the document is specifically an argument in favor of sex: "Now there is one test case which marks the difference between the hedonistic and ascetic conception of life better than any

48. Bourdieu, *Distinction.*
49. Grant Allen, *Fortnightly Review,* March 1894, 377–92.

other. I am not going to shirk it. . . . From beginning to end, there is no feeling of our nature against which asceticism has made so dead a set as the sexual instinct" (383–84). In lists comparable to those of *Physiological Aesthetics*, Allen argues that from the beautiful song of the bird to the pleasing physical properties of animals, flowers, and fruits, "every lovely object in organic nature owes its loveliness direct to sexual selection" (385). He goes on to attribute all our "higher emotions"—"our sense of duty, parental responsibility, paternal and maternal love, domestic affections . . . pathos and fidelity, in one word, the soul itself in embryo" (387)—to "the instinct of sex." Thus the reproductive body returns at the fin de siècle to haunt the consuming or pleasured body, in direct evolutionary descent: the highest pleasures derive from the most basic instinct to reproduce. Throughout the 1890s Allen's heterosexual aesthetic, with its beautiful body formed for sexual selection, was in cultural dialectic with other, perverse aesthetics. In some cases, as I have written, art for art's sake was allied with a defense of sex for sex's sake, or nonreproductive sex.[50] In other cases, the aesthetic was not beautiful at all but sublime and terrible, and its body was often abject, repulsive. We have come to call this Other body the "Gothic" body.[51]

Physiological aesthetics—aesthetics that calculated immediate pleasure—was pervasive in the fin de siècle, not just in Pater's *Renaissance,* in which he wrote that our object was "to get as many pulsations as possible into the given time,"[52] but also in Vernon Lee's "psychological aesthetics." (*Physiological* and *psychological* were used interchangeably.) Based on her reading of Allen, Lee experimented on the sensitive body of her lesbian lover, Clementina Anstruther-Thomson, which aesthetic experiments compromised the ethical aesthetics Lee had inherited from Ruskin and the missionary aesthetics the aristocratic Anstruther-Thomson had inherited from a tradition of women's philanthropy.[53]

With the notable exception of Marxist aesthetics, what survived physiological aesthetics was not the linkage with ethical or political purpose but the hierarchy implied in the end of aesthetic history. For

50. Gagnier, *Idylls of the Marketplace,* 137–76.
51. See Kelly Hurley, *The Gothic Body: Sexuality, Materialism, and Degeneration at the Fin de Siècle* (Cambridge: Cambridge University Press, 1996).
52. Walter Pater, *Selected Writings,* ed. Harold Bloom (New York: Signet, 1974), 17.
53. See Diana Maltz, "Engaging 'Delicate Brains': From Working-Class Enculturation to Upper-Class Lesbian Liberation in Vernon Lee and Kit Anstruther-Thomson's Psychological Aesthetics," in *Women and British Aestheticism, 1860–1934,* ed. Talia Schaffer and Kathy Alexis Psomiades (Charlottesville: University Press of Virginia, 1999), 211–29.

the hundred years since Allen, aesthetics has served to divide the
people between high and low culture, or elite, popular, and mass arts;
between those who fancy themselves making fine distinctions and
those whose tastes are tolerant. Aesthetics has flattered a few, humili-
ated or baffled a few more, but most in postmodern society are indifferent, believing *chacun a son goût*. As a symbol of the Good, or a
theory of production, or a record of human history, aesthetics has been
disempowered. When art becomes entirely individual or subjective,
Hegel had argued, it dissolves. Ironically, it dissolves into the wealth
of impressions of consumer society, "a means for the gratification of
the senses."

Until Morris, none of the aesthetic philosophers much considered
women, except as objects of beauty (Burke) or, more often, as incapable of the finest discrimination because of their propensity for interestedness (Kant). Occasionally they served as disembodied Idea
(Goethe's Eternal Womanhood leading upward), more often, popu-
larly, as embodied animal whose developing intellect could only
threaten its reproductive function. Although women were largely excluded from the economic realm by economists, they were largely relegated to it by aesthetic theorists, who found them too rooted in the
reproduction of daily life to be disinterested in the consumption of art.
Morris included women in the liberation of creative labor in *News
from Nowhere,* but only with *Orlando* (1928) did Virginia Woolf, taking account of gender, rewrite the history of aesthetics and aesthetic
man from a feminist perspective. When the novel abruptly ends in October 1928, Orlando has led an aesthetic life: a life of rich and varied
sensations, having experienced (in addition to an evident suspension
of mortality) both genders, an uninhibited sexuality, perpetual good
health, leisure, wealth, in short, a life freed from the realms of necessity. There is no "toil and trouble" in *Orlando,* an absence indicating
the liberation of aesthetics from production to pleasant sensation and
leisurely craft (see Orlando's sole product, the poem "The Oak Tree").

In the Renaissance, Orlando is a mediocre and melancholy male
poet, writing poems at night while his house guests revel.[54] In the eighteenth century, she is feminized, "bright-eyed" and "bright-cheeked,"
gossiping and pouring tea for Pope and Addison: infantilized Beauty.
The nineteenth century and the British Empire come in with a "damp"
productivity—domestic, grey, fertile, and heavy. Orlando submits "to
the spirit of the age, and takes a husband" (243). By the fin de siècle,

---

54. Virginia Woolf, *Orlando: A Biography* (London: Harcourt Brace Jovanovich,
1928), 104.

an urban Orlando walks the streets Engels called "atomistic," in which she sees "[e]ach man and each woman bent on his [*sic*] own affairs . . . past vast windows piled high with handbags, and mirrors, and dressing gowns, and fishing rods": handbags for women who shop, mirrors for their narcissism, dressing gowns and fishing rods for leisure (275–78). Now all the young writers publish paperbacks and puffery, and, "in the pay of booksellers, turn out any trash that serves to pay their tailor's bills" (ibid.). At this point, Orlando reflects on the "fulfillment of natural desire" (294) and bears a boy, the nineteenth century culminating in consumption, commodification, leisure time, and biologism.

The twentieth century arrives with automobiles, electric lights, department stores, and the voice of America on the radio. Just before the books ends, Orlando speeds out of London in a motor car back to her house in the country, exhibiting the fractured identity of modernism:

> After twenty minutes the body and mind were like scraps of torn paper tumbling from a sack and, indeed, the process of motoring fast out of London so much resembles the chopping up small of body and mind, which precedes unconsciousness and perhaps death that it is an open question in what sense Orlando can be said to have existed at the present moment. Indeed we should have given her over for a person entirely disassembled. (307)

Although Orlando cannot escape the atomic-atomistic age, she regains a centered self-image associated with the countryside, traditional landscape of the beautiful, when returned to that place of slow production and sensuous life:

> She had been working at [her poem] for close on three hundred years now. It was time to make an end. And so she began . . . thinking as she read how very little she had changed all these years. She had been a gloomy boy, in love with death, as boys are; and then she had been amorous and florid; and then she had been sprightly and satirical; and sometimes she had tried prose and sometimes she had tried the drama. Yet through all these changes she had remained, she reflected, fundamentally the same. She had the same brooding meditative temper, the same love of animals and nature, the same passion for the country and the seasons. (236–37)

This centered wholeness associated with country houses, however, was accessible only to those freed from necessity, or, as Woolf would say in the same year that *Orlando* was published, "for those with five hundred a year and rooms of our own."[55]

It was otherwise with Hardy. Contrary to *Orlando*'s freedoms and aesthetic tolerance, *Jude the Obscure* illustrates the intractable tensions in the period between ethical, political-economic, and physiological aesthetics. The latter probably predominates in the novel. From the beginning, Jude possesses a distinct temperament. Uncommonly sensitive to the sufferings of birds (34), pigs (36), rabbits (234), and women (289), he *expects* others to feel as he does. On being moved by a church hymn, Jude assumes that the composer will sympathize with his own ambition. He is shocked and disappointed to find, upon seeking him out, that the composer has given up music for trade (214–15).

Jude and Sue's uncommon "sensitivity" (305) is manifested not only in sympathy toward vulnerability but also in their mutual recoil from vulgarity. While Jude castigates himself for his innate and vicious attraction to women and spirits, he cannot help feeling aesthetically violated when Arabella reveals a hairpiece on their wedding night: he feels a sudden distaste for her, "a feeling of sickness," and fears that she might have "an instinct towards artificiality . . . might become adept in counterfeiting" (79). When Arabella sells his photograph before she emigrates, Jude perceives "the utter death of every tender sentiment in his wife" (93). He regrets their marriage, "based upon a temporary feeling which had no necessary connection with affinities that alone render a life-long comradeship tolerable" (90). He shares those affinities with Sue, who is "light and slight, of the type dubbed elegant" (109) and variously described as "uncarnate" (207), a "disembodied phantom, hardly flesh at all" (265, 413), and "a phantasmal bodiless creature" (279). The cruelty that Sue's bodilessness entails for her husbands is forgiven by Jude's agonized "all that's best and noblest in me loves you, and your freedom from everything that's gross has elevated me" (285). Sue demands this sublimation and continually condemns the carnal Arabella (Matter to Sue's Reason) as "low," "coarse," and "vulgar" (285, 287, 290). We might understand Arabella as instinctively acting upon Hume's famous dictum that "Reason is and ought only to be the slave of the passions, and can never pretend to any other office than to serve and obey them," in which a minimal reason relates means to ends but makes no claims concerning the rightness of ends.[56]

55. Virginia Woolf, *A Room of One's Own* (San Diego: Harcourt Brace Jovanovitch, 1957), 117–18. I have analyzed Woolf's views on economic and aesthetic individualism in *Subjectivities: A History of Self-Representation in Britain, 1832–1920* (Oxford: Oxford University Press, 1991), 36–39.

56. David Hume, *Treatise of Human Nature* (Middlesex: Penguin, 1969), 415.

Jude's communal feeling as a stonemason can no more be reconciled with these hierarchical tastes than his feeling for the laborer can be reconciled with his chastisement of the body. One aesthetic is productivist, the other is discriminatory and ascetic. Jude, the working man of taste, embodies the contradictions.

Maintaining this level of taste requires vigilant idealization, not only of Jude and Sue's own relationship as Shelleyan soulmates but of everything and everyone else. When Jude at nineteen agrees to marry Arabella, he comforts himself that "[h]is idea of her was the thing of most consequence, not Arabella herself" (78). He considers Oxford University in this sublimated vein:

> Through the solid barrier of cold cretaceous upland to the northward he was always beholding a gorgeous city, the fancied place he had likened to the new Jerusalem. . . . And the city acquired a tangibility, a permanence, a hold on his life. . . .
>
> "It is a city of light," he said to himself.
>
> "The tree of knowledge grows there," he added a few steps further on.
>
> "It is a place that teachers of men spring from and go to."
>
> "It is what you may call a castle, manned by scholarship and religion."
>
> After this figure he was silent a long while, till he added: "It would just suit me." (45)

Given Hardy's sympathy with determinism, it is hardly surprising that the son of Jude the idealist would inherit a tendency toward abstraction. Little Time "seemed to have begun with the generals of life, and never to have concerned himself with the particulars. To him the houses, the willows, the obscure fields beyond, were apparently regarded not as brick residences, pollards, meadows; but as human dwellings in the abstract, vegetation, and the wide dark world" (296). At the fair, Time says that he "should like the flowers very very much, if I didn't keep on thinking they'd be all withered in a few days!" (316). His instinct for abstraction comes to tragic conclusion when he acts on the Malthusian abstraction that children of the poor would be better off dead.

Yet the figure of Time raises one difference with physiological aesthetics that again shows how Hardy forecloses the aesthetic possibilities of his predecessors and of Woolf. This foreclosure is best illustrated by contrast with Pater. As mentioned above, Pater refers to aesthetic experience throughout his work as "the desire of beauty quickened by the sense of death." Mortality, our inevitable scarcity of time, gives us a passion for beauty: "We have an interval, and then our place knows us no more. Some spend this interval in listlessness, some in high passions, the wisest, at least among 'the children of this world,' in art and song. For our one chance lies in expanding that interval, in getting as many pulsations as possible into the given time" (61). Pater captures this sense of seizing the time in the wonderful last sentence of his essay on Leonardo da Vinci, in which he imagines the genius anticipating death: "We forget [antiquarianism]," writes Pater, "in speculating how one who had been always so desirous of beauty, but desired it always in such definite and precise forms, as hands or flowers or hair, looked forward now into the vague land, and experienced the last curiosity" (48). This aesthetic sense of loving the time, of spending one's interval in high passions or art and song, the passions of Woolf's *Orlando,* is forbidden in *Jude the Obscure.* Jude dies quoting Job, "Let the day perish wherein I was born. . . . Why died I not from the womb? . . . Wherefore is light given to him that is in misery?" (423–24). Hardy denies to Jude and Sue the aesthetic life of rich and varied sensuous experience, just as he has denied to them self-creation and autonomy and the value of their labor. In ethics, production, consumption, or taste, *Jude the Obscure* is an anti-aesthetic.

In the concluding pages of *History of Aesthetic,* Bosanquet quotes Hardy as representing a particularly modern aesthetic that leaves Burke's (and Woolf's) benevolent and sociable Beauty behind.

> Haggard Egdon [in Hardy's *Return of the Native*] appealed to a subtler and scarcer instinct, to a more recently learnt emotion, than that which responds to the sort of beauty called charming and fair. Indeed, it is a question if the exclusive reign of this orthodox beauty is not approaching its last quarter . . . human souls may find themselves in closer and closer harmony with external things wearing a somberness distasteful to our race when it was young. The time seems near, if it has not actually arrived, when the chastened sublimity of a moor, a sea, or a mountain will be all of nature that is absolutely in keeping with the moods of the more thinking among mankind. (467 n. 1)

Through Hardy, Bosanquet alludes to the end of Burke's and Woolf's bourgeois beauty, the beauty of order and civility, of the romanticized countryside, of stable hierarchical relations, and predicts the "terrible beauty" (Yeats) of modernity, a beauty that will evoke the feelings of the sublime, the overwhelming of the individual in the face of larger forces (Woolf's "person disassembled"). He correctly predicted the tropes of modernism: mass society, fascism, the terror of technological powers seemingly uncontrollable once unleashed.

The example of *Jude* takes us full circle, for of course *Jude the Obscure* is about desire: the desire to be free of one's class, one's gender, one's marriage and reproductive function. It is about the desire to live aesthetically the life of rich and varied sensations that Jude associates with the mental life and material beauty of Oxford. But it is ultimately an anti-aesthetic, showing how social institutions oppose the aesthetic life. Yet with hindsight we recall that just as *Jude* was revealed to the world, to cause the scandal that its demands on behalf of women and working people brought down on Hardy (such that he blamed it for his final abandonment of fiction), just then "labor" activists with their productivist ethics and sexual dissidents with their perverse pleasures were meeting in the social networks of Edward Carpenter, Olive Schreiner, Gertrude Dix, Eleanor Marx, and Amy Levy, to name just a few.[57]

This chapter has analyzed a plurality of aesthetics in Victorian Britain as a way to critique reified notions of "the Aesthetic." It is clear that in nineteenth-century Britain, aesthetic agendas were related to economic agendas in which key elements were the artist as creative or alienated producer, the man of taste or the critic as consumer, and the work as autonomous ("value") or commodified ("price"). If economics in the nineteenth century defined itself as the domain for the provision for the needs and desires of the people, aesthetics was in its most inclusive sense the apprehension and expression of the people's needs and desires at the level of sense, feeling, and emotion. In the next chapter I shall build on these historical foundations a concept of "practical" aesthetics.

57. See Sally Ledger, *The New Woman: Fiction and Feminism at the Fin de Siècle* (Manchester: Manchester University Press, 1997), esp. 35–61.

FIVE

Practical Aesthetics

Rolfe, Wilde, and New Women
at the Fin de Siècle

A current debate in literary and cultural studies centers on the relation of historicism to aesthetic evaluation. For a couple of decades,
historicists have delved deeply with little aesthetic evaluation, and aesthetic formalists have provided subjective evaluation without regard
for how audiences actually receive or consume the work. In this chapter, I explore the *functions* of the great aesthetic categories—the Sublime, the Beautiful, Taste, Form, and so forth—within specific material
conditions. In *Idylls of the Marketplace* I showed how the circumstances of Wilde's imprisonment, especially solitary confinement, en-
forced silence, bureaucratic centralization, and unproductive labor, informed the style and content of *De Profundis,* the long letter Wilde
wrote to Alfred Douglas from prison. Today I believe that aesthetic
knowledge saved Wilde's life, or at least his sanity, while he was in
prison, and I want to add this study of *De Profundis* to an examination
of other aesthetic moments as they arise in specific conditions. I am
asking, when we cannot change the world, what kinds of aesthetic
knowledge provide alternatives to the forces of brutalization, mechanization, or commodification? What are the pragmatics, or practical
functions, of aesthetics in everyday life, in this case in modern market
society?

Practical aesthetics concerns itself with humans as creative producers and with the conditions of creativity, sense, sensation, feeling, taste,
and emotion. It concerns the dulcet effect of beauty on society and
social relations, and it deals with the expression of everyday experience. Three case studies will demonstrate practical aesthetics: Frederick Rolfe's fantasy of exact exchange in social relations, Oscar Wilde's

An earlier version of this chapter appeared as "A Critique of Practical Aesthetics" in
Aesthetics and Ideology, ed. George Levine (New Brunswick, N.J.: Rutgers University
Press, 1994), 264–82.

abandonment of both production and consumption aesthetics in prison in favor of a Kantian beauty, and some New Women's criticisms of male aesthetes in pursuit of pleasure.

FREDERICK ROLFE: A DECADENT FANTASY
OF EXACT EXCHANGE

The difference between Aestheticism as presented by Ruskin, Morris, and Wilde and the English Decadence might be approached psychologically. Anyone who has moved in progressive or liberal circles—and here I include feminist circles—has witnessed the demoralizing case of the wannabe Progressive who is incapable of operating in conditions of uncertainty, risk, or vulnerability; incapable of living without authoritarian or hierarchical structures; incapable, in short, of living with change. Since risk, vulnerability, and instability are the inevitable conditions of progress, this psychological incapacity, no matter how fervent the conscious commitment, throws the wannabe liberal perpetually into contradiction between her emotional needs and her abstract desires. The nature of nurture as we have known it renders some people psychologically incapable of living with freedom.

This psychological contradiction is the secret of the Decadence. William Morris could immerse himself in the social without fear of loss of identity, and trusted his own body to judge value. Asserting, "I make no social distinctions; I didn't care twopence what they were," Wilde at least attempted to live life with the freedom of art. Both risked social position, exposed themselves to emotional instability, recognized their interdependence with others, and promoted—even precipitated—change. The Decadents, although they desired freedom from bourgeois constraints and conventions, at the same time required, even sought, control, stability, and distance from others. This contradiction leads to the hysterical and outrageous quality of the writing of Huysmans, Stoker, Conrad, and Rolfe, where the imaginative exploration of the horizons of desire culminates in recuperative and repressive closure. Feminist theorists from Simone de Beauvoir to Carol Gilligan and Nancy Chodorow through to Jessica Benjamin have described the personality with hard boundaries, unable to expose itself to the risk of others, a failure that has been associated, rather parochially perhaps, with the masculine need to differentiate the male self from the socially devalued mother. In the broad social arena—the society with hard boundaries, the modern militarized nation-state—the fear of undifferentiation manifests itself as fear of engulfment by the mass, of external invasion by barbarian hordes. The antidote to this social undifferentiation is to maintain hierarchy, to seek a social space in which everyone knows her place and where all social relations are predetermined. The personality or state with hard boundaries seeks immunization against contamination and an illusory autonomy from other personalities and states. It does not seek change but "scientifically" calculates "fair" exchanges. It sees risk in terms of sacrifice. In its hardest form, it attains the psychological condition of military hierarchy; in its unconscious and contradictory form, it achieves the psychological condition of decadents, for whom art is the only space—a tiny, safe space—of freedom.[1]

A classic Decadent text, in this sense, is Frederick Rolfe's *Desire and Pursuit of the Whole: A Romance of Modern Venice* (1909). Appropriated as a cult work in the 1960s, the novel has again fallen out of fashion except among aficionados of gay history. The subject of desire and pursuit is Nicholas Crabbe, an English expatriate and writer barely surviving in Venice. Like his namesake, he is hard on the outside but inwardly soft; the whole he desires and pursues is the ideal Love of Plato's parable. Crabbe requires from the beloved who will be his other half absolute loyalty, complete fidelity, and the physical attributes of a young Venetian sailor. These he finds in a sixteen-year-old female earthquake victim named Ermenegilda. Soft on the outside but inwardly firm, Ermenegilda is adopted by Crabbe as his gondolier, dressed and addressed as a boy (now called "Zildo") and consecrated to sharing Crabbe's fate in his adopted city. Having obliterated her sex—except in rare and poignant moments when Crabbe stumbles upon vestigial traces of her femininity, for example, a rag doll concealed in their pupparin—Crabbe and the narrator fervently establish perfect sympathy between Zildo and Crabbe, meaning, as a contemporary reader will quickly note, Zildo's sympathy with Crabbe, whom he/she always addresses as Master.

Their perfect sympathy is contrasted with Crabbe's uncompromising lack of sympathy with all of his compatriots—whether at home or in Venice. The imaginative investment inspiring half the text is the fantasy of perfect love with Zildo; that driving the other half—and it is equally impassioned—is a typically Decadent hatred of bourgeois English life: its materialism and spiritual shallowness, its lack of imagination and lack of appreciation of the "natural aristocrat" (Crabbe),

1. In 1959, Renato Poggioli characterized the decadent aesthete whose yearning for cultural salvation dwindled to the mere salvaging of beautiful tidbits. "Qualis Artifex Pereo! or Barbarism and Decadence," *Harvard Library Bulletin* 13 (1959): 135–59.

and its vulgar and tedious heterosexual domesticity. The objects of Crabbe's prolonged and eloquent vituperation are scarcely-veiled associates of Rolfe. W. H. Auden, who wrote the Foreword to the only edition of the novel still in print, describes Crabbe/Rolfe as the quintessential paranoid. I quote at length because the portrait could be of any number of fictive and real characters in the European Decadence.

A paranoid goes through life with the assumption: "I am so extraordinary a person that others are bound to treat me as a unique end, never as a means." Accordingly, when others treat him as a means or are just indifferent, he cannot believe this and has to interpret their conduct as malignant; they are treating him as an end, but in a negative way; they are trying to destroy him.

The "normal" person knows that, as a matter of fact, in most of our relations most of the time, we are doing no more than make use of each other, as a rule with mutual consent, as a means to pleasure, intellectual stimulus, etc., but keeps up the convention, both with himself and others, that we love and are loved for "ourselves alone," a fiction which is probably wise, for not only would social life be unbearable without it, but also the possibilities of genuine agape which, rare and delicate as they may be, do exist, would wither without its protective encouragement.

But it is a salutary experience also that, every now and then, we should have it stripped from us and that is what the paranoid does. His inordinate demand that we love him very much and his accusation when we do not that we hate him very much compel us to realise that we very rarely love or hate anybody; on the contrary, we can only stand each other in small doses without getting bored. The paranoid is the epitome of the bore. Crabbe was mistaken in thinking that the British colony in Venice hated him, but he was quite correct in thinking that they would be highly relieved to hear that he was dead.

Any paranoid is a nuisance, but a penniless one is a torment. The average person, if he has enough money in his pockets to be comfortable, will feel an obligation to help an acquaintance in a financial jam such as being unable to pay a hotel bill, but he hopes that will be the end of the matter and he certainly does not expect it to be taken too personally. Personally, however, is just how the paranoid takes it; he will never leave a benefactor alone because, to him, the important thing is not his hotel bill but the interest another has shown in him by paying it; consequently, he will soon create another crisis as a test and continue until the wretched benefactor can bear no more and the inevitable explosion occurs.[2]

We see that the loyal and true Zildo is merely a fantasy-reaction against the "betrayals" of the perfidious English, whom Rolfe/Crabbe never ceases to test and who never fail to fail the test.

To go somewhat beyond Auden's commonsensical ethos of self-interest, it takes a Crabbe to show us how very little most of us adhere to Kant's categorical imperative to treat others as ends in themselves rather than means to our own profit, pleasure, stimulation, or comfort. It takes a Crabbe to show us that while we use others we are nonetheless resentful when they take our use of them personally—as if it were our purpose to use them rather than simply our purpose to be profit-maximizing, pleasured, stimulated, or comforted. Those who are exploited for our gain only imagine that we have harbored malice aforethought. Our actions are selfish but not personal: it is a definition of modern anomie.

In the end, the beauty and loyalty of Venice and Zildo are the fantasy contrast to Crabbe's abuse and neglect at the hands of his compatriots. Since they will not justly give him his due, he starves to death. Rolfe depicts the homeless (in Italian, "without-roof") Crabbe wandering all night in the Field of Mars, dying of exposure in the public spaces of gorgeous Venice composing his magnum opus *Towards Aristocracy*. Even the title is an oblique and decadent reference to the properly aesthetic and socialist poem by Edward Carpenter, *Towards Democracy* (1883), reminding us of the precise intertextualities of Decadence and Aestheticism or aesthetic democracy. Carpenter, one of the more "out" homosexuals in nineteenth-century England, and one of the most genuinely democratic and progressive writers of the age, is the perfect foil to Crabbe/Rolfe, who must in the long run love a girl rather than a sixteen-year-old boy, because boys were historically autonomous pursuers of self-interest and not realistically capable of absolute and life-long devotion to middle-aged men with no money. They did not, like historical (and aristocratic) girls, "choose" to serve and then find that in their service was their "perfect freedom." (This explains the social and narratological bases of the conclusion, in which Zildo is gendered as female; whereas through most of the text, and as Rolfe's realistic object of desire, she is male.) Indeed the "out" and

---

2. Frederick Rolfe [Baron Corvo], *The Desire and Pursuit of the Whole* (New York: Da Capo, 1986), vi–vii.

open lovingness of an Edward Carpenter is the perfect contrast to the love-as-domination of the repressed Rolfe.

For most readers from Auden to the present, the troubling aspect of Crabbe's martyrdom at the hands of the treacherous but banal English is Crabbe/Rolfe himself. Although perspicacious about the faults of the English, Crabbe/Rolfe is utterly blind to his own. He often praises Venetian charity but is incapable either of accepting it or of getting a job, insisting always on his "right" to his own expropriated property. Obliterating Zildo's femininity, he never ceases to remind the reader of his own "abnormally masculine" physique and temperament. What Crabbe sees is a failure of nobility on the part of everyone but himself and Zildo, and what he demands from everyone, despite his ardent religiosity—Rolfe tried hard to enter holy orders and, failing, deceptively used Fr. (from Frederick) to signify "Father"—is the repentance that should be the Lord's. Seeing himself as a rebel of heroic, even sublime, proportions, he bears all the marks of the most conservative Englishness: love of hierarchy and of ritual for its own sake, obsession with private property (including the Beloved), general inflexibility, and a deluded self-sufficiency. While he protests that he wants (comm)unity (the desire and pursuit of the [w]hole), the novel chronicles the assertion of his independence—as an artist, an expatriate, and a lover: his boundaries, like the crab's, are armoured, impermeable.

Wilde told a story about love called "The Teacher of Wisdom." In it, a holy man seeks for the perfect knowledge of God as an object to be known by him. At the end of his life he has failed to know enough. When he gives up the search, he receives by this sacrifice the perfect love of God, or the gift of himself as a subject of God's love. Given Rolfe's rigid need to know and control the Other, the only way the relation of self to other can be reconciled with mutuality is to be magical, romantic. The fantastic Zildo reappears as a deus/dea ex machina, as, in fact, the principle of justice (but, as we shall see, a particular kind of justice). Finding Crabbe dead from starvation and exposure (or the negligence of Others), Zildo now repays his first sacrifice with one greater: she gives him her blood, proclaiming, "you get back what you give." As he had saved her from the earthquake, so she now saves him. At this moment, and for the first time, Crabbe and the narrator call her "she" rather than "he," and the desire and pursuit of the whole is crowned and rewarded by heterosexual love. Thus not risk, nor generosity, nor change (the values of the earlier, socialist aesthetes) rule Rolfe's world, but the firm principle of exact exchange: you get back what you give, measure for measure. Failing to be loved for himself alone ("true value"), Crabbe/Rolfe demands from beloved as well as benefactor exact exchange. (Below when I turn to Rolfe's biography, I shall consider how much this psychological structure has to do with his dealings with male prostitutes.) Moreover, what you give is returned to you in symmetrical gender relations—the male and the female, the hard and the soft. The formal disparity between the Venetian romance of the marvelous Zildo and the satirical realism of English finance at home and abroad also indicates the autonomy of the aesthetic that Ruskin, Morris, and Wilde had repudiated: only art (the dreamy boy-girl Zildo) can save Crabbe; for Rolfe, art is an escape from, not a transformation of, daily life.

Whereas Ruskin, Morris, and Wilde wrote for freedom, equality, and toleration, the Decadents may be characterized by their fear of the freedom of Others: of women (the New Woman literature and late-Victorian Gothic, which express the fear of undifferentiation from female or feminized bodies of various morphologies); of racial Others (the "heart of darkness" literature of the British recoiling from their own projections on Asia, Africa, and Latin America); of working-class Others (the East End poverty literature and naturalism that thrived in the 1890s); and national Others (the literature of expatriatism, whether in Venice, Mexico, or New Zealand). Indeed, the most salient characteristic of Decadence to surface in recent criticism is English writers' abjection—their fear of loss of boundaries—and their recuperative attempts to fortify the rigid boundaries of the self and British society against the barbarians at the gates. (Both the United States and Britain have gone through cycles of such Decadence, the most recent signified by irrational fears of "multiculturalism," "diversity," and "asylum fraud," the struggle over educational policy taking up where immigration policy leaves off.)[3] This decadent fear of the freedom of Others is a dominant strain in European and American modernism.

In its sublime or in its bathetic form, a "romance" is technically, generically, a search for the object of desire, whether the object is the Holy Grail, the beloved Beatrice, or a better world (the *Zukunftstaat*).[4] In Rolfe's case a search for the beloved is inseparable from finance, and this probably has something to do with his objects of desire having been male prostitutes. *The Desire and Pursuit of the Whole* was written while Rolfe was living on the margins of Palazzo Mocenigo Corner in Venice, as the penniless guest of Dr. and Mrs. van Somerens, car-

3. Donna Haraway discusses the history of American decadence in terms of fear of others in *Primate Visions* (New York: Routledge, 1989). See especially ch. 3, "Teddy Bear Patriarchy," 26–58.

4. For such generic definitions, it remains wise to begin with Northrop Frye's *The Anatomy of Criticism: Four Essays* (Princeton: Princeton University Press, 1957).

rying logs and separating cream for his board. He was evicted after eight months, when his hosts read his abuse of their hospitality in the manuscript. While composing the novel, Rolfe wrote a number of letters to benefactors in England in which we can see how his aesthetic was formed in part through pornography (literally, writing about prostitutes). In a number of letters Rolfe describes in detail his sexual activity with boys called "Amadeo" who "serviced" him gratis in exchange for Rolfe recommending them to his richer friends, for example, the benefactor correspondent.[5] In Letter 10 Rolfe wants to know if his "writing" (that is, pornography) gives his correspondent "pleasure," which he defines as consumed in "use":

> I want to know whether my writing makes my readers' imagination see and smell and hear and taste and feel what I describe.
> What he [Amadeo] would be in use I tremble to imagine.
> And not to be able to devour his beauty so freely offered now!
> There's a lot of lovely material utterly wasted and thrown away.

This "free" use or consumption of boys in pleasure is contrasted with the reproductive "waste" of women:

> He'll be like this till Spring, say three months more. Then some great fat slow cow of a girl will . . . drain him dry.
> Look at Fausto. That Jew is a begetter of offspring. He certainly isn't a source of pleasure. [In which Fausto's potency seems allied to his Jewishness.]
> Unless they are used and cultivated *now*, they will flower at Easter, fruit at midsummer, and be fallen by the autumn.

Just as Rolfe openly used his benefactors' money to buy presents for the boys whose services he cannot himself afford ("If only another letter comes from you all would be well. At least I could give [Piero] a day's pleasure" [Letter 15]), he also uses others' money to maintain rank—distinguish himself from others—that he could not sustain without it: "One reason why I'm so infinitely obliged to you for the P.O.'s is that it enabled me to tip the three remaining servants. If I hadn't been able to do that at Christmas, they would have treated me as one of themselves; and their insolent familiarity would have become

5. Frederick Rolfe, *The Venice Letters*, ed. Cecil Woolf (L. and A. Woolf Ltd. ed., 1909). I have read these letters in corrected proofs sent from Cecil Woolf to the Wyndham Lewis scholar Alan Munton, but have not been able to lay my hands on a copy of the published volume. The proofs constitute a selection of letters numbered 1 through 25 plus notes by Woolf. The pornographic letters are primarily 7, 8, 13, 14, 15, 16. References in the text are to numbered letters.

intolerable" (Letter 12). "Being able to supplement my gently haughty demeanor with tips," Rolfe writes, "has so far saved me from undue arrogance" (ibid.). While Rolfe enables unity with the object of desire through the help of others, he also maintains distance from the less desirable through the same agency of others. The male prostitutes "service" him and his friends; the servants serve his sense of personal distinction. While Rolfe fantasizes pleasures in use distinct from productivity and reproduction, his actual relations are pathologically mediated by monetary exchange. He needs patrons so that he may patronize boys and distinguish himself from servants. His *aristos* was heavily subsidized.

However one estimates the romance of Zildo or the realism of Rolfe's financial dealings with patrons and publishers, another aspect of Rolfe's novel also resonates with the concerns of practical aesthetics. Auden refers to Rolfe's artistically embodied love for Venice: Rolfe knows Venice like an infant knows the body of its mother. Yet Rolfe's love for Venice is uniquely powerful because it is a passion for a *city* on the part of a man with no *domus*—a homeless, indeed a starving, man—who is also (with his boy prostitutes) without domesticity. This part of the novel is also true: Rolfe was for long periods homeless and starving. He writes the sufferings of those who sleep on the streets; who watch helplessly the disintegration of their clothes, beginning with underwear; who, experiencing mental and physical agony and loneliness, contrive "to present to the world a face offensive, disdainful, utterly unapproachable" (281). Rolfe chronicles how the homeless live by bread alone, until they can stomach only a handful of water, taken surreptiously at night from public lavatories. He tells what it is like to sicken and die alone.

Just beyond this vale of tears there is always the daily life of tranquil Venice, described in the prose with reverent detail yet with a reluctance to give up distinctions of taste, which are invoked in the following passage by "plebians," "pathetic designs," and "cheap chrysanthemums." The destitute Crabbe

> slowly paced along cypress-avenues, between the graves of little children with blue or white standards and the graves of adults marked by more sombre memorials. All around him were patricians bringing sheaves of painted candles and gorgeous garlands of orchids and everlastings, or plebians on their knees grubbing up weeds and tracing pathetic designs with cheap chrysanthemums and farthing night-lights. Here, were a baker's boy and a telegraph-messenger, repainting their father's grave-post with a

tin of black and a bottle of gold. There, were a half a dozen ribald venal dishonest licentious young gondolieri, quiet and alone on their wicked knees round the grave of a comrade.[6]

These two images, of human vulnerability and our consequent interdependence, as figured here in the homely pieties of daily life and death, were images that Auden himself would associate with Italy in his hymn to the unheroic but tolerant life of the senses, "In Praise of Limestone" (1948).

In that poem of dissolving landscapes that begins in the Yorkshire of Auden's childhood and ends in the Italy of his mature desire, the young male "never doubts / that for all his faults he is loved,"[7] and the child is forgiven for wishing "to receive more attention than his brothers" (115). The "band of rivals"—not really competitors, but more like brothers in athletic games—cannot "conceive a god whose temper-tantrums are moral / and not to be pacified by a clever line / Or a good lay."

> Accustomed to a stone that responds,
> They have never had to veil their faces in awe
> Of a crater whose blazing fury could not be fixed [. . .]
> Their eyes have never looked into infinite space
> Through the lattice-work of a nomad's comb. (115)

What they do, instead, is seek at their own expense the attention of others: "ruin a fine tenor voice / For effects that bring down the house."

Auden contrasts these pleasure-seekers, these hedonists, with saints, Caesars, and ascetics ambitious to control self or others, beckoned by "Immoderate soils where the beauty was not so external . . . and the meaning of life / Something more than a mad camp" (116). But he imaginatively rebukes the scientist for "his concern for Nature's / Remotest aspects" (116). Italy's forgiving, inconstant, capricious landscape, "made solely for pleasure" and friendship, without duty or purpose, makes "a further point": "The blessed will not care what angle they are regarded from, / having nothing to hide."

The blessed are the beautiful who do not count for much, who do not calculate exact exchange, whose perspective and values are not absolute. As Auden says and Rolfe could only dream of, what could be more like a good mother's tolerance, forgiveness, and flexibility than limestone? Yet economists such as Gary Becker find it "puzzling" (in

6. Rolfe, *Desire and Pursuit of the Whole*, 281–82; see also Letter 4.
7. W. H. Auden, *Selected Poetry of W. H. Auden* (New York: Vintage, 1971), 114–17.

a chapter called "The Economic Way of Looking at Life") that parents in Western countries tend to bequeath equal amounts of their wealth to different children.[8]

AN AESTHETIC LIFE: OSCAR WILDE'S *DE PROFUNDIS*

Art is not a mirror but a crystal. It creates its own shapes and forms.
—Letter to More Adey from Reading

Wilde's Reading Gaol figure for art is not limestone but a crystal creating its own shapes and forms. The modern judgment of *De Profundis* was always that it was an "aesthetic" document, made to appear even more so by Robert Ross's initial suppression of the parts in which Wilde mentioned Douglas. Consider the reviews from 1905 when it was first published with all reference to Douglas suppressed:[9] "A shining light of literary purity reflected from a dark background of insincerity and depravity. . . . Odious pretentions. . . . Oscar Wilde was a poser to the last" (1905). "This is not sorrow, but its dextrously constructed counterfeit. . . . [Wilde] grew to be incapable of deliberately telling the truth about himself or anything else" (1905). "There was something about Wilde's personality that renders it difficult for the reader to believe in his sincerity" (1908). When the unexpurgated letter was finally published in 1962, reviews continued in the same vein: Wilde was "almost unable to call up the language of sincerity" (1962). "The veil of artifice is seldom lifted" (1962). "Wilde was totally devoid of an interior life" (1962). "Wilde creates the myth and legend of himself . . . a mingling of artificial high comedy and grotesque and lurid melodrama" (1962). "He may never really have existed, except as a performance" (1962). One cannot help but think that if these phrases were said of Wilde today they would serve as terms of praise rather than blame. Indeed, the last links the modern to the postmodern response, in which the idea of essence has been supplanted by that of performance. A few years ago, Jonathan Dollimore attributed to Wilde an antiessentialist concept of human nature and a critique of sincerity and subjective depth, as if the charges of Wilde's reviewers simply ex-

8. Gary S. Becker, *Accounting for Tastes* (Cambridge: Harvard University Press, 1998), 156.
9. For full references to the reviews cited, see Regenia Gagnier, *Idylls of the Marketplace: Oscar Wilde and the Victorian Public* (Stanford: Stanford University Press, 1986), 231–32.

pressed his own considered philosophical views.[10] In our most recent theories of performativity, attributes or qualities such as human nature or gender are not expressions of a soul within but performances that when repeated take on the appearance of nature.

Within Victorian aesthetics, Wilde's works seem to run the gamut of aesthetic possibilities: the "Soul of Man Under Socialism" considers both the conditions of artistic production and the work's consumption in mass society; *Salomé* and *Dorian Gray* primarily lend themselves to hedonics, or consumption models of pleasure and taste; and *De Profundis*, written in prison, must abandon aesthetics of production and pleasure to achieve the ethical reconstruction of the self. This multiplicity suggests that rather than *a* Wildean aesthetic, aesthetics were, for Wilde, a performance that altered in kind with his audience and location.

To take another example, Wilde specifically produced an aesthetic of glamour in his plays, which, he pointed out repeatedly in his letters, was literally inconceivable in prison. With this prefatory anthropological or pluralist understanding of what aesthetics might mean today, I return to *De Profundis*, its ethical aesthetic, and its gendering mechanisms, bearing in mind that both the aesthetic and the gendering may not be essences but performances realizable only under specific conditions. It may be that there is no one Wildean aesthetic: there is only Wilde at home (displaying his taste), Wilde on stage (displaying his glamour), Wilde on the streets (engaged in acts of creative production or consumption), or Wilde in gaol (reconstructing ethics). There is no one Wildean gender or sexuality, only Wilde at home with Constance and the boys, Wilde at the Savoy feasting with panthers, or Wilde in Reading Gaol reimagining a boy whose red rose-leaf lips made for music of song take on in anger "the froth and foam of an epileptic fit."[11] My argument is that just as aesthetics means wresting aesthetic effects from everyday life—seizing moments of sense, feeling, emotion, or taste—so gender and sexuality are less properties of individuals than effects of relationships that change over time.[12]

10. See Jonathan Dollimore, "Different Desires: Subjectivity and Transgression in Wilde and Gide," in *Critical Essays on Oscar Wilde*, ed. Regenia Gagnier, 48–67.

11. Oscar Wilde, *De Profundis*, in *The Portable Oscar Wilde*, ed. Richard Aldington and Stanley Weintraub (New York: Penguin, 1981), 538; see also *The Letters of Oscar Wilde*, ed. Rupert Hart-Davis (New York: Harcourt Brace and World, 1962), p. 326. All references to *De Profundis* will be to the Penguin *Portable Oscar Wilde*.

12. This view is in line with the less essentialist contemporary views of gender and sexuality, such as queer theory, or theory less inclined toward fixed identity politics than gay male or lesbian studies. See in particular Joseph Bristow, "'A complex multiform creature'—Wilde's sexual identities," in *The Cambridge Companion to Oscar Wilde*,

The problem for Wilde in *De Profundis* was how to reconstitute the ego after its sublime confrontation with abjection in prison. In Kant the sublime is a psychological condition in which the self is overwhelmed by magnitude or number but then reconstituted through Reason and an act of human will. There is much of magnitude and number in *De Profundis:* the mechanical "system" of prison centralization that runs over the prisoners like a juggernaut, the countless minutes of waiting and watching, the magnitude of the tragedy of Wilde's fall into ignominy, the calculations of the moneys or books lost through Douglas's extravagance or carelessness or thoughtlessness, the immensity of sorrow itself, of *lacrimae rerum,* all the tears of the world, as Wilde calls them when he writes of his mother's dying while her son is in gaol. Yet granting that the letter itself is an instance of the sublime, of the ego reconstituting itself as an act of will after its confrontation with abjection, I want to focus on how Wilde in gaol experienced the aesthetic of the Beautiful.

This was precisely in contrast to an abject image of Alfred Douglas. Traditionally the characteristics associated with the Beautiful were civility, sociability, and form (as opposed to formlessness and abjection). The effect of the Beautiful is to remove the selfish desires, to calm, to soothe, to bring the self's warring passions and interests into harmony and to harmonize the self with others. Wilde contrasts Robbie Ross's tact and taste in love and literature with Alfred Douglas's "world of coarse uncompleted passions, of appetite without distinction, desire without limit, and formless greed." Throughout the letter Wilde is obsessed with the formlessness he associates with Douglas and his life with Douglas, and with the form he wants to create for himself and his future life. In the famous passage that begins "I was a man who stood in symbolic relations to the art and culture of my age" (579–81), his life before Douglas had form, and it produced form in others' lives. "I awoke the imagination of my century so that it created myth and legend around me: I summed up all systems in a phrase and all existence in an epigram" (580). Notice here that the forms Wilde claims to

---

ed. Peter Raby (Cambridge: Cambridge University Press, 1997), 195–218; Bristow, *Sexuality* (London: Routledge, 1997); Bristow, *Effeminate England: Homoerotic Writing After 1885* (New York: Columbia University Press, 1995); Gregory Woods, "The Futures of Gay Literature" (paper presented at the Gender and Sexuality seminar of the Brandenburg Symposium of the British Council, Potsdam, 12–18 September 1998); and see Woods, *A History of Gay Literature: The Male Tradition* (New Haven: Yale University Press, 1998); Alan Sinfield, *The Wilde Century: Effeminacy, Oscar Wilde, and the Queer Moment* (New York: Columbia University Press, 1994).

have produced are precisely cultural and literary forms: myth, legend, phrase, and epigram. With Douglas, he lost his form, in his own terms spent his genius, wasted his youth, grew careless of the lives of others, took pleasure and passed on, was dominated and frightened (580–81). Now in prison, his life has been one of feeling without form: "wild despair, and abandonment to grief . . . terrible and impotent rage . . . anguish that wept aloud; misery that could find no voice; sorrow that was dumb" (581). He quotes Wordsworth's Sublime imagining of the formlessness of suffering: "Suffering is permanent, obscure, and dark / And has the nature of Infinity" (581). The worst thing he can say of Douglas, to contrast with Robbie's taste and tact in love and literature, is that Douglas's letters lacked form. He recalls reading one, "in the middle of its mire, wondering with infinite sadness how you could write letters that were really like the froth and foam on the lips of an epilectic" (628), and he contrasts this with the memory of one of his own letters to Douglas, which was "like a passage from one of Shakespeare's sonnets" (538), the red rose-leaf lips made for music of song, representing Beautiful form, now transformed by Douglas into the image of abject formlessness. Here Wilde also matches the formlessness of Douglas's loss of self-control with his own "infinite"—that is, sublime, formless, overwhelming—sadness in prison.

De Profundis is obsessed with form:

What the artist is always looking for is that mode of existence in which soul and body are one and indivisible . . . in which Form reveals.

. . . In which the soul is made flesh, and the body instinct with Spirit.

Truth in Art is the unity of a thing with itself: the outward rendered expressive of the inward. (592, 607, 593)

Wilde introduces the figure of Jesus as precisely this, the incarnation in which form reveals, whose outward life is expressive of the inward, who gave voice to the formless cries of the oppressed (599). Jesus's life, as narrated by Wilde, is "the most wonderful of poems" (599), unmatched in Greek tragedy, Dante, Shakespeare, or Celtic myth. Wilde's two-page summary of the life of Christ culminates in praise of the form of the Mass as a drama (601).

Every part of *De Profundis* is infused with this will to form, including my favorite passage in all of Wilde, that on the Savoy dinners, in which every artistic element demands symmetry, reciprocity. In this passage, repayment of debt becomes a figure for perfect inner and

outer form: the outer forms of politeness, civility, and communal interdependence and the inner form of conduct, ethics, and Kantian practical reason.

The Savoy dinners—the clear turtle-soup, the luscious orto-
lans wrapped in their crinkled Sicilian vine-leaves, the heavy
amber-coloured, indeed almost amber-scented champagne—Da-
gonet 1880, I think, was your favourite wine? all have still to be
paid for. The suppers at Willis's, the special *cuvée* of Perrier-Jouet
reserved always for us, the wonderful *pâtés* procured directly
from Strasburg, the marvellous *fine champagne* served always at
the bottom of great bell-shaped glasses that its bouquet might be
the better savoured by the true epicures of what was really exquisite in life—these cannot be left unpaid, as bad debts of a dishonest *client.* Even the dainty sleeve-links—four heart-shaped moon-
stones of silver mist, girdled by alternate ruby and diamond for
their setting—that I designed, and had made at Henry Lewis's as
a special little present to you, to celebrate the success of my second comedy—these even—though I believe you sold them for a
song a few months afterwards—have to be paid for. I cannot
leave the jeweller out of pocket for the presents I gave you, no
matter what you did with them. . . . And what is true of a bankrupt is true of everyone else in life. For every single thing that is
done someone has to pay. (650–51)

In calling the passage Kantian I emphasize its aesthetico-ethical dimension. The essential elements of Kantian aesthetics were that the
Beautiful was a symbol of the moral good and that the moral good
was to free oneself from one's selfish desires so that one might act in
such a way that one's actions could be the basis of general action. The
theory was essentially bourgeois in that it related to the ethical construction of an autonomous subject who subjected his immediate desires to the social good, and in that way Wilde's high bourgeois trading
in wine and expensive jewelry is part of the civil culture of property
that Kant wrote about in his *Anthropology.* There, taste alone could
not make a morally good man (the subject is male in Kant), but it could
prepare him for the moral good by leading him to please others (see
chapter 4).

Yet though this aesthetico-ethical love of form is bourgeois, it is
not the formal*ism,* or the fetishism of formal aspects of art, that most
twentieth-century critics think of as such. It is not, for example, the
preoccupation with form that Bourdieu associates with the "taste" of
twentieth-century French lovers of high culture. Wilde specifically calls

formalism by the name of Philistinism, which he repudiates, and which he also associates with Douglas. As the Savoy dinners passage shows, form for Wilde is certainly sensuous, as in the exquisite pleasures of the dinners, but it is also ethical (in his story he must pay for them) and social (he must pay the jeweller for the sleeve-links of silver mist). Indeed, one might say that Wilde's attitude to form in *De Profundis* is best indicated by the difference between his treatment of creditors there and in *The Importance of Being Earnest*. In the original four-act version of *Earnest,* when Algy is "attached" for an outstanding bill of £762 at the Savoy, he breezily responds, "Pay it? How on earth am I going to do that? You don't suppose I have got any money? How perfectly silly you are. No gentleman ever has any money." The contrast with the Savoy dinners passage suggests that outside prison an aesthetic of debt points to irony, pleasure, and consumption, whereas in prison an aesthetic of debt points to conduct and ethics.

Wilde makes the distinction between substantive form ("someone has to pay") and empty formalism ("How on earth am I going to pay it?") through the figure of Jesus, who resisted what Wilde calls "stereotyped" form (612). He "had no patience with the dull lifeless mechanical systems that treat people as if they were things, and so treat everybody alike" (613). He "exposed the tedious formalisms so dear to the middle-class [!] mind with utter and relentless scorn" (614). The function of Wilde's Jesus, with his sympathetic imagination (612) and poetic justice (613), is the same as that of Rolfe's Zildo with respect to the perfidious English in Venice: to oppose the formalisms of "mechanical people, to whom life is a shrewd speculation dependent on a careful calculation of ways and means" (617)—this last quotation being a concise condemnation of the formalism of economic rationality. Indeed, in its hatred of mechanical systems and ethically neutral instrumentalism, the passage recalls Carlyle, the century's hater of formalism and neutrality par excellence.

In one of the angrier passages of the letter, Wilde tells Douglas that he "despises" him most because in urging him to sue Queensberry for libel Douglas had led Wilde to appeal to Philistine formalism.

The one disgraceful, unpardonable, and to all time contemptible action of my life was my allowing myself to be forced into appealing to Society for help and protection against your father . . . you brought the element of Philistinism into a life that had been a complete protest against it. . . . He is the Philistine who upholds and aids the heavy, cumbrous, blind mechanical forces of Society. (625)

Whereas Douglas in the letter lurches from total loss of self-control, abject panic, indulgence, and excess to empty formalism, epitomized in the laws he "forced" Wilde to appeal to, Wilde and Jesus are informed, formed by sympathy, and have the power to move others. We learn from Jesus as we learn from art: "He is just like a work of art himself. He does not really teach one anything, but by being brought into his presence one becomes something" (617). Jesus, like the Beautiful, is useless but transformative. To him Wilde contrasts Douglas, who was seemingly immune to informing form, "Don't you understand now that your lack of imagination was the one really fatal defect of your character?" (549). Yet Christ was "all imagination" (598 and passim).

Wilde is not just concerned with form in the letter; he is also concerned with the letter's form. The letter itself must be formed and re-formed, in order to compose its author. Wilde says that he writes the letter so that he can forgive Douglas and go on without bitterness (579). That is, forgiveness, like the Kantian Aesthetic, is a psychological process relating to the subject, not the object, and the writing of the letter is a form of action in the ethical construction of the self. In the classic theory of moral sentiments that informed Victorian psychology, one learned moral conduct through continuously evaluating the actions of others until one had internalized the moral virtues, both the "feminine" ("civilized") virtues of sympathy, benevolence, and mercy, and the "masculine" ("savage" or "aristocratic") virtues of duty and self-restraint. In exploring both sympathetic outpouring and self-restraint, Wilde achieves the range of moral virtues. He repeats this performance in "The Ballad of Reading Gaol," in which he has second thoughts about the sensual excesses of the body, while simultaneously making an effort of sympathy with the man about to die for murdering his wife.

Because this preeminently *social* activity—judging conduct by means of the conduct of others—must be enacted in isolation, through writing, Wilde's pronouncements here about *style* have a degree of sincerity and urgency beyond those elsewhere in his corpus. The ethical reconstruction of the self must happen in writing, and the writing is meant to display the masculine economy that Pater had claimed for the perfected individual style. "Self-restraint, a skilful economy of means, *ascesis,* that too has a beauty of its own," wrote Pater, "*Surplusage!* [the writer] will dread that, as the runner on his muscles" (110–11). Wilde writes:

> As for the corrections and *errata,* I have made them in order
> that my words should be an absolute expression of my thoughts,

and err neither through surplusage nor through being inadequate. . . . As it stands, at any rate, my letter has its definite meaning behind every phrase. There is in it nothing of rhetoric. Wherever there is erasion or substitution, however slight, however elaborate, it is because I am seeking to render my real impression, to find for my mood its exact equivalent. Whatever is first in feeling comes always last in form. (642)

Although Wilde's utterance here is provoked *in extremis,* we can recall from the previous chapter the history of masculine autonomy behind such repudiations of rhetoric, from Smith to Mill to Pater.

Nonetheless, this hard, gemlike individual style achieved with difficulty, the style that *is* the individual man, is ultimately eclipsed by a classic notion of the Beautiful, which, unlike the objects of mere taste (distinction), is impersonal, not private property but shared by all. Kant had made natural objects the essence of the Beautiful because art objects were conducive to egoism or individualism. Whereas taste had to do with individualism and private property, the Beautiful excluded self-interest and ownership. When one viewed a sunset, one's judgment was not clouded by desire for possession or envy of others: there was enough for all equally. In a passage that I used to think was sentimental but now believe to be one of literature's great instances of aesthetic imagination, Wilde writes of "those things that are meant as much for me as for anyone else—the beauty of the sun and moon, the pageant of the seasons, the music of daybreak and the silence of great nights" (586). He now reserves the term *beauty* for natural beauty, which he associates with his freedom:

> I tremble with pleasure when I think that on the very day of my leaving prison both the laburnum and the lilac will be blooming in the gardens, and that I shall see the wind stir into restless beauty the swaying gold of the one, and make the other toss the pale purple of its plumes so that all the air shall be Arabia for me. . . . I know that for me, to whom flowers are part of desire, there are tears waiting in the petals of some rose. . . . There is not a single colour hidden away in the chalice of a flower, or the curve of a shell, to which, by some subtle sympathy with the very soul of things, my nature does not answer. (654)

This natural beauty is a symbol, as Kant said, of the morally good: "Behind all this Beauty, satisfying though it be, there is some Spirit hidden of which the painted forms and shapes are but modes of manifestation, and it is with this Spirit that I desire to become in harmony"

(654). Refusing a philosophy of taste or pleasure, associated by this time exclusively with individualism and subjectivism, Wilde opts for the "universal" symbols of aesthetics: sunrise and sunset, the songs of birds, the flowers.

In sum, *De Profundis* rejects mere taste: "One who is entirely ignorant of the modes of Art in its revolution or the moods of thought in its progress . . . may yet be full of the very sweetest wisdom" (511). Or, "Charming people such as fishermen, shepherds, ploughboys, peasants and the like know nothing about Art, and are the very salt of the earth" (625). Indeed, it is Douglas who represents mere *taste:* "Your interests were merely in your meals and moods. Your desires were simply for amusements, for ordinary or less ordinary pleasures" (514). Or, "as your persistent grasp on my life grew stronger and stronger, [my] money was spent on little more than the pleasures of eating, drinking, and the like. . . . You demanded without grace and received without thanks" (516). Or, "Out of the reckless dinners with you nothing remains but the memory that too much was eaten and too much was drunk" (517).

De Profundis is informed by a history of aesthetic thought and feeling and an aesthetic love of form; yet it repudiates formalism and despises taste as a mean thing. Now, one might say that yes, *De Profundis* is about substantive, even Kantian, form; but after all it is only a performance. The beautiful images, the aesthetic feelings, serve Wilde in a theatrical or performative humiliation of Alfred Douglas made from Wilde's equally theatrical or performative position of ethical superiority. We have also seen that it is a gendered performance: Douglas is the formless, abject feminine castigated by Wilde the self-regulating man of reason. Or Douglas represents feminine matter to Wilde's masculine informing form. To which we might rejoin, yes, Wilde's aesthetic in *De Profundis* is a performance, one that is certainly at variance with other aesthetic performances elsewhere in his works.

This brings me to the relation of this aesthetic reading of *De Profundis* to my reading of the letter in *Idylls of the Marketplace* (1986), where I argued that it was determined by the material conditions of the prison. First, prison conditions of unproductive labor rendered prisoners unproductive, while the deprivations of incarceration (obviously) limited pleasure or taste. In Reading Gaol, Wilde was neither a producer nor a consumer: he was limited under the conditions of solitary confinement to working on the self. In *Idylls of the Marketplace* I included much testimony to this effect by other prisoners. As one twentieth-century prisoner put it, in memorably Platonic terms that resonate for others who have been in solitary confinement, "In solitary there is just you and your self. Then watch out, self." This means that in the 1890s the aesthetics available outside prison, creative labor (that gave rise to productivist aesthetics) or consumption (that gave rise to philosophies of taste), were unavailable inside. What was available was the inner psychological process that Kant described, the relating of perception to concept resulting in the free play of imagination that was the symbol of a greater freedom. Excluded from all ordinary practices of production and consumption, Wilde was inevitably drawn to the one aesthetic possible in prison at that time, the Kantian aesthetic, which in all its magnificent abstraction works only on the self.

I also pointed out in my early work on prison literature how central-ized prison systems are conducive to grand theories and claims to "see it all," and *De Profundis* also displays these. Such is Wilde's elaborate reading of Jesus, whose significant attribute is his autonomy, or inde-pendence of context in time or space, such that he should have been crucified by "tedious middle-class minds" not unlike those known to Wilde at the fin de siècle. Imaginative freedom independent of context is necessarily the condition of imprisonment. Which leads me to con-clude, again, that performances of all kinds—gender, ethical, and aesthetic—are inevitably grounded in specific material conditions.

NEW WOMEN AND MALE LEISURE

At a recent conference on Wilde, the feminist critic Elaine Showalter regretted that Wilde and some of the late Victorian feminists had made so little common cause. This section is an attempt to think through this lack of solidarity, though its optic is one of difference and tension rather than regret. Whereas the male Aesthetes often proposed aes-thetic models of consumption, taste, and pleasure, women in the aes-thetic movement, especially in the more popular, or applied, forms of aestheticism, such as the decorative arts and suburban literatures, were more conscious of their roles as reproducers of daily life and as produc-ers subject to audience demand. A new volume on women in British Aestheticism edited by Talia Schaffer and Kathy Psomiades, like a re-cent exhibit in Manchester on the women Pre-Raphaelite painters, shows how critical women could be of male so-called Decadents.[13] Es-says by Ann Ardis, Annette Federico, and Edward Marx show that the women artists and writers often sided with male "Counter-Decadents"

13. Talia Schaffer and Kathy Psomiades, eds., *Women and British Aestheticism* (Charlottesville: University Press of Virginia, 1999). Unless otherwise cited, the essays named below are included in this volume.

in negating the Decadent negation of bourgeois life. Their work in country cottages, London suburbs, or the empire popularized aestheticism for broader audiences while simultaneously expressing the desires of subordinated groups for ideals beyond production and reproduction. Thus what Ardis calls Anne Page's "elegantly aging self" in Netta Syrett's *Anne Page* (1909) rejected the antibourgeois stance of Wilde and company but created an aesthetic life in a Warwickshire garden untrammeled by husband or children. Or Marie Corelli, probably the best-selling of all Victorian novelists, negotiated the conflict between the artistic value of autonomous literature and the cash value of literary commodities by a complex narrative "trade" between aestheticism and popular fiction. In Edward Marx's accounts of Sarojini Naidu and Violet Nicolson ("Laurence Hope"), the popular demand for "exotic" literature created opportunities for women writers "who possessed direct knowledge of the empire"; and Marx proposes a history of women's readership, or literary consumption, in our analyses of Decadent exoticism.

As the art historian Alison Matthews has put it, although aestheticism may function as an elite form of consumerism, in which aesthetic rhetoric conceals structural inequalities of class, race, or gender and differential access to luxury goods,[14] in the cases just mentioned consumption is also driving the production of women and other marginal writers. In Talia Schaffer's reading, "Lucas Malet"'s (Mary St. Leger Kingsley Harrison's) *History of Sir Richard Calmady* (1901) provides a highly self-conscious, literary critique of late Victorian commodification and consumption in the character of a crippled, emasculated aristocrat who cannot engage in "productive" activity himself but who ultimately devotes his life to helping the victims of industrial accidents. It would seem that the women of Aestheticism were consistently sensitive to the manifold politics of aesthetic production and consumption. If they sometimes reinforced gender and heterosexual stereotypes of production and reproduction while countering the excesses of pleasure-driven male aesthetes, they also confronted their implication in commodity culture more directly than did some of the male aesthetes.

It is a useful thought experiment to consider how William Morris's socialist, productivist aesthetic looks when its actual *products* are compared with Mary Eliza Haweis's. Both Haweis and Morris dealt in book production, typesetting, fashion, and furniture design; both were

14. See also Linda Dowling, *The Vulgarization of Art: The Victorians and Aesthetic Democracy* (Charlottesville: University Press of Virginia, 1996), chapter 3 on Morris.

deeply influenced by medievalism; and both produced commodities that suburbanites could use to beautify their homes. Is it Morris's work, his status as a socialist activist, or his gender as a craftsman that distinguishes him from Haweis as a home decorator, or does his socialist practice only make his participation in a high-end niche market all the more ironic? Another way of putting the point is, was the manifestly productivist aesthetic of Ruskin and Morris always implicated in consumer culture, their aestheticism an "elite form of consumerism," as Matthews has it, but its commodification displaced onto women? Already, at the height of mid-Victorian productivism, Matthew Arnold uneasily acknowledged that his time was an age of criticism, or consumption, rather than creation, or production ("The Function of Criticism at the Present Time" [1865]), to be answered by Wilde in "The Critic as Artist" (1891) that criticism-consumption was indeed a higher form than creation or production. It is arguable that the commercialism so resisted by Morris and Arnold, from their very different but equally elevated platforms ("machinery" in Arnold and "exploitation" in Morris), was typically displaced onto the products of women or homosexuals, resulting in the ultimate trivialization of the latter's creative labor. Such an analysis builds on Lyn Pykett's, which describes how women's writing was coded as mass culture in relation to male expressions of individuated artistic genius.[15]

These observations indicate the kinds of tensions that arose within aestheticism as women's productive activity, often relegated to "applied arts" like home decoration, began to challenge the art world, in which women themselves were commodified as aesthetic objects. If we understand aesthetics not as philosophically monolithic but as a diverse if often overlapping group of claims made for art and culture, each with particular motivations and specific audiences in a web of social relations, such tensions emerge between and within aesthetics. In this web, those who were aesthetic objects for the consumption of others, like women, might become aesthetic subjects, agents, or producers; conversely, those who had been aesthetic subjects, like the aesthete, the man of taste, or the critic, might be objectified, in a society in which commodification applied as easily to people as to goods, with all the accompanying psychological repercussions.

Sally Ledger's *The New Woman* (1997) is helpful in showing the tensions between the New Woman in both her fictional and real forms and other social and cultural movements of the fin de siècle: the New

---

15. Lyn Pykett, *Engendering Fictions: The English Novel in the Early Twentieth Century* (London: Edward Arnold, 1995).

Woman in tension with socialism, with naturalism, with imperialism, with Decadence, with urbanism, with modernism, and with mass culture.[16] I shall now discuss the New Woman's relation to the Decadence in the light of two of the aesthetic models that have concerned us, one conceiving people as producers, reproducers, and creators, the other conceiving them as consumers or creatures of taste and pleasure—productivist aesthetics and hedonics.

Consumption or Pleasure

Ledger cites Olive Schreiner's 1899 essay "The Woman Question" for Schreiner's attack on male homosexuals as products of what she called the Female Parasite, despised by Schreiner as the idle woman, the woman who did not labor (except to reproduce "effete and inactive males"). Schreiner explictly uses the term *decay* to describe these men and opposes their consumption of leisure to her ethos of productive labor:

> Only an able and labouring womanhood can permanently produce an able manhood; only an effete and inactive male can ultimately be produced by an effete and inactive womanhood. The curled darling, scented and languid, with his drawl, his delicate apparel, his devotion to the rarity and variety of his viands, whose severest labour is the search after pleasure; . . . this male whether found in the late Roman empire, the Turkish harem of today, or in our northern civilisations, is possible only because generations of parasitic women have preceded him. More repulsive than the parasitic female herself, because a yet further product of decay, it is yet only the scent of his mother's boudoir that we smell in his hair. (cited in Ledger, 76)

Here Schreiner's valuing of labor led to an attack on male *consumers* while it simultaneously attacked the Female Parasite for *producing* them. The Female Parasite, or bourgeois woman, reproduced pleasure-seekers but, locked into the cycle of reproduction, could not fully devote herself to pleasure.

Elsewhere Ledger refers to the feminist attacks on male pleasure that led to the passing of the Criminal Law Amendment Act, which brought Wilde down; but even then the social purity movement left women with little voice to express their own sexuality. Ledger further shows how social purity activism ultimately forced lesbians such as

---

16. Sally Ledger, *The New Woman: Fiction and Feminism at the Fin de Siècle* (Manchester: Manchester University Press, 1997).

Radclyffe Hall to submit to the discourses of male sexologists. These sexologists had anatomized Wilde as much for his aesthetic *taste* as his—to use an anachronism—"sexual preference." Here we use the terms *taste* and *preference* as economists had begun to use them by the end of the century, as individualized consumption patterns, the choices one makes in the satisfaction of needs and desires. In fact it is notable that the feminist New Women who were so critical of the male consumer or Decadent devoted "to the rarity and variety of his viands, whose severest labour [was] the search for pleasure" rarely spoke of their own choices at all, but only of the constraints on choice. So it was that by the time of Radclyffe Hall, sexual choice had also become a constraint, biologically determined. This was something that the male aesthetes had tried hard to resist.[17]

Production and Reproduction

As Rita Felski and others have argued (see Ledger, 97), the male aesthetes also resisted stylistic reproduction, or realism, by means of an antirealist decadent style that self-consciously performed its femininity in relation to the more masculine realism of mid-Victorian fiction (but see above for Rolfe's and Wilde's respective "realism" in penury and prison). This stylistic femininity, as expressed in *The Desire and Pursuit of the Whole* or *The Picture of Dorian Gray* (1890), contrasts with the embodied realism of women within the text, like Sybil Vane, in whom Dorian loses interest the instant she steps from her role as an actress into life. It seems clear now that the great age of literary realism was also that of industrial production and Malthusian reproduction. The New Woman novelists who were still committed to realism and to its late Victorian efflorescence in naturalism—Ella Hepworth Dixon, Mary Cholmondeley, and Margaret Harkness—were those most committed to the production and reproduction of daily life. On the other hand, the life of the consumer, of intense sensation, of what Pater called the "flood of external objects pressing on us with a sharp and importunate reality" and the "swarm of impressions" they ignited in the desiring brain, contributed increasingly to the fevers of the Decadence and modernist streams of consciousness.[18] I shall discuss below how it also contributed to the longed-for disembodiment of the male aesthete and Decadent.

17. Martha Vicinus has recently argued that Hall's deterministic attitude toward lesbianism could be opposed to the more ludic, "queer" sexuality represented in Djuna Barnes. See *Romantic Friendship: Lesbian Identities, 1800–1930* (forthcoming).

18. Walter Pater, conclusion to *The Renaissance*, in *Selected Writings*, ed. Harold Bloom (New York: Signet, 1974), 59–60.

A story in Hubert Crackanthorpe's *Wreckage* (1893) illustrates the wishes and struggles ignited as women's activities gained power in the marketplace, especially in relation to aesthetic production and consumption.[19] Titled "A Conflict of Egoisms," it is the story of two ambitious but monadic individuals who marry as if to escape their respective solitudes. (See Pater's description of "the individual in his isolation, each keeping as a solitary prisoner its own dream of a world" ["Conclusion," 60].) The man is a famous writer described in terms of a detachment that would come to seem Jamesian (James wrote approvingly of Crackanthorpe's clinical style):

> All by himself, in a quiet corner of Chelsea, he lived, at the top of a pile of flats overlooking the river. And each year the love of solitude had grown stronger within him, so that now he regularly spent the greater part of the day alone. Not that he had not a considerable circle of acquaintances; but very few of them had he admitted into his life ungrudgingly. This was not from misanthropy, sound or morbid, but rather the accumulated result of years of voluntary isolation. People sometimes surmised that he must have had some great love trouble in his youth from which he had never recovered. But it was not so. In the interminable day-dreams, which had filled so many hours of his life, no woman's image had ever long occupied a place. It was the sex, abstract and generalised, that appealed to him; for he lived as it were too far off to distinguish particular members. In like manner, his whole view of human nature was a generalised, abstract view: he saw no detail, only the broad lights and shades. And, since he started with no preconceived ideas for prejudices concerning the people with whom he came in contact, he accepted them as he found them, absolutely; and this, coupled with the effects of his solitary habits, gave him a supreme tolerance—the tolerance of indifference.[20]

The female protagonist is a subeditor, eventually the editor, of a ladies' weekly. Success in her work leads—in a familiar economy—to free time, enhanced taste for personal comforts (new rooms, new clothes), the idle reading of "sentimental novels," and finally desire for

---

19. I am grateful to Monica Borg for pointing out how closely Crackanthorpe's story reflects the concerns of my recent work. I refer readers to Borg's own excellent work on Crackanthorpe in her Ph.D. dissertation (in process, English Department, University of Birmingham).

20. Hubert Crackanthorpe, *Wreckage* (London: William Heinemann, 1893), 57–58.

a man. Attempting to acclimatize herself within her rapid progress from necessity to leisure, Letty moves from being a producer of literature, to a consumer of romance, to a nonproductive literary muse for (or a critic of) her husband's work—a role that also leaves her unsatisfied. After their marriage, he speeds up literary production in order to escape from her need for affection, she is driven mad by the frustrated desire to communicate with him, and he finally drops dead just before he planned to jump to his death from the banks of the Thames.

The son of a well-known feminist, Crackanthorpe himself committed suicide at the age of twenty-six by throwing himself into the Seine, avoiding a divorce action in which he would have been accused of infecting his literary wife with venereal disease. His stories were highly praised in the 1890s for their psychological and sexual frankness, and they attracted the attention of the early British school of psychoanalysis. The self-styled Counterdecadent Richard Le Gallienne called them "little documents of Hell."[21] For our purposes, the story illustrates, with stages of aesthetic development and hierarchies of taste familiar to the Victorian fin de siècle, the complex psychological circuits of production, reproduction, and consumption that were so central to Aestheticism and the Decadence. It also illustrates the gender valences and gender threats that came to bear on the production and consumption of aesthetic commodities and, perhaps most important, the isolated, monadic nature of egos in conditions of competition. "A Conflict of Egoisms" describes male-female relations in modern society as well as atomistic individuals in modern conditions of work and the pursuit of leisure.

The Urban Migration

The master narrative of political economy tells us that our labor was alienated when we were torn from the land and propelled to the cities with their divisions of commodified labor, divisions and commodifications that would eventually make obsolete the original division—the division of labor in biological reproduction. At the beginning of the nineteenth century 20 percent of the British population lived in towns; by the end of the century 20 percent lived in the country. Ledger quotes Judith Walkowitz on the way in which the women who flooded the streets of the city confronted the men who were increasingly left behind in their idleness: the "stare of the prostitute repeatedly challenged the glance of the *flaneur* in the great metropolis of the *Fin*" (Ledger, 153).

---

21. Cited in *The 1890s: An Encyclopedia of British Literature, Art, and Culture,* ed. G. A. Cevasco (New York: Garland, 1993), 684.

Although he may in reality have been scrambling to make a living, the Decadent *flaneur* represented himself as outside the circuits of production and reproduction, consuming the spectacle of the city, wandering aimlessly amid the New Women striding purposively past him to work, or to work the streets. The stare of the woman working the streets, the stare that said "a fair bit of work for a wage," shames and frightens the flaneur, whose *glance*—codeword for flirtation—reveals itself as unproductive, aimless, effete, a by-product of more leisured existences.

In a typology of flaneurs, flaneuses, and other urban pedestrians, Deborah Parsons has distinguished the Paterian-Jamesian line of collectors and hoarders, the consumers of the sights of the city, from the women who walk to work and their divergent aesthetic standpoints.[22] Parsons's study shows not only the more *active* engagement with the city on the part of the women walkers but also the effects of the urban migration on perspective. The wide philosopher's view of the countryside that led to universalist and objective aesthetics of the Beautiful is replaced by the subjective perspectives of the city, seen only in angles obstructed by buildings or traffic or through the self-conscious social status of the perceiver, the latter very much a perspective constructed within social relations in which women's perspectives were increasingly prominent.

Both the male Aesthetes and the New Women participated in the modern perspectivism of the city, but the male Aesthetes tried harder to hold on to universal conceptions of the Beautiful, the coveted interpretation of which enhanced their status as Aesthetes. Their self-representation then as idle consumers of urban aesthetics was to some extent an image produced in crisis, under the shadow of women's mobility and productivity. One might recall Arthur Symons's unwitting demonstration of this flaneur attitude, not toward women but toward working people (producers), in his impressionistic account of Edgware Road in *London: A Book of Aspects,* privately printed in 1909:

> As I walk to and fro in Edgware Road, I cannot help sometimes wondering why these people exist. Watch their faces, and you will see in them a listlessness, a hard unconcern, a failure to be interested. . . . In all these faces you will see no beauty, and you will see no beauty in the clothes they wear, or in their attitudes in rest or movement, or in their voices when they speak. They are

22. Deborah Parsons, "Flaneuse or Rag-Picker?: Women Walking the Cities of Modernity" (Ph.D. diss., Birkbeck College, 1998).

human beings to whom nature has given no grace or charm, whom life has made vulgar.[23]

Here the working poor are aestheticized, that is, consumed by the man of taste for his aesthetic satisfaction, while they are simultaneously excluded from the world of aesthetes, or taste. The effect would be perfected in T. S. Eliot's descriptions of the urban crowd in *The Waste Land* (1922).

The Division of Labor

As we have seen, Victorian feminists from the Mills to Schreiner argued that the alienation, or commodification, of labor was not all bad for women, slaves, or Jews. Sexual and racial domination were yet worse, in the progressive terms of the age, than the exploitation of the wage, which could liberate women, slaves, and Jews into contractual social agency. I conclude this section with what Victorian anthropologists called the original division of labor in the sexual act. Although both male Aesthetes and New Women claimed to be progressive, they differed in key ways. Male Aesthetes thought that progress lay in the liberation from sexual roles, an end to which much of their fictive role-playing inclined. If Angelique Richardson is right that a significant aspect of the New Woman, most notably in Sarah Grand's formulation, sought to replace both romantic and passionate love with "eugenic" love, or love for the race, then this love as a form of citizenship is modeled on the more deterministic political-economic "stages of development." Richardson quotes Grand: "Love, like passion, may have its stages, but they are always from the lower to the higher. And as it is in the particular so it is in the general; it prefers the good of the community at large to its own immediate advantage."[24] Eugenics was the biologization of class, saving the bourgeoisie from the degenerate barbarism of the aristocracy and the primitive savagery of the urban working classes. It also saved women from male sexual aggression.

Chapter 3 discusses how the division of labor as understood under political economy—as contingent on technological development—became biologized in the course of the nineteenth century, so that by the end of the century so-called noncompeting groups based on class and to a lesser extent on race were seen to be fixed and inherent. Richard-

23. Cited in Karl Beckson, *Arthur Symons: A Life* (Oxford: Clarendon, 1987), 242.
24. Angelique Richardson, "The Eugenization of Love: Darwin, Galton, and New Woman Fictions of Heredity and Eugenics" (Ph.D. diss., Birkbeck College, University of London, 1999), 174.

son demonstrates that Grand was not alone among New Women in her advocacy of eugenic love. Women themselves were key contributors to the biologization of the division of labor at the fin de siècle. Not only did they often join the Counterdecadents in countering the Aesthetes' artifice (whereas only in their greatest trials, like Wilde's, did the male Aesthetes fail to resist biology). The New Women eugenicists were also distinctly different in purpose from Grant Allen and his sublimation of romantic sexual love in "The New Hedonism."[25] Whereas Allen specifically contrasted his New Hedonism, or the philosophy of pleasure and pain, with the Old Asceticism, which he associated with the work ethic and self-restraint, Grand's eugenization of love was not guided by pleasure or sensation but rather (as in the homophobic quotation by Schreiner above) by self-sacrifice in the service of the state. Richardson discusses how Grand's pronatalism extended in her fiction to an emphasis on creative production and to the pathologizing of French literature as "vain, hollow, cynical, . . . *barren*."[26] This is counterdecadence with a vengeance, at the levels of both art and life.

We may conclude this chapter with this question of the biological dimension of the New Woman, for if further research shows that it was widespread then it would necessarily oppose her to the Decadents, who resisted biological determinism while devoting themselves to physical sensation. This would mean that New Women had to control their reproduction for the state while Decadents were inclined to avoid reproduction altogether in favor of the life of choice and preference.

Sex and Freedom

Right up to our own contemporary sociobiology and evolutionary psychology, biological destiny tends to point to social unfreedom. The question is, was there something profoundly contradictory between the freedom that the male Aesthetes wanted in the aesthetic life—the consuming life of Paterian aestheticism "burning with a hard gemlike flame" that had to do with the "passage and dissolution of impressions, images, sensations" that eventually led to "that continual vanishing away, that strange, perpetual weaving and unweaving of ourselves" (Pater, 60)—and the embodied self-control of reproductive powers linked to New Womanism? The Aesthetic men wished to unravel and wear away their bodies in the pursuit of pleasure, while the New Women shored up theirs as productive vessels. In a now-famous

25. Grant Allen, "The New Hedonism," *Fortnightly Review,* March 1894, 377–92. See also chapter 4.

26. Angelique Richardson, "The Eugenization of Love: Sarah Grand and the Morality of Genealogy," *Victorian Studies* (winter 1999–2000): 244.

sentence from the second wave of feminism, Ti-Grace Atkinson said, "I do not know any feminist worthy of that name who, if forced to choose between freedom and sex, would choose sex. She'd choose freedom every time."[27] When Grand, Schreiner, and other New Women rejected sex for pleasure in favor of pronatalism, were they choosing biological sex as a higher destiny, or a Kantian freedom in perfect service to the state? Were they choosing a kind of Kantian autonomy in the face of the apparent heteronomy, the being buffed about by desire, of male Aesthetes and consumer society? Or were they choosing something else altogether?

At several points in this study we have seen women as self-identified producers and reproducers in tension with men as pleasure-seeking consumers. Without limiting the variety of New Women at the fin de siècle, who certainly were not confined to pronatalists or eugenicists, we might want to ask whether control of reproduction was not a *precondition* for—in their terms—"higher" choices that women might determine for themselves. Such a formulation would be consistent with political economy from Malthus to Mill to Schreiner but might constitute women's particular contribution to formulations of individual choice at the fin de siècle, distinct from the image of female consumer of domestic or luxury goods that began to be popularized at that time. Here, too, is another tension: that between women's autonomy as represented in their own literature and women's subjection to commodity culture as represented by advertisers who sought to use women for their own ends.

27. Cited in Catharine A. Mackinnon, "Sexuality," in *Theorizing Feminism: Parallel Trends in the Humanities and Social Sciences,* ed. Anne C. Hermann and Abigail J. Stewart (Boulder, Colo.: Westview, 1994), 277.

Practical Aesthetics II

On Heroes, Hero-Worship, and
the Heroic in the 1980s

Universal History, the history of what man has accomplished in this
world, is at bottom the History of the Great Men who have worked here
—Thomas Carlyle

A modern fashion in the nineteenth century led writers to reflect on
the most recent of pasts: the French Revolution obsessed the novelists
and essayists of the 1820s and 1830s; the Hungry 1840s obsessed the
novelists of the 1850s and 1860s; the 1880s, those of the 1890s, or the
fin de siècle. "There is always something rather absurd about the past,"
wrote Max Beerbohm in 1895 in an essay in *The Yellow Book* called
"1880": "To give an accurate and exhaustive account of the period
would need a far less brilliant pen than mine."[1] "The period of 1880
must have been delicious" (275), he wrote (he was born in 1872), and
he characterized it as the age of commodification, when "the spheres
of fashion and art met." Earlier, Beerbohm had also characterized his
own decade, the 1890s, in the pages of *The Yellow Book* as the age of
cosmetics, surfaces, and gambling.[2]

In the spirit of historical summaries of the most recent of pasts, this
chapter is about the 1980s, another decade of gambling and surfaces.
It may not emerge as the classic essay on the 1980s, but it offers us an
opportunity to reflect on what we went through in that decade. Although the terms in which it represented itself in all its books called
"Money" described individual heroes and sublime growth, this chapter
juxtaposes those stories with stories of institutions, the structures of
government, banking, and law that enabled, empowered, and protected them. It was, as Beerbohm said of the previous fin de siècle, a complicated age.

In literary and cultural studies in the United States, the 1980s were

1. Max Beerbohm, "1880," *The Yellow Book,* January 1895, 275–83, see 283.
2. Max Beerbohm, "A Defense of Cosmetics," *The Yellow Book,* April 1894, 65–82.

the best of times and the worst of times. The fashion for theory and abstraction elicited more genius and innovation than literary studies probably ever had, diversifying the discipline beyond recognition. On the other hand, as the language of fashion, innovation, and diversification suggests, the practitioners of the discipline took to acting more and more like Economic Man, throwing themselves on the market as often as several times a year to increase their salaries (maximization), increase their expense accounts (hedonism), or decrease their teaching loads (toil and trouble, burdensome labor). Enormous disparities and injustices were created as economistic deans competed to meet outside offers (the market price) to self-promoting faculty; students were abandoned when professors turned into "conference junkies" and began spending most of their time "doing research"—in some cases even refusing to talk with students, who might market their ideas before they could. Department chairs catered to "star" faculty at the expense of others, ignoring the fact that in most cases the "star" was born precisely with its commodification, its putting itself repeatedly on the market. Every assistant professor on a tenure track is now required to publish at least one book to achieve tenure, and every maximizing tenured professor produces a book every few years, which, though no doubt contributing to a more democratic academe, has led to a glut and devaluing of academic work and the literal impossibility of a scholar ever really covering a field—to say nothing of the quality of the "product." Faced with an ever-increasing supply of "tenure books," some formerly respected academic presses, guaranteed a market at least in libraries, publish anything, but in ever-smaller print runs. The "marketplace of ideas" (Mill) in the study of culture has never been so well stocked, but this comes at the cost of its total institutional "restructuring" (a 1980s term) as a marketplace.

In Britain, American-style competitive individualism is a consequence of a different market strategy: corporatism. The Research Assessment Exercises that currently dominate British academic life were begun in the 1980s ostensibly to increase academic productivity: the government, which funded virtually all British higher education, began to fund selectively institutions with demonstrable research cultures. Thus as student numbers increased dramatically in the 1980s and 1990s, government funding was actually reduced. Because RAEs are discipline-based, each department is competing with every other in its discipline for a higher research rating, on which funding for its university depends. (Recall that both Mill and Jevons envisioned workers and employers uniting in competition against other firms, thus eroding class divisions.) Ambitious departments "raid" top researchers from competitors to increase their ratings. Although RAEs have without a doubt increased competitive productivity among academics, perhaps even exceeding the American tenure system, they are also over time creating an atmosphere of competitive individualism, even star systems, in institutions that before exhibited comparative collegiality.[3] This chapter will say no more about the academic marketplace per se, but it will show its coherence with the larger society.

The Victorian comedy *Money* (1840) by Edward Bulwer-Lytton concludes with the protagonist's rhapsody on "the everlasting holiness of truth and love."[4] But a chorus consisting of all the cast immediately rejoins:

GRAVES: But for the truth and the love, when found, to make us tolerably happy, we should not be without—
LADY FRANKLIN: Good health;
GRAVES: Good Spirits;
CLARA: A good heart;
SMOOTH: An innocent rubber; [that is, a carefree game, in which nobody gets hurt]
GEORGINA: Congenial tempers;
BLOUNT: A pwoper degwee of pwudence;
STOUT: Enlightened opinions;
GLOSSMORE: Constitutional principles;
SIR JOHN: Knowledge of the world;
EVELYN: And—plenty of Money.
      Curtain. (120)

The Victorians were not apologetic about their materialism. The play, a melange de genres between a Restoration comedy of manners and Dickens, mixes cynicism and sentimentality. The characters quip the truisms of market society—"Men are valued not for what they *are*, but what they *seem* to be" or "Benevolence is a useful virtue, particularly when you can have it for nothing"—while the plot consists of a sentimental domestic comedy. On balance, the play does not rank truth or love above money or an innocent rubber: all "utilities" are objectified, commensurable, fungible. As Victorian reviewers obligingly noted, such theater would spoil nobody's supper.

3. See Regenia Gagnier, "American in Britain," special issue on Anglo/American feminisms in *Women: A Cultural Review* 10, no. 2 (August 1999): 206–12, and Gagnier, "'The Disturbances Overseas': A Comparative Report on the Future of English Studies," in special issue on cultural studies in *Victorian Literature and Culture* (1999): 467–74.

4. Edward Bulwer-Lytton, *Money*, in *Nineteenth-Century Plays*, ed. George Rowell (Oxford: Oxford University Press, 1990), 45–120.

Immediately following what was called in contemporary artistic circles "Enlightenment Thursday," when Prime Minister Margaret Thatcher resigned in 1990, the playwright Howard Brenton began a review of the arts in the 1980s, "If there is one insight that comes from the most noted novels, television drama series and plays of the 1980s, it is that during the decade we were overtaken by something malevolent. It may seem exaggerated, but it was as if some kind of evil was abroad in our society, a palpable degradation of the spirit."[5] Writing of the way the arts registered the evil, Brenton continued:

Television gave us Alan Bleasdale's *The Boys from the Blackstuff*, about the loss of the dignity of work, and Troy Kennedy Martin's *Edge of Darkness*, about our loss of the trust of mother nature. They are two very different works, but they were both shot through with profound anxiety, which, typically of eighties' writing, the authors could not quite articulate. None of us could: human evil, unlike the glamorous religious evil of Milton's Satan, is banal, grotty and everyday. (25)

In citing two works of fiction that "brilliantly caught the ethos of the Thatcher years," Brenton described Salman Rushdie's *Satanic Verses* ("actually an attack on contemporary manifestations of human evil and a 1980's classic") and Martin Amis's *Money* (1984), about which more below. In the theater, he cited Caryl Churchill's *Serious Money* (1987), dramatizing a "black hole of amorality in the public world of the day, into which traditional liberal values were sucked away without a trace."

Brenton went on to describe the results of management-driven productivity goals as applied to artistic activity: theatrical producers and movie people packaged "product," and the originally socialist Arts Council became a politically censorious production agency that developed an Orwellian "artspeak." Theater companies had to deliver "assessments of achievement of financial performance targets" and attended "brain-melting seminars on subjects such as 'the development of a donor constituency.'" The council was increasingly cautious about "idiosyncratic self-expression." Letting the market decide, Brenton argued passionately, was antithetical to the "economics of the madhouse of the imagination."

The crash came, according to Brenton, in 1988, when beggars appeared in numbers on the streets:

5. Howard Brenton, "The Art of Survival," *Guardian Weekly*, 9 December 1990, 25–26.

What people in public life said on television about the country seemed finally to lose any relation at all to what it was like to live in it, or to walk down any street. Again and again Thatcher and her ministers claimed success, in torrents of figures. *Everything* was better and "up by 11 percent." This unreality reached a surreal apogee in Thatcher's farewell speech in the House of Commons. She seemed to think her premiership had established a Utopia that we had been living in for the past eleven-and-a-half years: surprising news. (26)

The issue is not whether it is detrimental or disastrous to the arts to be dependent on the market, although this is a present concern in both the United States and Britain, but how culture responds to the situation described by Brenton: a glamorous public discourse of conservative values such as nation, family, growth, and wealth, and a lived experience of social disharmony and hard times.

The leveling of values or utilities in market society, apparent in Bulwer-Lytton's *Money,* is a formal as well as a thematic achievement in Caryl Churchill's *Serious Money,* first produced in March 1987 at the Royal Court Theatre. At the play's height, London's financial district, The City, bused stocks and bonds traders to the theater, presumably for the instruction it provided. In the play, whose slight plot is a mystery concerning the suicide or murder of an inside trader, each character recites in verse what he or she does on "the Street," explaining in detail to the audience the technical terms of 1980s stocks and bonds: *raider, arbitrage, takeover, target company, leveraged buyout* (*LBO* or, in Europe, *management buyout* or *MBO*), *white knight, greenmail, futures, poison pills, shark repellent,* and so on.[6] Like Brecht,

---

6. *Arbitrage:* originally the exploitation of differences in the price of the same commodity in different markets, the term has come more generally to mean buying cheap and selling high, especially of stocks or bonds. In the 1980s, arbitrage often included "parking" (see text).

Futures: a contract to buy some commodity or security at some specified point in the future, at a predetermined price.

Greenmail: the buying back of a raider's block of stock at a premium, or higher price than the going market price, discriminating against other shareholders.

LBO or MBO: when a group of investors, often the corporation management, buy up the publicly owned stock and use the company's own assets as collateral to borrow the money.

Poison pill (Share Purchase Rights Plan): poisons the value of the raider's investment when he or she is forced to swallow it by certain events, e.g., a special issue of stock that when a hostile bidder completes the takeover converts into the rights holders' right to buy two shares of the acquired company's stock for the price of one, raising the cost of acquisition to forbidden levels.

Raider: initiator of a bid to take control of a company.

Churchill wants to educate the audience viscerally as well as cognitively: written in verse with calculated voice overlaps, in which several conversations often take place at once, the content of the dialogue is impossible to follow. Very often it's all just noise, sounding like the floor of the stock market itself at trading time. The play's rapid pace, again like the stock market, makes understanding impossible, and this formal effect is part of the pedagogy.

Jake Todd, who sold trade information to an American arbitrager (Marylou Baines), is found dead. His last act was to pass on information concerning a classic takeover of a target company called Albion (or, allegorically, Britain). The CEO of Albion could have responded with a classic LBO, but instead he acquires a white knight. In the meantime, an old-fashioned jobber has blown the whistle to the Department of Trade and Industry (DTI). Before Jake can be called as a witness, he kills himself or is murdered.

As in Bulwer-Lytton, the characters are cynical, and women and people of color are as immoral as white men. Scilla, the dead man's sister, interrupts her mourning long enough to explain to the audience the trade in financial futures. The Peruvian businesswoman Jacinta Condor withdraws her money from the country while Peru is held hostage to the IMF. The banker Zac distributes clean urine samples and condoms, cynically profiting from the war on drugs and AIDS. Nigel Ajibala, an importer from Ghana, agrees, regarding Third World debt, that the philanthropic concert organizer of Live Aid

> Bob Geldof was a silly cunt.
> He did his charity back to front.
> They should have had the concerts in Zaire.
> And shipped the money to banks over here. (68)

Despite the refrain that "sexy greedy *is* the late eighties," the characters cannot have sex. They are too tired after trading (104). The traders on the floor prefer to tell misogynistic jokes. The personal assistant of the arbitrager Baines, buying large quantities of stock cheap and selling them dear, says he's learned everything from Marylou: "Do others before they can do you" (108, which reminds one of another memorably

---

Shark repellents: legal devices intended to repel raiders, e.g., staggered boards, special voting rights, and white knights.

Target company: company threatened by a hostile bidder.

White Knight: a third party invited to acquire the target company and "save" it from the hostile bidder.

The text used for quotations is Caryl Churchill, *Serious Money* (London: Methuen, 1987).

sadomasochistic tag from a film in the 1980s: "It is all about ass: you either kick it, or lick it").

The arts are implicated in the cynicism when they are associated with the ruthless raider Corman. He hires a public relations agent to create a public persona for him as other than a profiteer. She says that she'll present him as "bad and glamorous," advising him to sponsor the elite arts and display his "taste." The chairman of the target company "sponsors provincial / Orchestras. You need the National / Theatre for power, opera for decadence, / String quartets bearing your name / for sensitivity and elegance" (91).

In the end, we learn, the Tory government itself killed Jake "because another scandal just before the elections would have been too much fuss" (109). A cabinet minister threatens to cut the raider off from the banks, so he cancels the deal and receives a knighthood, a piece of the tunnel under the Channel, and the chairmanship of the board of the National Theatre. (Ivan Boesky, one of the 1980s' best-known arbitragers, who was convicted, imprisoned, and personally fined $100 million, ostentatiously served on theater boards.) A couple of Old Gentlemen of the City, including the dead man's father and the one who originally blew the whistle to the DTI, are scapegoated, go to prison, and are forgotten. Britain is going the way of America; women are as corrupt as men; financial elites of the Third World sell out their dying countries. Brenton wrote that "Thatcherism, like all authoritarian dogmas, was brightly coloured":

> Writers were trying to get at the darkness, the social cruelty and suffering behind the numbingly neon-bright phrases—"the right to choose," "freedom under the law," "rolling back the state." It was as if a hyperactive demon was flitting about amongst us, seeking with its touch to turn everything into a banal conformity, a single-value culture with one creed—"by their sales returns ye shall know them." (25)

It would come to be an allegory of the Information Age. With its deafening noise and blinding staging, *Serious Money* explained the techniques of 1980s finance while simultaneously ensuring that the explanations could not be heard. Mill's "marketplace of ideas" in *On Liberty,* in which through unconstrained debate Truth would eventually become apprehensible, had been replaced by knowledge without power and information without knowledge.

This is also the story of John Self, the protagonist of Martin Amis's *Money,* the yuppie—another 1980s term: young upwardly mobile professional—duped by the brave new world he so greedily embraced.

The British film director Self pursues pleasure in New York and London. The son of a publican, his ambition is "to make lots of money."[7] Addicted to junk food, pornography, and "hand-jobs," Self is torn between two women, Selina Street, who cares only for his money, and Martina, who "sees nothing in [him] but [him]self." Martina is cultured, sensitive, and vulnerable; she gives him *1984*, the classic representation of the terror of the information age. Selina is "authentically corrupt, seriously vulgar, intensely twentieth century" (323). Although she makes him sick, he can't give her up. He is addicted to Selina as he is to America, "the land of opportunity, vigorously mongrel"—in the technical economic sense of addiction that denies diminishing marginal utility: the more you have of a thing the more you want it.[8] For Self, who came of age in a Britain dominated by the markers of social class, believes, like Richard Branson—the real-life entrepreneur and proprietor of the Virgin empire—that "money is so democratic. You even things out for me and my kind" (225). The novel is a prescient interrogation of the widely publicized advice Ivan Boesky gave in his commencement address to the University of California School of Business Administration in 1985: "Greed is all right. Greed is healthy. You can be greedy and still feel good about yourself."

Yet early on, the British Self begins to fall apart (disassemble). Out of the street noise (both Wall Street and Selina Street), he longs for, and eventually becomes obsessed with, "a human voice." He seeks a "human touch" and wants to "cuddle down" (109), to break out of "the world of money" into "the world of thought and fascination," but he cannot. (In the last essay he ever wrote, "Civilisation in the United States" [1888], Matthew Arnold concluded that for all its social, political, and economic successes, the United States had failed in "humanness" and "interestingness," the great sources of interestingness being distinction and beauty.)[9] Self grapples with his disintegration in "Room 101," which in *1984* is where each prisoner faces the thing she fears most and in this case is his suite in an exclusive Manhatten hotel. He begins to abuse homeless people and imagine their reprisals. Conned by a ruthless film industry, he loses his women, money, and job; he fucks his father's wife, a porno queen, only to learn, after being badly trounced, that the publican he thought was his father was not his father after all. He attempts suicide, but ends up penniless with a

7. Martin Amis, *Money: A Suicide Note* (London: Jonathan Cape, 1984), 92.

8. See Gary S. Becker, *Accounting for Tastes* (Cambridge: Harvard University Press, 1998), 50–76, and the appendix below.

9. *Matthew Arnold,* ed. Miriam Allott and Robert H. Super, Oxford Authors Series (Oxford: Oxford University Press, 1986), 489–504.

fat nurse who alternately cuddles and beats him when he gets out of line: a very British ending to a very American tale.

The moral of the novel is that John Self cannot teach himself self-discipline, self-respect, or how to love beyond self-interest.[10] Without the elite training that the British historically developed to form "character," Self pursues formless self-gratification by pursuing money in the United States, "the vulgar, the mongrel." It is too fast for him; in fact, its cheap thrills are killing him, and Self obsessively dreams of a body transplant in California. The conclusion, in which a woman passing by the penniless Self in the street innocently tosses 10p in his cap, is an allegory of unaccommodated man, finally stripped down, without either inner or outer resources, mortified.

Clearly, the British interpretation of John Self's dissolution is an indictment of Thatcherite culture: of the unthinkable notion that working- or lower-middle-class lager louts could ever achieve "the world of thought and fascination" rather than (simply) "the [vulgar] world of money." The novel was marketed as being "about what happens when people don't have Culture, and how impossible that makes it for them to understand what is going on" (from the dustjacket). Although Martin Amis (the character as well as the author; see note 10) is as repelled by Self's wasted and wasteful, abused and abusive "lifestyle" as the baffled and uncomprehending Self himself, Amis has reserves of "Culture" that allow him "to understand what is going on." What is going on—as John Self follows the American dream all the way to the California coast in what the dustjacket calls its "low-life high-life . . . with its futile focus on gratification," and, in Churchill, the City follows Wall Street in its electronic and immoral transfers of wealth, and, in Brenton, Thatcher follows Reagan in market rhetoric—is "Culture" giving way to anomie. (Thatcher famously said, "there is no such thing as society.")[11] Yet for all the critical distance Amis brings to bear on America, including the novel's stylistic self-reflexivity, American pleasures are "addictive": since *Money* Amis has often been accused in the British press of spending too much imaginative and other time in the United States.

Is the British cultural indictment of American market values, which we have seen from at least the 1840s (see chapters 2 and 3), merely snobbism—upper-middle-class (that is, "cultured") Britain lamenting that America did not, in its mongrel democracy, follow the *Budden-*

10. This "moral" does not take into account the novel's self-reflexivity, which is expressed in the frequent appearance in the text of the author, Amis, who colludes with the producer Fielding in the fleecing of John Self.

11. Interview with Margaret Thatcher, *Woman's Own* (31 October 1987), n.p.

brooks model and evolve a hierarchy of tastes commensurate with its wealth? A particularly poignant representation of American anomie at the top is Brent Wade's *Company Man* (1992), the story of a black man who has succeeded in corporate America. William (or Billy or Bill, depending on, for example, the race of his interlocutor) Covington has ascended the management ranks of Varitech. He is a black Republican, has the ear of the CEO, lives in an established and affluent Baltimore neighborhood, drives a red Jaguar XJ6, and has a beautiful and educated wife. After a decade in the company he finds himself wearying of the corruption and insensitivity of corporate life and a crisis builds: he becomes impotent, and he is pressured to spy on the company's black machinists, who are planning a strike to protest the company's move to Mexico. The crisis comes not in the form of Bill's values, for they are those of the company (profit, wealth, status in the hierarchy), but rather in the form of his personal identity, which, unlike his values, cannot, it seems, be entirely mapped onto his corporate persona. Surrounded by white rules and white ignorance of the things that were part of his precorporate history (including the concerns of the black machinists), his crisis finally erupts in the form of a question, "Who are you? I whispered inside myself." [12]

The lack of "Culture" here is specifically the lack of black American culture:

> You must understand that I had spent my entire career avoiding situations where my race would put me at odds with my race, or my employer. And to a degree I had achieved that. The result was, however, that I had no real credibility as a black person at Varitech. I was not known by them, I had not associated with them, I had never gone out of my way to cultivate an awareness of myself as a black person. And the whites seemed to appreciate that. I had avoided association with black professional groups (the kind white upper management gives supportive lip service to and most white employees despise and label racist) and black professionals who were considered sensitive. (You see, to be labeled "sensitive" is the kiss of death for blacks in corporate America.) (180)

Prior to the crisis, in which Bill shoots himself with permanent but not fatal effect, he had reflected upon the way corporate life discouraged sensitivity to others, to any community but the corporation. This sensitivity to one's place among others, to one's accountability toward oth-

---

12. Brent Wade, *Company Man* (Chapel Hill: Algonquin, 1992), 205.

ers, is what is called "dignity" in the black community, represented in
Company Man by Billy's father-in-law (Dr. Bond), a southern civil
rights leader. In this sense, the company can bestow status on a black
man but not dignity:

> I don't believe I could ever make Dr. Bond appreciate how diffi-
> cult it is to sustain a sense of dignity in the corporate world—
> and stay employed. Men and women of Dr. Bond's generation see
> the doors open they fought to have opened and then look upon
> the likes of me with embarrassment. They have little understand-
> ing for what lies beyond that ivory threshold. Dr. Bond works for
> himself, a black man serving a grateful black community. They
> allow him a brevet standing and then look in awe upon the fruits
> of what they've tithed: the house, the German cars, the position
> as racial spokesman. His dignity is packaged in the communal
> strength of belonging to a culture that recognizes him as a native
> son. (For the culture that wouldn't recognize him, he has his
> [Afrocentric] library.) (48)

Although perhaps new in black American literature, awareness of the
hollowness within the heart of the firm is not new to literature, going
back well before Thomas (The Senator) Buddenbrook's revelation at
the top that what he called "the practical life of the merchant" was
shameless, cruel, and empty.

Through these and other media the culture industries of the 1980s
said that elite whites lacked "culture" (any resources that are not material or for immediate consumption) and that elite people of color
lacked their "cultures" (or the resources of their personal history, kin-
ship, family, communities).

WE ARE ALL GAMBLERS ONCE MORE

The world was more than ordinarily alive because of Melmotte and his
failures.
—Anthony Trollope

Someone once said that artists are like the canaries the miners used to
hang in the mines to warn of noxious gases—and artists have now begun
to look at the frenzy of the 80s. That suggests to me that it is late in the
era, for when the canaries start to sing, something is about to happen.
—PBS host Adam Smith

In his *Lectures on Aesthetics* (1835) Hegel defined art and culture as
the ways that societies represented themselves to themselves and

thereby constructed their identities.[13] The acclaimed nonfiction accounts of corporate wealth and ruin from the 1980s and the related accounts of the deregulated savings and loan industry appeared as a whole after the fiction, but they read like novels and arguably show how a culture "represents itself to itself": *Takeover, The Roaring '80s, The Predators' Ball, Liar's Poker, Other People's Money, Inside Job, Barbarians at the Gate, The Big Fix: Inside the Savings and Loan Scandal,* and so on.[14] Most prominent are individuals—which is significant, given the structural powers discussed below—the characters, or *players* (a 1980s term distinguishing those who have power within an institution from those who have not). Moira Johnston opines in *Takeover* that "after the failure of utopianism in the 1960's" (7) Americans wanted to feel good about their materialism, and so they subscribed to vulgarized versions of the Invisible Hand, glamorizing the ruthless Economic Men who taught that greed was all right, greed was healthy, you could be greedy and still feel good about yourself.

The raiders (James Goldsmith, Carl Icahn, T. Boone Pickens), arbitragers (Ivan Boesky), and investment bankers (Michael Milken) are portrayed variously as Renaissance men (*Sir* James Goldsmith) or instances of the American immigrant's dream, in which uncouth brilliance overcomes WASP elitism. Goldsmith, "an entrepreneur of Renaissance vision and dimensions," who took over Crown Zellerbach, was frustrated with "the gentrifications of the middle class that had stripped it of the lusty mercantile spirit that had built the British empire" (*Takeover,* 25). Boone Pickens posed as the champion of shareholders against decadent management and was mythologized as the little guy who made good from the oil patch of Oklahoma. Michael Milken, brilliant but unconnected, nerdy and ascetic in lifestyle but with an insatiable desire for the power wealth bequeathed, provided the spectacle for others, enabling them, like Trollope's financier Mel-

13. G. W. F. Hegel, *Introductory Lectures on Aesthetics,* trans. Bernard Bosanquet (London: Penguin, 1993), 35–36.

14. James Ring Adams, *The Big Fix: Inside the Savings and Loan Scandal* (New York: John Wiley, 1990); Connie Bruck, *The Predators' Ball: The Inside Story of Drexel Burnham and the Rise of the Junk Bond Raiders* (New York: Penguin, 1988); Bryan Burrough and John Helyar, *Barbarians at the Gate: The Fall of RJR Nabisco* (New York: Harper and Row, 1990); Moira Johnston, *Takeover: The New Wall Street Warriors* (New York: Penguin, 1986); Michael Lewis, *Liar's Poker: Rising from the Wreckage on Wall Street* (New York: Penguin, 1989); Paul Zane Pilzer with Robert Deitz, *Other People's Money: The Inside Story of the Savings and Loan Mess* (New York: Simon and Schuster, 1989); Stephen Pizzo, Mary Fricker, and Paul Muolo, *Inside Job: The Looting of America's Savings and Loans* (New York: McGraw-Hill, 1989); Adam Smith, *The Roaring '80s: A Roller-Coaster Ride Through the Greed Decade* (New York: Penguin, 1988).

motte, to live "the way we live now": the notorious annual Predators' Balls in Beverly Hills in the mid-eighties, officially called the Drexel High Yield [that is, "Junk"] Bond Conference. Connie Bruck, senior reporter for *The American Lawyer* and award winner in business and financial journalism, develops the view in *Predators' Ball* that the outsider Milken broke the back of New England's trade aristocracy.

Investment bankers were traditionally a pedigreed class who underwrote university club connections. Corporate managers were fraternity brothers whom somebody liked. Milken, on the other hand, was an outsider:

> He married his high-school sweetheart. He left New York for California when it was unthinkable that someone who aspired to success on Wall Street should do so. He moved back to his old neighborhood in the unfashionable San Fernando Valley, where he remained after accumulating his hundreds of millions of dollars. He brought his brother and high school friends into his group. . . . Perhaps as a consequence of that, one can still see vestiges today of the oddness that always set him apart, making him slightly misfitted for any group but the one he eventually created. He was, after all, the teenager who slept only three or four hours a night, who was not the football player but the cheerleader, who in L.A. and Berkeley in the sixties not only never smoked or drank or experimented with drugs but did not even drink carbonated beverages. He was the new Wharton student, made fun of by his pipe-smoking Ivy League classmates, but vowing he would be number one in his class. He was the Jew at the blueblood Drexel Firestone, segregated off in a corner of the trading floor. He was the bond trader at Drexel Burnham who, even as he began making millions trading his strange bonds, still looked so strange, with his shirt-and-tie combinations that made him the brunt of others' jokes, with his dreadful [wig]. . . . He was the Drexel junk-bond trader from *California,* no less, who, when he asserted to a roomful of investment bankers and lawyers in '83 that he could raise $4–5 billion for Boone Pickens' Mesa-Gulf bid, which Pickens was having trouble financing, was greeted by snickers from the men from Cravath, Swaine and Moore, and Lehman Brothers, the aristocrats of the Street. (*Predators' Ball,* 355)

According to Bruck, Milken beat the WASPs with a consuming passion for power and empire. There are stories of his Air Fund, the "highly confident letter" (Drexel was "highly confident" that it could

raise a given sum necessary for its client to take over the target company), in which Drexel pretended it had a billion-dollar bank line; of
Milken's starting work at 4:30 A.M. and, when everyone was tired,
moderating fantastic "what if?" sessions that led to phone calls that,
that very night, became done deals. There are stories of his omni-
science, his omnipotence, until, in desperation, his lawyers begin to
refer to him as "a national treasure" and he, to play the role, ostenta-
tiously applies himself to sorting out Latin American debt. There are
stories of an empire built on Milken's belief that people worked hardest
when they were part of a collective enterprise and not distracted by
romance or wealth—by anything, that is, that one might work for, the
literally fascistic notion of the social body or corporation as end in
itself. "Driven by limitless greed," his "lifestyle" was nonetheless a
model of asceticism, and he subsumed all pleasure to work (one of
Arnold's Philistines), until in 1988 he was betrayed by his friends, who
buckled under a force more powerful than he—the U.S. government.
Even then, according to the legend, he believed that he was paying the
price not for having broken the laws of fair commerce but for having
scaled the fortress of corporate America and having deposed the rich,
credentialed, and powerful, for having led, in short, the revolt of an
underclass. Milken called his junk bonds "a way to finance the dispossessed"—a clear case of the Invisible Hand at work: "By pursuing his
own interest he frequently," said Adam Smith of the Butcher, "pro-
motes that of the society more effectually than when he really intends
to promote it."

In 1986, Milken's personal "compensation" was $714.8 million.
In September 1988, the Securities and Exchange Commission (SEC)
charged Milken, his associates, and Drexel with trading on inside information, manipulating stock prices, filing false disclosure forms with
the SEC in order to disguise stock ownership, filing fraudulent offering
materials, keeping false books and records, and, most shocking, de-
frauding their own clients. (At Drexel Milken said, "If we can't make
money off our friends, who can we make money off of?" [*Predators'
Ball*, 360].) He was convicted with the help of his friend Ivan Boesky,
with whom he had had a long-term reciprocal stock-parking arrangement. (*Parking* refers to one investor's holding stock for another in
order to conceal its true ownership. It typically involves the holder's
being guaranteed against losses, and it violates a number of SEC prohibitions.)

Milken was sentenced to ten years in a federal work camp, three
years' probation, and community service of 1,800 hours a year for an
undetermined duration. He agreed to pay $600 million in fines and

restitution to defrauded investors. He was released from prison in early 1993, having served twenty-two months. He was released from a half-way house a month later. After he was paroled, he taught a course in the UCLA Business School, which was marketed on video, performed court-ordered community service, and funded research on prostate cancer. The author of the *New York Times Magazine* article that reported Milken's enterprise in medical finance seemed impressed by this latest—perhaps even his last—venture in self-interest. The article referred to Milken's cancer as a "hostile takeover."[15] Milken still denied that he had been involved in insider trading. Drexel was bankrupt and out of business.

Like Milken, the raider-heroes of the 1980s allegedly saw "value," or profit, where others saw only social relations, or people working, saving, and spending. The raider-heroes looked at assets as dynamic entities to be endlessly manipulated into vehicles for maximized profit, heedless of the quality of products or the welfare of employees or of the communities built around firms. The heroes wanted instant financial gratification. Carl Icahn was said to tolerate "no restrictions on his conduct . . . he was guided only by his economic interest" (*Predators' Ball,* 169). The raider went for the target instinctively, like a predatory insect. Asked by a member of a congressional panel why he had chosen TWA as a target, Icahn responded, "Do you ask Willie Mays why he jumped a certain way for a ball? Or . . . McEnroe why he holds the racket a certain way?" (ibid., 172). They intimidated the old guard. At one point, elite corporate defenders feared reprisal for even attempting to repel them: since a number of the raiders were Jewish, stopping them might be construed as corporate anti-Semitism (ibid., 205).

The national story was also heroic. Word was that we live at the end of the age of oil. America is in transition from a rusting industrial economy to a new day of technology, especially information technology (anticipating Bill Gates, the Microsoft hero of the 1990s, whose personal fortune exceeds the combined GNPs of forty-eight of the poorest countries in the world). Since the Great Depression, industry had been fettered by regulation, taxation, antitrust laws, and a vigilant Supreme Court. A "free-market" spirit began to take hold by the late 1970s and was fanned by Reaganism. Takeovers were to be the answer to America's perceived failure to compete in international trade. Raiders would oust lazy, stupid managers, the "organization men" in the "gray flannel suits" of yesterday, increase productivity, and give share-

---

15. "Michael Milken Fights a Hostile Takeover," *New York Times Magazine,* 5 June 1994, 34–37.

holders the dividends they deserved.[16] Balance sheets and boardroom tips were replaced by high-tech research into "undervalued assets." In a cruel, though certainly unconscious, parody of Walter Benjamin's Angel of History, the president and CEO of RJR Nabisco, Ross Johnson, who waged war on an entrenched and cautious management, expressed his contempt for the accountant as "a man who puts his head in the past and backs his ass into the future" (*Barbarians at the Gate*, 13). Reviving social Darwinism, the new motto was "Organisms necessarily change." The Wall Street warriors brought with them a love for continuous restructuring and reorganization, and the "organisms" reproduced themselves in strange ways, even through perverse autoeroticism. By the mid-1980s Drexel was often on all sides of a transaction, financing raiders while simultaneously financing the target companies, as in Icahn's takeover of TWA. Milken cultivated what he called a "synchronicity" (otherwise known as "conflict") of interest, underwriting debt securities, owning them, owning those issuers' equity, and placing others' debt with those companies. Drexel did, as Milken claimed, further the democratization of capital to small companies, but it also financed the buyouts of those same companies.

The buyouts provided their own tragic stories. Debt was the edifice on which the empires arose. When interest rates climbed and cash flow declined, Drexel was the first to fall. Relatively well-run companies were laid waste; assets and workers were passed, as one commentator memorably put it, from hand to hand like carpets at a bazaar. An RJR Nabisco employee once allegedly left the instructions, "if my boss calls, ask him for his name and number" (*Barbarians at the Gate*, quoted on the dustjacket). Great names were besmirched, and many employees paid with their jobs. The kinder and gentler founder of the National Biscuit Company (Nabisco) had had a dream for a workers' cooperative and had produced in Oreos and Ritz crackers the best-selling biscuits in the world; Reynolds Tobacco had made workers shareholders and, although antiunion, had provided better than union wages, virtually free health care, and at-cost housing and food—until Ross Johnson took over.

In *Knights, Raiders, and Targets: The Impact of the Hostile Takeover* (1988), Louis Lowenstein, director of the Columbia Center for Law and Economics and formerly chief executive officer of Supermarkets General, and Edward S. Herman of the Wharton School studied

---

16. See the classic nonfiction and fiction works on postwar corporate culture: William H. Whyte Jr., *The Organization Man* (New York: Simon and Schuster, 1956) and Sloan Wilson, *The Man in the Gray Flannel Suit* (New York: Simon and Schuster, 1955).

fifty-six target firms that succumbed to hostile takeovers in the period 1975 to 1983. They concluded that "after the takeover, the bidders performed well below the level of either the bidders or their targets during the years before the bid."[17] Contrary to the raiders' claims, efficiency gains did not drive the takeover market. Rather, the raiders just stripped the companies' assets.

In the preface to *Liar's Poker*, Michael Lewis, a bond trader at Salomon Brothers, characterized what *Business Week* called "the wild and colorful era when the markets ran amok" as a "modern gold rush. Never before have so many unskilled twenty-four-year-olds made so much money in so little time as we did this decade in New York and London" (*Liar's Poker*, 9). Lewis describes how the best minds of his generation wasted their educations taking their degrees in economics:

> There was one sure way, and only one sure way, to get ahead, and everyone with eyes in 1982 saw it: major in economics; use your economics degree to get an analyst job on Wall Street; use your analyst job to get into the Harvard or Stanford Business School; and worry about the rest of your life later.
>
> . . . At Harvard in 1987 the course in the principles of economics had forty sections and a thousand students; the enrollment had tripled in ten years. At Princeton, in my senior year, for the first time in the history of the school, economics became the single most popular area of concentration. And the more people studied economics, the more an economics degree became a requirement for a job on Wall street.
>
> There was good reason for this. Economics satisfied the two most basic needs of investment bankers. First investment bankers wanted practical people, willing to subordinate their educations to their careers. Economics, which was becoming an ever more abstruse science, producing mathematical treatises with no obvious use, seemed almost designed as a sifting device. The way it was taught did not exactly fire the imagination. I mean, few people would claim they actually *liked* studying economics; there was not a trace of self-indulgence in the act. Studying economics was more a ritual sacrifice. I can't prove this, of course. It is bald assertion, based on what economists call casual empiricism. I watched. I saw friends steadily drained of life. I often asked oth-

17. "The Efficiency Effects of Hostile Takeovers," in *Knights, Raiders, and Targets,* ed. J. Coffee, L. Lowenstein, and S. Rose-Ackerman (New York: Oxford University Press, 1987), 211–40. Cited in Lowenstein, *What's Wrong with Wall Street: Short-Term Gain and the Absentee Shareholder* (New York: Addison Wesley, 1988), 137.

erwise intelligent members of the prebanking set why they studied economics, and they explained that it was the most practical course of study, even while they spent their time drawing funny little graphs. They were right, of course, and that was even more maddening. Economics *was* practical. It got people jobs. And it did this because it demonstrated that they were among the most fervent believers in the primacy of economic life. (24–25)

In human capital theory, the theory of credentialism holds that formal education simply provides a sifting device for employers: a certain degree certifies trainability for the firm.[18] Taking their degrees in economics as it is currently practiced showed Wall Street that students had little interest in intellectual or ethical issues, that they were willing to subordinate their education to economic gain. They were therefore maximally employable. Lewis, who took his degree in art history, believed that "the chief economic purpose of art history was clandestinely to lift the grade-point averages of the economics students" (25).

In the 1980s the meaning of work and its place in people's identity changed.[19] The End of the Oil/ Beginning of the Information Age story read like this. At the end of World War II, the United States emerged with one-half the productive capacity of the world, enormous technological innovation, and an expansion of plant capacity that greatly increased productivity. Its major "competitors"—for this is the language in which media economics had come to see international relations— had been bombed back into the nineteenth century and would not reemerge as competition until the 1970s. Trade unions were strong; about one-third of all workers were unionized and perhaps 80 to 90 percent in major industries such as automobiles, steel, chemicals, and coal. These unionized workers shared the profits of firms, so that the years 1945–1965 have been called by economists "the golden age of capitalism."

On the other hand, there was manifest tension between the excitement of war and a peace with boring jobs (see *The Man in the Gray Flannel Suit* [Sloan Wilson, 1955] or the classic film *The Best Years of Our Lives* [1946]), and considerable anxiety over American affluence: was the United States growing soft? John Kenneth Galbraith's *The Af-*

18. Mark Blaug, *The Methodology of Economics: Or, How Economists Explain,* 2d ed. (Cambridge: Cambridge University Press, 1992), 214.

19. For a more extensive discussion of the different meanings of work that have developed since Adam Smith and the introduction of wage labor, see Regenia Gagnier and John Dupré, "On Work and Idleness," *Feminist Economics* 3 (1995): 96–109 and John Dupré and Regenia Gagnier, "A Brief History of Work," *Journal of Economic Issues* 30, no. 2 (June 1996): 553–59.

fluent Society (1958) argued that the nation's economic problems were solved but Americans' lives needed to be made more meaningful through a redistribution of wealth. Lyndon Johnson's presidency proposed the Great Society and the war on poverty (until the surplus was absorbed by the war in Vietnam), and the civil rights movement was under way. The division of labor had been challenged during wartime by women's active participation in what were previously "men's jobs," and this ensured continuing tension along gender lines. William H. Whyte Jr., the editor of *Fortune,* launched a jeremiad against the homogeneity of civic culture, the complacency of corporate man, the "social ethic" of the new suburbs, and the lack of romantic, rugged individualism, especially the lack of (Schumpeterian) entrepreneurs. (See also David Reisman's *The Lonely Crowd* [1950], with its other-directed Americans, as opposed to the [mythic] inner-directed self-maximizers of the nineteenth century.)[20]

Whyte's classic *The Organization Man* (1956) was an indictment of the corporate mentality that made secure workers loyal to low-risk-taking firms. The responses to the deficiencies it popularized— the "downsizing" and "restructuring" for "efficiency," "productivity," and "flexibility" so prominent in economic discourse since the early 1980s—have fostered another culture of work. The shift for most workers, as reported in the business press, was from the security of the 1950s and 1960s to the uncertainty of the 1980s and 1990s. One particularly telling article in a series in *Fortune,* "The End of the Job," contrasts the changes in the job since Whyte.[21] Today, more workers are temporary, part-time, and contingent, less loyal to employers and less happy with their jobs. Because firms seek flexibility, even workers with relatively high-paying jobs work under constant threat of unemployment and must continually educate themselves for new positions. They must work without supervision, work in teams, be project-oriented, change their hours and days of employment, and be able to relocate.[22] Some economists have recently argued against home ownership as a disincentive to worker mobility. Women and people of color, especially women of color, are often at the low-paying periphery of core high-tech industries such as the electronics industry in the Silicon

20. In *Gentlemen Capitalists: The Social and Political World of the Victorian Businessman* (Stanford: Stanford University Press, 1992), H. L. Malchow debunks the myth of the Victorian entrepreneur, showing how Victorian capitalists were aided by and embedded in family, social, institutional, and political circles.

21. William Bridges, "The End of the Job," *Fortune,* 19 September 1994, 62–74.

22. See also Bennett Harrison, *Lean and Mean: The Changing Landscape of Corporate Power in the Age of Flexibility* (New York: Basic Books, 1994).

Valley, working in conditions of exploitation and insecurity reminiscent of the nineteenth century. In the classic article on how the population was disciplined into wage labor, Edward P. Thompson drew our attention to specialists who provided "ideological orientations" in "structuring a labour force" in industrializing countries in Africa and Latin America.[23] One could document a similar ideological stratagem for the "restructuring" of market economies in the past two decades.

Those who benefited from this restructuring of work also redefined work in a manner peculiar to themselves. In classical political economy the justification of capitalism was that it entitled one to the fruits of one's labor and abstinence, the worker's labor and the abstinence of the capitalist, who employed others rather than consumed her own wealth. What is abstinence to an arbitrager or bond dealer? What is labor when it amounts to electronic bleeps on a screen? What is abstinence when it lasts a microsecond before the next deal? What does it mean to be personally "compensated," as Michael Milken was, by $714 million a year? When Carlyle wrote in "On Heroes" in 1840 that Universal History was at bottom the History of the Great Men who had worked here, he had a very different idea of work.

In the 1990s, Microsoft's Bill Gates—with a personal fortune of $59.5 billion (£35 billion), history's richest man—took on the U.S. government in a case as definitive of the information age as John D. Rockefeller's was of the industrial age.[24] Standard Oil once supplied kerosene to virtually every house in the United States. It was broken up by the same antitrust authority now after Gates. Gates is represented by friends as a successful businessman who has made his fortune by innovation and price-cutting. To his competitors, he is a ruthless monopolist who stifles innovation. In a world where cultural capital no longer has the value it once held, he may not, like Rockefeller, mellow into a patron of the arts.

Gates, like Rockefeller and Milken, is typically represented as an individual, a Schumpeterian entrepreneur with Keynesian "animal spirits" taking on superpowers. Two other heroes surfaced in the late 1990s: the Nobel Prize–winning economists Robert Merton and Myron Scholes. Grand wizards of finance theory, they joined with one of the protagonists of *Liar's Poker* (one of Salomon Brothers' "Big Swinging Dicks," John Meriwether) and a former vice-chairman of the Federal Reserve as partners in the spectacularly misnamed hedge fund

---

23. Edward P. Thompson, "Time, Work-Discipline, and Industrial Capitalism," *Past and Present* 38 (1967): 56–97, esp. 92–94.

24. "A World Wide Tangled Web," *The Guardian,* 17 October 1998, 2.

"Long-Term Capital Management." (A hedge fund is a pool of speculative capital, free of almost all regulation. The LTCM was misnamed in two senses, for it was proved to be short-term, high-risk gambling. Rather than hedging one's bets against loss, the fund leveraged $4 billion to borrow $1 trillion, approximately the GNP of China, betting that their models would not break down in practice. They did, and their peers in government and banking put together a "bailout fund" of $3.5 billion.) Rockefeller produced oil; Gates produces information access across the world; Merton and Scholes destabilize the world's economy. The rise and fall of LTCM suggest that the heroes of the 1980s and 1990s are were less Schumpeterian entrepreneurs than a financial elite at the center of political, financial, and legal institutions. We now turn to these.

NEVER HAVE SO FEW OWED SO MUCH TO SO MANY: THE SAVINGS AND LOAN STORY

In the 1930s, '40s, and '50s, American savings and loans were a working-class economic experiment, the repository of millions of small savers' wealth, representing a collective dream of home ownership and children's college education. Depression-era regulations on interest-rate limits led to a withdrawal of deposits due to high inflation and a 162 percent cost of living increase between 1965 and 1980. Money market funds—large pooled deposits—offered higher interest and contributed to the exit from thrifts after 1965. In order to save the industry the government deregulated it, and in 1972 savings and loans began to allow brokered deposits. By 1979, there was an industry crisis. The Deregulation Act of 1980 removed interest-rate limitations on depositors' funds, and savings and loans were receiving 8 or 9 percent interest on long-term mortgage loans while unable to attract depositors at less than 16 percent. In 1982, thrifts were allowed to lend to speculators in real estate, land, barbecues, junk bonds, and so on, in addition to residential mortgage seekers. Yet whereas the fixed interest rates of the 1933 Glass-Steagall Act had required no special skills for supervision, deregulation did, and they were not sufficiently in place. Comparing the "political betrayal of the public" to the crimes of Laval and Quisling, James Ring Adams summarized the rest thus:

> The accidents of history and a series of understandable but ill-conceived policies helped turn federal deposit insurance for the savings and loan industry into a virtually unlimited government subsidy for fraud. A network of experienced swindlers stood

ready to exploit the opening. . . . The criminals who plundered the country's banks and thrifts succeeded in draining off their billions and tens of billions because they could buy political protection. United States senators and representatives pressured the bank regulators on behalf of large contributors. They often made no discernible effort to understand the concerns of the regulators and even less effort to judge the moral character of the people giving them the money.

The result has been serious, endemic corruption, in the precise meaning of that word. . . . Several statehouses have been implicated. And the political milieu in Washington has become so degenerate that many of its elected officials don't even realize that they are corrupt.[25]

Twenty of the twenty-four most insolvent thrifts in Texas in 1987 were owned by real estate developers who bought their way into the industry following deregulation in 1980 and knew nothing about financing homes for ordinary citizens. The consensus in the literature seems to be that the Texas "Cowboys" were crude and unrefined (lavish parties reported in the Sunbelt were quaintly called "marketing strategy"), while the California "Gamblers" were slick and modern, playing computerized roulette with junk bonds and mortgage-backed securities. Federal deposit insurance kept Milken, Drexel, and the junk bond market afloat. The Federal Deposit Insurance Corporation (FDIC) and the Resolution Trust Company filed a $6.8 billion claim in the Drexel bankruptcy, charging that "Drexel and those acting in concert and conspiracy with it have willfully, deliberately and systematically plundered the S&Ls" (Adams, 288–89).

Given momentary grace by accounting rules that registered losses as gains, thrift owners called in political favors when obfuscation became impossible. By 1987, the industry, including its politicians, accountants, lawyers, and real estate owners, was just trying to keep quiet until the cost was high enough to necessitate a taxpayer bailout. The stories of crime (murder as well as fraud), spending extravagance, and the traffic in women are included in great detail in reportage such as Adams's *The Big Fix,* Pizzo, Fricker, and Muolo's *Inside Job,* and Pilzer and Deitz's *Other People's Money.* The protagonists are shocking only in their lack of concern for the public funds that were entrusted to them. Otherwise they are utterly banal—small, collective figurines that supported the heroes and superfirms such as Drexel. An outdated system unfit for new freedoms; a regulatory framework wholly inade-

25. Adams, *Big Fix,* viii–ix.

quate to supervise those freedoms; an industry using its political clout; greedy congressional patrons blindly following campaign contributors: the only thing extraordinary about the story is that the financial speculators of the "wild and colorful era" of the 1980s, the wildest of the Wild West, were entirely ensured by the United States government, so that at last count every American—man, woman, and child—will pay several thousand dollars of the variously reported but certainly twelve-figure debt.[26]

The global economist Paul Krugman compared the bailout to the crisis of Third World debt—only national losses to the S&Ls are much greater:

> During the 1980s, there were two major financial crises. One of them was very exciting and romantic and you could talk global. That was the Third World debt crisis. People were swarming over that issue; everyone wanted a piece of it; everyone wanted to

26. In a pamphlet titled *Crime and Punishment in the S&L Industry: The Bush Administration's Anemic War on S&L Fraud* (1990), the consumer and environmental advocacy organization Public Citizen's Congress Watch urged criminal prosecution as well as regulatory and civil measures. The Resolution Trust Corporation found fraud in 60 percent of the savings and loans seized by the government in 1989; these institutions were looted for the direct financial benefit of officers, directors, or major stockholders. Between August 1989 and May 1990, 440 savings and loans were seized, the cost of resolution averaging $123 million per failed institution. By June 1990, out of 17,000 criminal referrals, 346 were sentenced to serve time. In 1989, the average length of a prison sentence for defrauding an S&L was 1.89 years (those convicted of more conventional bank robbery are sentenced to an average of 9.4 years in prison).

Under the Bush administration, the Justice Department was reluctant to convict, and the Treasury Department refused to freeze the assets of those being sued, so that by the time they were convicted they had no possibility of making restitution. Public Citizen condemned the Bush administration for the failure of the Justice Department's accountability; for allocating few resources to the prosecution of management, complicitous lawyers, accountants, and appraisers; for failing to preserve civil RICO (the Racketeer Influenced and Corrupt Organizations Act, the single most effective tool to combat pervasive forms of white-collar crime); and for not authorizing qui tam (whistleblower's) suits for S&L fraud. The Congress Watch concluded that "[f]inancial fraud flourishes in an atmosphere where sophisticated criminals know they will probably not be caught. More than any other type of criminal, white-collar swindlers calculate the possibility of punishment and gain. . . . It will be cause for justifiable outrage if the Adminstration continues its lack of commitment to white-collar crime enforcement in the middle of the biggest taxpayer rip-off in history" (Sherry Ettleson and Thomas Hilliard, *Crime and Punishment in the S&L Industry* [Washington, D.C.: Public Citizen's Congress Watch, June 1990], 12–13).

The elections of 1992 distracted attention from the issue again, but during Clinton's first economic open forum in December 1992, the alarming growth of the deficit was attributed in large part to the ongoing S&L bailout. In both cases of corporate takeovers and the gutting of the S&Ls, economic abstractions obscured material crises and politics supported the obfuscation.

be involved, wanted their names on plans to solve it. Economists, including me, were writing innumerable analyses.

There was also this dull, boring other financial issue involving savings and loans that was going on in unglamorous places like Texas and Oklahoma. Nobody was interested in that, and it turns out we lost about 10 times as much on savings and loans as we did on third world debt repudiations.[27]

The S&L debacle illustrates the adequacy of "public choice" theory, the political theory based on economic models of rational choice, to democracy-as-we-know-it in the United States. In most applications of this theory, it is assumed that isolated individuals act out of self-interest, the public is unorganized and uncommitted, power is therefore wielded by interest groups, politicians are motivated by the wish to seek and keep office, and voters are skeptical, apathetic, and under-educated or uninformed. Choice theorists take this state to be the best democracy can be, based on the premises of economic rationality, whereas critics see it as a perversion of democracy as it ought to be.[28]

Now, if we return to the culture industry, it is noteworthy that in the three works discussed above—Churchill's *Serious Money*, Amis's *Money*, and Wade's *Corporate Man*—the structuring device is a murder or an attempted suicide. The comprehensiveness of this lethal perspective on market society in the 1980s is suggested by a virtual parody of financial elitism under Reaganism, the very successful black film *New Jack City* (1991), in which enterprising young black men introduce a new product on the street, crack cocaine, and take over the Carter apartment building, driving out the tenants. They restructure the plant into two major divisions: the "drug store," where the product is manufactured, and the Enterprise, where it is, in part, consumed. The look of the film is somewhere between a petty dictator's (Nino Brown's associates wear paramilitary-style—with an eighties emphasis on "style"—uniforms) and business as usual (they have weekly board meetings where they sit at long conference tables discussing marketing strategy). The film shows a black underclass's adaptation to the dominant ideology of the 1980s, what one critic has called a "crypto-Keynesian youth employment program." The UCLA economist Paul Bullock has observed that "the last rational option to Watts youth—

27. Paul Krugman, "Krugman Debunks U.S.-Japan Economic Competition," *Campus Report* (Stanford University), 7 September 1994, 4.

28. For a full account of public choice theory, see Dennis Mueller, *Public Choice* (Cambridge: Cambridge University Press, 1979). For a critique, especially from a Deweyan perspective, see Margaret Jane Radin, *Contested Commodities* (Cambridge: Harvard University Press, 1996), 211–23.

at least in the neoclassical sense of utility-maximizing economic behavior—is to sell drugs."[29]

In another underclass film mirroring high finance in the 1980s, Edward James Olmos's *American Me* (1992), Chicano drug culture in California provides a Milkenesque study of masculine ascesis. Unlike *New Jack City,* in which the drug culture is glamorous and commercial, Chicano culture is portrayed without frills—this film is about stark power between men. As Milken said that romance, display, and leisure activities simply impeded the work of making money, so Nuestra Familia distinguishes itself from Italian drug dealers who "exhibit their wealth" through conspicuous consumption. The parts of life whose ends might be *served* by wealth are absent: "Made in Folsom" (the productivist theme of the film, which in large part takes place in the prison), the protagonist, Santana, never knew or cared about southern California's women, beaches, or entertainment (which attracted effete British like Amis's John Self, who was seduced by pleasure). Santana does not know how to make love to women but assumes on the basis of his experience in prison that anal rape is the norm. As in the ascetic image of Milken, life is about power, not possession for use or pleasure. Foucault's theories of power, institutions, the body, and the carceral capture the film's aura, showing the convergence of high theory and mass culture in the 1980s.

American Me appeals to the same myth of economic individualism as the stories of "democratic" opportunity in the market, the assault on corporate elitism symbolized by the Jewish financiers. Far from ethnic or racial essentialism, Santana is probably the son of a white sailor who raped his mother; his main partner is white, an "honorary" or performative Chicano; the soundtrack marking the passage of time in prison is black (Motown), and so forth. The drug industry, the main source of jobs in postindustrial Los Angeles, is portrayed as an equal opportunity employer.

In contrast to such representations of underclass wealth and power were films such as *Boyz 'n the Hood* (1991) and *Straight out of Brooklyn* (1991), which depicted the hopeless deterioration and lack of choice of these communities. Reflecting the high proportion of young black men currently involved with the criminal justice system, Oliver Stone's *South Central* (1992) tells the story of three generations of an incarcerated family. The film, like others of the black self-help genre, is an urgent intervention attempting to break the cycle of fatherlessness

---

29. Quoted in Mike Davis, *City of Quartz: Excavating the Future in Los Angeles* (New York: Verso, 1990), 30.

among black boys. Often in the 1980s such media products were targeted as indicating a "lack of values" in the cities.

In *The Way We Never Were,* the sociologist Stephanie Coontz attempted to counteract American nostalgia, fed by the culture industry, for a golden age of the family. In one chapter she provides an instructive economic history of the black family in the United States.[30] The economic and political gains of the postwar period allowed many poorly educated black Americans to find blue-collar jobs in which they could work up to a level of security and seniority that permitted them to establish families, buy homes, and contemplate sending their children to school for longer periods. Coontz points out that this is the traditional route to mobility for all social and ethnic groups in U.S. history, especially migrants to the cities: first income security, then investment in education.

In the 1970s government cutbacks and national economic restructuring fell with special force on the blue-collar occupations and urban regions that had seemed only a few years earlier to offer the best opportunities for black people. Deindustrialization or mechanization especially affected industries such as steel and auto manufacture in northeastern and midwestern cities, where blacks had made the greatest gains.[31] Between 1979 and 1984, one-half of the black workers in durable-goods manufacturing in the Great Lakes region lost their jobs. Black male employment fell from 80 percent in 1930 to 56 percent in 1983. The average real income of young black men fell by almost 50 percent between 1973 and 1986. The biggest losers were unskilled or uneducated black men who could once by very hard work make an adequate income to support a family. By 1986, the average black high school dropout earned 61 percent less than he had in 1973.

Since the 1970s, the demoralizing effects of growing poverty and unemployment have been magnified by "hyperghettoization." For all sectors of the black population except college graduates—a relatively small proportion of the black American population—gains have stagnated or reversed since the mid-1970s, while between 1976 and 1985 the percentage of black students going on to college from high school dropped from 34 to 26 percent. Simultaneously, the poverty rate for black heads of household who graduated from high school but did not

30. Stephanie Coontz, *The Way We Never Were: American Families and the Nostalgia Trap* (New York: Basic, 1992), 234–54.

31. Paul Krugman has recently challenged the predominance of deindustrialization (as in Coontz), emphasizing instead increased productivity through mechanization. The consequences of both, of course, are unemployment. See Krugman, "Krugman Debunks U.S.-Japan Economic Competition," 4–5.

attend college climbed from 18.7 percent in 1978 to 27.8 percent in 1987. The number of blacks who are desperately poor—with incomes 50 percent below the poverty line—has increased by 69 percent since 1978, and the number of blacks living in areas of the city where almost all their neighbors are also poor has increased by about 20 percent.

This magnification and concentration of poverty is associated with dramatic social and familial changes: declining life expectancy for black Americans (an unprecedented trend in a modern industrial nation); infant mortality rates twice as high as those for whites; extensive (45 percent) childhood impoverishment; soaring homicide rates for black teens; and a majority of black children born to single mothers. Coontz links these phenomena not to a black "culture of poverty" but to the deteriorating economic and social position of lower-income black men.

Recording an anecdote of violence among ghetto children, Coontz writes:

> The consequences of behaviors and attitudes such as these are chilling, but so are the consequences of not rejecting mainstream values when people have no way of living up to them: self-contempt, depression, even insanity and suicide. In fact, embracing dominant values has sometimes had negative effects in the context of the pressures on African Americans. The black men most likely to leave their families when faced with unemployment or income loss are those who subscribe most firmly to the idea of a self-reliant male breadwinner. Middle-class blacks who believe in a color-blind meritocracy experience tremendous stress when they encounter setbacks; some studies show that blacks who let themselves off the hook by admitting the obstacles posed by racism are better able to maintain work and educational commitment in the face of reverses than those who believe in the ethic of individual achievement. (250)

Whereas 1980s ideologues claimed that weak family ties and an absence of "family values" created black poverty, Coontz adduced a range of examples to show that black family ties are so strong that they often hamper individual economic mobility. Black Americans who do attain upward mobility, often by resisting such demands, have higher rates of guilt and depression than stable or downwardly mobile blacks, in large part because of their sense that they have failed in their obligations to kin and community. This is the story of Billy Covington's breakdown in *Company Man*.

Coontz's research shows with heartbreaking clarity that black

America was, in short, scapegoated in the 1980s to cover up a national economic restructuring attributed in the media to a handful of heroic white male entrepreneurs but in fact supported at all levels by legal, financial, and political establishments. Deprived of their means to make a living for themselves and their families, black men were "culturalized," or stereotyped as a class. Given the face of crime and poverty, this "class" was the flip side of the face of successful individualism—the Milkens, Boone Pickenses, Goldsmiths. Between them, they lulled a nation into apathy toward a colossal redistribution of its wealth.

On Labor Day of 1990, the Economic Policy Institute issued *The State of Working America*.[32] It was taken to be an important assessment of the country's material welfare after a decade of Reaganomics. Using figures adjusted for inflation, the report said that the bottom 40 percent of families had lost income in the 1980s; families in the middle gained only slightly, largely due to the income of "working wives"; and the top brackets made out like bandits. Reasons for the polarization, in effect a national redistribution of wealth, were that wages and salaries stagnated and transfer payments dwindled while capital income (interest, dividends, capital gains, and rent) soared. Hourly wages fell more than 9 percent from 1980 to 1989 and fringe benefits fell almost 14 percent, the decline hitting mainly blue-collar and service workers. The real value of public assistance (transfer payments) also declined, so that the poorest one-fifth of the population, who rely on it to supplement or substitute for low wages, declined further into poverty. Contrary to economic theory, the decline in wages did not lead to an increase in employment but rather accompanied a decrease.

At the next level, the middle fifth, or quintile, of families gained 2.3 percent in income during the 1980s; the second-richest quintile gained 7 percent, and the richest quintile gained almost 29 percent. The richest one percent of Americans gained almost 74 percent.

These figures refer to before-tax income. Almost all the federal tax breaks since 1977 have gone to the top 10 percent of U.S. households. The poorest 90 percent of the population are paying a higher federal tax than in 1977. If we turn to wealth rather than income, the disparities are even more startling. In 1983, the top 2 percent of households claimed 14 percent of all income but owned 54 percent of all financial assets; the bottom 90 percent claimed 67 percent of income but owned

32. Economic Policy Institute, *The State of Working America,* 1990–91 ed. (Armonk, N.Y.: M. E. Sharpe, 1991). The following discussion of its findings is also indebted to *Left Business Observer,* 14 September 1990, 4–5.

14 percent of the wealth (152–53). The editors of the EPI report comment that in addition to blacks and other minorities having lower incomes than whites, they also "lag even further behind in the accumulation of wealth. The wealth of a typical black family is just a fraction of the wealth of a typical white family *at the same income level*" (155, emphasis in original).

In no other rich country did real wages decline during the 1980s; nowhere outside the Third World do anything like a quarter of all children—half of all black children—live in officially defined poverty. A report by the Joint Center for Political and Economic Studies concluded that poverty in the United States was more widespread, severe, and long-lasting during the 1980s than it was in other Western industrialized democracies and that the United States did least to help its poor.[33] The study found that, in contrast to government programs in Great Britain, the Netherlands, and France that pulled more than one-half of poor households above the poverty line, U.S. tax and transfer programs lifted no poor households out of poverty.

When the government shifted the tax burden downward, America's working poor lost. Yet commentators expressed more surprise over the decline in prospects of young middle-class families, particularly those whose education ended after high school. Even with wives and children working outside the home, the median income of families headed by high school graduates dropped by almost 10 percent in the 1980s, while that of families headed by college graduates increased by more than 10 percent. This transfer of earning capacity and wealth from high school graduates raised the income differential between them and college graduates from 16 percent to 33 percent. One commentator made the education policy explicit:

> A four-tier education system is creating four American classes in the 1990's: the underclass, with less than a high school education; high school graduates, who are being squeezed out of the middle class as work requirements demand more education; middle-class graduates of public universities; and the children of the rich, being trained and slotted for leadership in a private university system priced far out of the reach of most other families.[34]

Government lobbying for "choice" in education will be seen in light of this economic segregation. The main point, however, is that al-

33. "U.S. Ranked Worst in Study of 80's Poverty," *San Francisco Chronicle*, 19 September 1991, 1.
34. Richard Reeves, "How Reaganomics Took America Back to 1947," *San Francisco Chronicle*, 19 September 1991, editorial page.

though the serendipitous heroes of high finance and villains of the S&Ls were seen as individuals and entrepreneurs, and "black culture" was blamed for poverty and crime, the main story of America in the 1980s was an economic restructuring supported by the state's legal, political, and economic institutions that led to a massive redistribution of wealth.

THEY KNEW THE PRICE OF EVERYTHING AND THE VALUE OF NOTHING

If the tax laws of the 1980s redistributed the wealth upwardly, the Federal Reserve's interest rates benefited the creditors who owned the money and harmed those who owned only their own labor: this is what Marx meant when he ironically called economics the science of wealth *and* renunciation, the wealth of the capitalists and the renunciation of the workers. In the early 1980s the Federal Reserve under Paul Volcker raised interest rates in order to stop inflation, thus limiting resources to people without wealth and giving a boon to those who owned the money. In the chapter "Slaughter of the Innocents" of his *Secrets of the Temple,* William Greider explained how the monetary policy hurt those who had the least.[35] As factories closed, "the decision makers, at every level, would reply, correctly, that they were merely agents of the larger logic that governed the political economy. Given the premise of maximum net gain, the choices were required of them. To entertain alternatives, one would have to challenge the underlying principles themselves, to question the dependent relationship between work and capital, to reject the natural supremacy of profit over intangible human cares" (453). The 1981–1982 recession engineered by the Federal Reserve dealt out personal rewards and punishments in an inverted pyramid: the least suffered most and vice versa. The increase in per capita income was attributable not to wages but to interest. Over the three years since the Federal Reserve had launched its anti-inflation initiative in 1979, there had been an explosive surge in the income families derived from interest payments on their financial assets. The contrast in economic fortunes was stark: industrial production shrank from its 1979 peak by nearly 12 percent, while personal income from interest grew by 67 percent. The real economy languished while finance fathered forth.

35. William Greider, *Secrets of the Temple: How the Federal Reserve Runs the Country* (New York: Simon and Schuster, 1987). The following discussion of the Federal Reserve is from Greider, 453–81.

Greider views the Federal Reserve's policy of high interest rates as an implicit government program for redistributing incomes whose magnitude by 1982 was approximately as great as all of the government's other income-transfer programs combined. The flow of money distributed to various beneficiaries through Social Security, veterans' pensions, welfare, and the rest came to $374 billion, about the same as the income distributed to wealth holders through high interest rates, $366 billion. The billions in government checks sent to the poor, the elderly, and disabled beneficiaries generated an endless social debate over whether the recipients were "deserving." No questions were raised, however, about the windfall in interest income for the well-to-do, though much of this vast redistribution was also attributable to government policy. Interest income was considered the just entitlement of capital, the reward that was due, under any circumstances, to industrious citizens who had managed to store up financial assets. Greider quotes Veblen as saying that the abstraction of money values was given priority over tangible needs of flesh and spirit.

Surprisingly for a Washington insider, Greider provides a gender analysis—one recalling the masculine ascesis of *American Me*. "The Federal Reserve was ruled, after all, by the masculine mystique. This was not simply because nearly all of its senior officers were men. The very purpose of the central bank was anchored in a sense of manly duty: the obligation to make hard and unpopular choices, unswayed by the passions of the crowd. One was expected to exercise a cool rationality. To be strong and stoical in the face of public abuse. To avoid the emotionalism that might contaminate judgment or reveal weakness" (462). In *American Me,* manly ascesis was demonstrated when brother killed brother because duty to Nuestra Familia required it, or when Santana went stoically to his death at the hands of the new, dominant gang. The one woman on the Federal Open Market Committee, which determines the regulation of the money supply, Nancy Teeters, argued repeatedly during the liquidation on behalf of the "social fabric." The other governors could not easily entertain the possibility of changing the rules rather than accepting continuing social disintegration. They sought the "right" decision by deliberating over the economic abstractions of the money formulas. In Henry Wallich's phrase, they were supposed to "have the guts to take the pain." Teeters kept reminding them that it was not they who would take the pain; the "renunciation" would be on the part of the lower-income working population. "In the male-dominated orthodoxy, particularly in economics, Teeters's concerns were dismissed as emotional, female, as evasion of hard facts." Yet it was, Greider concludes, the masculine approach itself that was a form of evasion, as in Dickens's *Hard Times,* a way to ignore complex social realities by focusing solely on "a system of mathematical abstractions" (468).

Christopher Lasch has explained why even those who are adept at deconstructing abstractions have yielded the commonwealth to the Gradgrinds and Bounderbys, the Greenspans and Milkens:

> In their ability to escape into a world of their own, most of those in the upper fifth of the income structure—the "symbolic analysts," as Robert Reich calls them, the people who make their living by managing information—should probably be called rich. They have less and less experience of the difficulties that afflict ordinary people. Membership in employer-sponsored health plans protects them from the danger of being wiped out by an unexpected medical disaster. They live for the most part in neighborhoods unthreatened by crime—often in compounds heavily policed by private security guards. They send their children to private schools and are not directly affected, therefore, by the collapse of public education. . . . The politically active segment of the population—the people who keep up with the news, who follow politics, vote, and read the *New Republic,* the *Atlantic,* and the *New York Times*—have little incentive to change anything, least of all the distribution of resources.[36]

It is, of course, always dangerous to analyze the present or the very recent past. For years economists will continue to debate whether the theater of the 1980s was economic tragedy, farce, or the heroic defeat of Keynesianism.[37] No doubt it would be safer to respond as Chou Enlai did when asked to comment on the consequences of the French Revolution: "It's too soon to tell." Yet it was the discourse of wealth in the face of poverty in the 1980s, and of individualism in the face of mobilized institutional powers, that initially led the cultural historian to reflect on the history of economics. The final chapter is on the Theatre of the Homeless.

36. Christopher Lasch, "Politics and Culture," *Salmagundi* nos. 98–99 (spring–summer 1993): 6.

37. For the defense of economic policy in the 1980s by those who made it, see *American Economic Policy in the 1980s,* ed. Martin Feldstein (Chicago: University of Chicago Press, 1994).

SEVEN

Practical Aesthetics III

Homelessness as an "Aesthetic Issue"

[T]hey breed like rabbits; and their poverty breeds filth, ugliness, dishonesty, disease, obscenity, drunkenness, and murder. In the midst of the riches which their labour piles up for you, their misery rises up too and stifles you. You withdraw in disgust to the other end of the town from them; you appoint special carriages on your railways and special seats in your churches and theatres for them; you set your life apart from theirs by every class barrier you can devise; and yet they swarm about you still: your face gets stamped with your habitual loathing and suspicion of them: your ears get so filled with the language of the vilest of them that you break into it when you lose your self-control: they poison your life as remorselessly as you have sacrificed theirs heartlessly. You begin to believe intensely in the devil. Then come the terror of their revolting; the drilling and arming of bodies of them to keep down the rest; the prison, the hospital, paroxysms of frantic coercion, followed by paroxysms of frantic charity. And in the meantime the population continues to increase.
—Bernard Shaw

So long as any particle of the matter of abundance remains in any one hand, it will rest with those, to whom it appears that they are able to assign a sufficient reason, to show why the requisite supply to any deficiency in the means of subsistence should be refused.
—Jeremy Bentham

The most dangerous creation of any society is that man who has nothing to lose.
—James Baldwin

This chapter will focus on the situation in California, first because the chapter was written in California, where the author lived for the

An earlier version of this chapter appeared as "The Two Nations: Homelessness as an 'Aesthetic Issue'" in *Stanford Humanities Review* 3:1 (February 1993): 34–53; and as "Homelessness as 'An Aesthetic Issue': Past and Present" in *Homes and Homelessness in the Victorian Imagination*, ed. Murray Baumgarten and H. M. Daleski (New York: AMS, 1998), 167–86.

first forty-three years of her life and therefore has had the opportunity to mark the evolving spirit of the age, and second because many take California to be the cutting edge of U.S. social trends. In the 1960s and 1970s California was in the vanguard of new social movements, in the 1980s it was the home of Reagan Republicanism, and in the 1990s it led postliberal attacks on affirmative action and immigration. The human geographer Edward Soja describes its centrality in a chapter called "It All Comes Together in Los Angeles":

> Employment and production in high technology industries have expanded to make Greater Los Angeles perhaps the world's largest "technopolis," with more engineers, scientists, mathematicians, technical specialists—and more high security cleared workers—than any other urban region. An even greater expansion in low-paying service and manufacturing jobs (with a booming garment industry leading the way) and an explosion in part-time and "contingent" work (flexibly organized to meet changing labour demands) has ballooned the bottom of the labour market to absorb most of the nearly two million new jobseekers (mainly immigrants and women) entering the market over the past twenty years. . . . Los Angeles [is] the financial hub of the Western USA and (with Tokyo) the "capital of capital" in the Pacific Rim. The region also contains the largest node of government employees in any American city outside Washington, DC; and the twin ports of San Pedro and Long Beach are now amongst the largest and fastest growing in the world in terms of imports and exports. Today they handle nearly half of the trans-Pacific trade of North America. And lest it be forgotten, the Los Angeles region has, since the Korean war at least, been the primate region in the country in the receipt of defence contracts for weapons research and development, the foremost arsenal of America. . . . One can find in Los Angeles not only the high technology industrial complexes of the Silicon Valley and the erratic sunbelt economy of Houston, but also the far-reaching industrial decline and bankrupt urban neighbourhoods of rust-belted Detroit or Cleveland. There is a Boston in Los Angeles, a Lower Manhattan and a South Bronx, a São Paulo and a Singapore. There may be no other comparable urban region which presents so vividly such a composite assemblage and articulation of urban restructuring processes.[1]

1. Edward W. Soja, *Postmodern Geographies: The Reassertion of Space in Critical Social Theory* (London: Verso, 1989), 192–93.

The author is aware that some of the descriptions below, such as that of the Theatre of the Homeless, will be surprising and even shocking to readers less familiar with daily life in the Golden State, which is often imagined a paradise. For some of us who have loved its sublime open spaces, literally in terms of its geography and figuratively in terms of its diverse populations and erstwhile public life, it may be a paradise lost.

THE GREAT ENCLOSURES

The front page of the 1 August 1991 *San Francisco Chronicle:*

> The homeless issue is "one of a multitude of issues we consider in designing any building," said architect Piero Patri. . . . "Hills Plaza has no hidden nooks and crannies. When we were planning it, we thought where to locate the security desks so there would be easy surveillance. But the homeless aren't a security issue; frankly, it's more aesthetic," he said.

That article was written when "the problem of homelessness" was considered the number one issue in San Francisco's mayoral race.[2] What does it mean to say that homeless people are an aesthetic problem? The patent meaning of the quotation is that homeless people are eyesores, not a species of the beautiful. They are not objects that inspire disinterested pleasure in spectators—or especially, as San Francisco's business community fears, in tourists. People begging on the streets in the fog may make tourists spending money on luxury items feel uncomfortable. (Or they may in fact seek them out: the economist Gary Becker has argued that some people "gain utility," or feel superior or lucky, in contrasting themselves with those less fortunate.[3] In such a theory, the aestheticization of poverty discussed in this chapter would maximize the self-esteem of the more advantaged.) Furthermore, homeless people actually mar the cityscape that propertied San Franciscans and tourists would otherwise find to be an object of disinterested pleasure. This perception reflects a shift in thinking about the city: San Francisco is conceived to be less a home for its citizens than an aesthetic object to be consumed by its visitors, a situation common enough in tourist economies of the third world, but relatively new in the United States.

2. See *San Francisco Chronicle,* 26 September 1991, 1.
3. Gary S. Becker, *Accounting for Tastes* (Cambridge: Harvard University Press, 1998), 233.

In addition to marring the cityscape, homeless people, as the architect's words remind us, cause the cityscape to be reworked in a manner that itself may be unaesthetic. The architect speaks of plazas that can henceforth have no nooks or crannies (so much for Ruskin's cathedral) and of buildings that must house "security desks for easy surveillance." The article describes some of the elements of homeless-proof architecture: "metal bars with spikes . . . bolted down to lower-level windows so people cannot sit or sleep on the ledges"; public benches "designed with multiple armrests so people cannot stretch out"; bus shelters with "hard, narrow fitting seats to discourage people from sleeping"; planters outside public buildings that are made too tall for homeless people to sit on the ledge; shrubbery in Golden Gate Park pruned down "so police and gardeners can see whether anyone is bedding down"; "fences raised around other public places"; "gates added to storefronts in neighborhoods that never before had them"; and special plant for private security guards and electronic surveillance.

From the second quarter of the eighteenth century to the first quarter of the nineteenth, nearly four thousand parliamentary acts allowed politically dominant landowners to appropriate more than six million acres of English land, extending cultivation but also concentrating land in the hands of a minority. This historic enclosure of public space resulted in the dispossession of small owners and tenants, henceforth landless and in many cases, leading to the Poor Law Amendment Act of 1834, homeless. It was not, as Raymond Williams points out, that the enclosures were a radical disruption of some mythic common or traditional life, for the process had been going on since the thirteenth century and had first reached a peak in the fifteenth and sixteenth centuries. Rather, the enclosures of the eighteenth and nineteenth centuries signified "merely" a drastic reduction of the common people's breathing space. When the pressure of a social system is great, writes Williams, one feels it necessary to find a breathing space, a fortunate distance, from the immediate and visible controls.[4] In the economic system of agrarian capitalism, what the common people had until the eighteenth- and nineteenth-century enclosures was just such a breathing space, a marginal day-to-day independence, a freedom.

In the chapter "Fortress L.A." of his *City of Quartz,* the cultural historian Mike Davis writes of the restless search in Beverly Hills and other affluent neighborhoods for "absolute security," of residential architects borrowing design secrets from overseas embassies and military

---

4. Raymond Williams, *The Country and the City* (New York: Oxford University Press, 1973), 107.

command posts. This gives rise to the privatization of the police function, in which homeowners hire armed guards at four to seven dollars
per hour. Ironically, the guards tend to be poor people of color, precisely the types the affluent homeowners want to keep out.[5] ("Frantic
coercion," Shaw called it, "the drilling and arming of bodies of them
to keep down the rest.")[6] The so-called new economic rights support-
ing this imbrication of the police function into the built environment
are not extended to homeless people. In the catacombs of San Francisco freeways, Caltrans workers periodically empty out and destroy
the belongings of homeless people who are away from "home" for
their day's work of collecting recyclables. Each of the alcoves in the
terraced tiers of retaining wall, we are told by one Caltrans worker, "is
like a little room. . . . Some had cooking stoves at the rear of the 25-
by-15-foot alcoves that also served as fireplaces . . . and each had its
community toilet."[7] While vandalizing their piteous belongings and
thus establishing that homeless people have no economic rights, American cities also attack their civil rights. The homeless activist Richard
Kreimer was repeatedly offered settlements of up to $600,000 if he
would stop challenging Boston's public libraries in the courts to maintain his reading privileges. He said, notably, that he would not, for any
amount, settle for the suspension of his civil rights. He cost the city
several hundred thousand dollars in legal fees.

One San Francisco judge recently went against the grain by striking
down California's anti-begging law of 1891, ruling that the law violated the free speech rights of the poor. When city officials maintained
that begging was not a form of expression protected by the First
Amendment, U.S. District Judge William H. Orrick Jr. countered that
"when the homeless seek alms, they convey a message to society: that
extreme poverty exists in the midst of affluence. It is a disturbing message, but that doesn't mean that the Government may silence the
poor."[8] Yet in discussing how homeless people have been systematically criminalized in the past decade, the criminologist Gregg Barak
cites the specific crimes with which homeless people in San Francisco
may be charged: delaying a police officer and obstructing sidewalks,
and violations of San Francisco Park Code prohibitions on camping,
sleeping, and parking. In Las Vegas, it has recently become a misde-

5. Mike Davis, *City of Quartz: Excavating the Future in Los Angeles* (New York:
Verso, 1990), 248.

6. Bernard Shaw, "The Economic Basis of Socialism," in *Democratic Socialism in
Britain*, ed. David Reisman (London: Pickering and Chatto, 1996), 4:20.

7. *San Francisco Chronicle*, 18 September 1991, A13.

8. *San Francisco Chronicle*, 26 September 1991, 1.

meanor to "solicit employment."[9] Given such attempts to obscure and silence them, the actual condition of people living on the streets is worth remembering. In his recent ethnography of homeless people, Steven Vanderstaay cites the necessity to keep moving as the major trauma of homeless people, whose lives are filled with trauma: "Ushered out of department stores, bus stations, libraries, even churches and synagogues, asked to move along by local police after a moment's respite on a park bench, homeless people with nowhere to go are often forced to spend their day getting there. Walking, remaining upright, and endlessly waiting become all-consuming tasks, full-time work."[10] It reminds one of an 1890s story by the Londoner and cockney street specialist Edwin Pugh in which a poor woman is hounded by the policeman's "bull's-eye" until she finally disappears in the catacombs of the Thames; yet she mused, then, "why the laws of England have ordained that no one shall sleep in the streets by night, whilst everyone is at liberty to sleep in the streets by day."[11] One hundred years later, the daylight has also been appropriated.

In dealing with the aesthetic problem of the homeless, San Francisco, named after the patron saint of poor people and beggars and with a history of tolerance, has not transformed the cityscape to the extent that Los Angeles, the City of Angels, has. Davis observes the buying up and closing off of public space. In state- or federally subsidized downtown areas, elite shopping malls, often underground but always enclosed and guarded, provide "soft" environments with enticing pedestrian corridors. Outside, the erstwhile "public space" is made as unlivable as possible for the urban poor. Davis lists the Los Angeles Rapid Transit District's new barrel-shaped "bum-proof" bus benches, which have a minimal surface to make sitting uncomfortable and make sleeping impossible; the aggressive deployment of outdoor sprinklers in parks, in front of businesses, and on sidewalks; locked and spiked enclosures protecting the refuse of markets and restaurants; and a planned shortage of public lavatories (233–34).

From the 1840s, the Victorian critic of art and society John Ruskin claimed that in a city's architecture one could read a society's values. Davis describes the *auteur* architect Frank Gehry's "vandal proof" li-

9. Gregg Barak, *Gimme Shelter: A Social History of Homelessness in Contemporary America* (New York: Praeger, 1991), 81.

10. Steven Vanderstaay, ed., *Street Lives: An Oral History of Homeless Americans* (Philadelphia: New Society Publishers, 1992), 2.

11. See my *Subjectivities: A History of Self-Representation in Britain, 1832–1920* (Oxford: Oxford University Press, 1991), ch. 3, "Representations of the Working Classes by Nonworking-Class Writers," esp. 131–33.

brary, the Frances Howard Goldwyn Regional Branch Library in Hollywood, as "the most menacing library ever built" (239), with fifteen-foot security walls of stucco-covered concrete block, antigraffiti barricades covered in ceramic tile, a sunken entrance protected by ten-foot steel stacks, and stylized sentry boxes on each side. Contrary to public libraries' traditional slogan, that reading will set you free, the Goldwyn Library intimidates and excludes the public with the weight of steel and stone.

Like twentieth-century Ruskins, we can read in San Francisco's and Los Angeles's architecture the closing off of public space and the consequent imbrication of the carceral in *all* our lives, the eclipse of civil rights by property rights, and the growth of what the Victorians called "the abyss," the socioeconomic distance between the rich and the poor.

Aware of the alienation of these groups from one another, Victorian England called the rich and the poor the "two nations." Before he became prime minister, the novelist Benjamin Disraeli described them thus: "Two nations; between whom there is no intercourse and no sympathy; who are as ignorant of each other's habits, thoughts, and feelings, as if they were dwellers in different zones, or inhabitants of different planets; who are formed by a different breeding, are fed by a different food, are ordered by different manners, and are not governed by the same laws: *The Rich and the Poor.*"[12] Like many of the Sentimental novelists, who believed that the problems of political economy could be solved by sympathy (then thought to be as innate as its opposite sentiment of self-interest), Disraeli was a master of juxtaposition, typically counterpointing scenarios of dispossessed tenants and hungry workers with voluptuous breakfasts in the manor house. The Sentimentalists believed that such contrasts would ignite a chain of "moral sentiment." After the Loma Prieta earthquake of 1989, the *San Francisco Chronicle* alluded to Dickens's *Tale of Two Cities* to contrast the Thanksgiving dinners provided for two kinds of homeless. The first was "in the soup kitchens of the seedy Tenderloin," feeding five thousand chronically homeless people.[13] At the second, former residents of the posh Marina District "enjoyed their free holiday meal at the Palace of Fine Arts." These "guests" of the city were individually invited, their names provided by the mayor's office. Their tables were set with pink and white linen, crystal, and silver cutlery. Another Victorian contrast was occasioned by the Oakland-Berkeley fire of 1991, nearly two years

---

12. Benjamin Disraeli, *Sybil, or the Two Nations* (London: Oxford University Press, 1926), 67.

13. *San Francisco Chronicle,* 24 November 1989, A2.

to the day after the earthquake, in which more than three thousand expensive homes and a number of rental accommodations for the less advantaged burned to the ground. Statutes against rent-gouging were immediately drawn up on behalf of people who had lost their costly homes in the hills, but they did not apply to renters of apartments, thus ensuring that only the most needy could be exploited.

If one were a Victorian novelist, one might contrast the diners at the Palace of Fine Arts with the children raised in the welfare hotels of the 1980s that temporarily housed their families, children who may never have seen a kitchen table. In another ethnography, one of homeless children, Judith Berck cites a fourteen-year-old boy who described the disorientation of leaving the hotel: "When we first moved out, my younger brothers and sisters, they'd never seen a kitchen table before. [So] one of them wouldn't sit at the table—he sat on the floor like we had to at the hotel. . . . My six-year-old sister, instead of washing dishes in the sink, she washed them in the [bath]tub, because she was so used to that." [14] One of America's most distinguished living novelists, Tom Wolfe, in writing of the 1980s (*The Bonfire of the Vanities* [1987]) and 1990s (*A Man in Full* [1998]) has focused precisely on such contrasts. In *A Man in Full* Wolfe interweaves the fates of Charlie Croker, an Atlanta corporate developer, and Conrad Hensley, a father of two laid off from the Croker Foods freezer unit in Oakland, California. In labeling his own novels "Victorian," Wolfe refers as much to their preoccupation with the interdependence of rich and poor as to their sprawling form.

Some contemporary human geographers would call such Disraelian juxtapositions "functionally interdependent." Soja maps just such contrasts in Los Angeles. Today the regional economic product of southern California is larger than the gross national product of all but ten countries; by 1987, California had surpassed Britain and Italy to become the world's sixth largest economy, with a total output of goods and services worth $550 billion. Yet the practical difference between economic "growth" and human welfare provides another Disraelian-Wolfean contrast: [15]

> Juxtaposed against indicators of rapid aggregate growth in the regional economy are equally startling indicators of decline and economic displacement: extensive job loss and factory closures

14. Judith Berck, *No Place to Be: Voices of Homeless Children*, with a foreword by Robert Coles (Boston: Houghton Mifflin, 1992), 54.

15. For the historical process by which economists' notion of "growth" came to be divorced from practical considerations of welfare, see chapter 1.

in the most unionized sectors of blue-collar industry and a steep decline in the membership of industrial labour unions; deepening poverty and unemployment in those neighbourhoods left behind to fend for themselves in a growing informal or underground economy; the multiplication of industrial sweatshops reminiscent of the nineteenth century; the intensification of residential segregation in what has always been a highly segregated city-region; unusually high rates of violent crime, gang murders, and drug use, as well as the largest urban prison population in the country. A particularly acute housing crisis has been boiling for many years, reversing the long trend toward increasing home-ownership and inducing an extraordinary array of disparate housing strategies. Perhaps as many as 250,000 people in Los Angeles County are living in transformed garages and backyard buildings, with half as many crowded in motel and hotel rooms hoping to save enough to pay the required security deposits on more stable but out of reach rental accommodations. Many are forced to "hotbed," taking turns sleeping on never-empty mattresses, while others find accommodation in cinemas which obligingly reduce their charges after midnight. Those even less fortunate live on the streets and under the freeways, in cardboard boxes and makeshift tents, pooling together to form the largest homeless population in the United States—another "first" for Los Angeles.[16]

In similar fashion, in Letter IV to *The Morning Chronicle* (30 October 1849), the Ur-ethnographer Henry Mayhew had observed the irony of the London docks, where enough wealth was amassed "to stay the cravings of the whole world" yet "you have but to visit the hovels grouped round about all this amazing excess of riches, to witness the same amazing excess of poverty. If the incomprehensibility of the wealth rises to sublimity, assuredly the want that co-exists with it is equally incomprehensible and equally sublime."[17] The sublime in Kant overwhelmed the spectator by its magnitude or number but was finally conquered by the idea of reason, of the self-sufficiency of humanity as a moral agent.[18] Soja's sublime "excess of poverty," a postmodern "abyss," has yet to evoke much moral response, though Wolfe's literally

16. Soja, *Postmodern Geographies*, 192–93.
17. Henry Mayhew, *The* Morning Chronicle *Survey of Labour and the Poor: The Metropolitan Districts*, 6 vols. (Sussex: Caliban Books, 1980), 1:80–81.
18. Immanuel Kant, *Critique of Judgment* (Indianapolis: Hackett, 1987), "Analytic of the Sublime," 97–140.

Stoic (à la Epictetus) solution is one individualistic response to economic excess.

Nor is Soja's comparison to nineteenth-century sweatshops frivolous. *Hotbedding* is of course a Victorian term, used often by Mayhew in *The* Morning Chronicle *Survey* and Marx in *Capital* to describe the technique whereby manufacturers increased production by having workers share beds on the premises, "the day-shift getting into beds that the night-shift had just quitted" and vice versa.[19] Repeatedly the human geographers point to Los Angeles's apparel manufacturing industry. Of the 125,000 jobs in the sector, 80 percent are held by undocumented workers, 90 percent of them women and girls, conditions recalling Mayhew's wretched needlewomen and slopworkers, who were "reduced to literal beggary and occasional prostitution by the low price given for their labour."[20] "Unionization rates," writes Soja, "are low and infringements of minimum wage, overtime, child labour, and occupational safety laws are endemic. Sweatshops that provoke images of nineteenth-century London have thus become as much a part of the restructured landscape of Los Angeles as the abandoned factory site and the new printed circuit plant" (208). In San Francisco, tuberculosis, or "consumption," a nineteenth-century disease, has infected one-third of the population of homeless shelters, and HIV, the AIDS virus, almost one-tenth, ensuring that many homeless people will avoid "like the plague" the already crowded shelters.[21] And, by way of contrast, no Dickensian or Disraelian character could be more stereotypically unself-conscious than a resident of the elite suburban community of Mission Viejo in southern California, who describes the criteria of membership in the development thus: "You must be happy, you must be well rounded and you must have children who do a lot of things. If you don't jog or walk or bike, people wonder if you have diabetes or some other disabling disease."[22]

In an important study of the systemic economic causes of the "New [post-1980] Homelessness," Gregg Barak describes day labor services that exploit the needs of homeless people in order to supply business with cheap and temporary labor (subminimum wage, no benefits).[23]

19. Karl Marx, *Capital* (New York: International, 1967), 1:758.

20. Mayhew, Morning Chronicle *Survey,* 1:189 and passim. For the sufferings of the needlewomen, see esp. 223–46.

21. *Campus Report* (Stanford University), 10 August 1994, 1; *San Francisco Chronicle,* 12 August 1994, A20.

22. Soja, *Postmodern Geographies,* 231, citing the *Los Angeles Times,* 22 August 1984, 1, 26–27.

23. Barak, *Gimme Shelter,* 36–39.

Mayhew described such "hiring out" in 1849, when appeals were made not in Spanish accents but in Irish:

> All are shouting. Some cry aloud [the hiring foreman's] surname, some his christian name; others call out their own names, to remind him that they are there. Now the appeal is made in Irish blarney, now in broken English. Indeed, it is a sight to sadden the most callous, to see *thousands* of men struggling for only one day's hire, the scuffle being made the fiercer by the knowledge that hundreds out of the number there assembled must be left to idle the day out in want. To look in the faces of that hungry crowd, is to see a sight that must be ever remembered. Some are smiling to the foreman to coax him into remembrance of them; others with their protruding eyes eager to snatch at the hoped-for pass. For weeks many have gone there, and gone through the same struggle, the same cries, and have gone away, after all, without the work they had screamed for. (1:71)

In 1990–91, the Center for the Study of Families, Children, and Youth at Stanford University conducted the most comprehensive examination to date of homeless families, children, and teens. Nine studies, conducted in Santa Clara and San Mateo Counties, provided the perspectives of homeless parents, formerly homeless parents, parents at risk of homelessness (that is, very poor families), homeless children, homeless teenagers living on their own, homeless families applying for any form of social service, service providers, school personnel, and low-income people. The studies displayed certain similarities with Mayhew's findings a century and half earlier. First, homeless children are not privileged with childhoods. They worry about things that most children do not consider, like paying bills and their parents' search for employment. A formerly homeless mother called her two-and-one-half-year-old daughter "a 35-year-old midget. She's aware of too much."[24] This recalls Mayhew's account in *London Labour and the London Poor* (1864) of the eight-year-old Watercress Girl, "so young that her features had scarcely formed themselves, talking of the bitterest struggles of life, with the calm earnestness of one who had endured them all."[25] Said Mayhew, "I did not know how to talk with her. . . . All her knowledge seemed to begin and end with watercresses, and

24. Sanford M. Dornbusch et al., *The Stanford Studies of Homeless Families, Children, and Youth: Preliminary Report* (Stanford: The Stanford Center for the Study of Families, Children, and Youth, 1991), 22.

25. Henry Mayhew, *London Labour and the London Poor,* 4 vols. (London: Griffin and Co., 1864), 1:157.

what they fetched." When asked whether the children cried when they washed the cress before dawn on icy winter mornings, the girl answered realistically, "No, it's no use."

The Watercress Girl had left school when the master abused her. Today, according to the Stanford studies, most homeless children are enrolled in schools, but lack of privacy and bad weather impede their ability to do homework. Elsewhere I have discussed the literal enlightenment of Alexander Somerville, a son of itinerant farm laborers in the Borders between Scotland and Wales in the first decades of the nineteenth century. Somerville's enlightenment was not a metaphor (the mirror of self-consciousness or the lamp revealing the truth of nature) but the difficult appropriation of light that allowed him to learn to read: "My father and mother had a window consisting of one small pane of glass, and when they moved from one house to another in different parts of Berwickshire they carried this window with them, and had it fixed in each hovel into which they went as tenants."[26] Children in the Stanford studies told the researchers that their families' rooms at shelters were usually too crowded with furniture, parents, and siblings to study. Children whose families did not have a shelter room of their own said they studied in a family car, a closet or restroom, a shelter's television room, or on the streets (*Stanford Studies*, 27).

Writing of her impoverished childhood in 1950s London, the historian Carolyn Steedman considered the significance to her sense of self of the school lunches provided by the welfare state.

I think I would be a very different person now if orange juice and milk and dinners at school hadn't told me, in a covert way, that I had a right to exist, was worth something. My inheritance from those years is the belief (maintained always with some difficulty) that I do have a right to the earth. . . . Being a child when the state was practically engaged in making children healthy and literate was a support against my own circumstances. . . . It was a considerable achievement for a society to pour so much milk and so much orange juice, so many vitamins, down the throats of its children, and for the height and weight of those children to outstrip the measurements of only a decade before. . . . What my mother lacked, I was given; and though vast inequalities remained between me and others of my generation, the sense that a benevolent state bestowed on me, that of my own existence and the worth of that existence—attenuated, but still there—demonstrate in some degree what a fully material culture might offer in

26. See Gagnier, *Subjectivities*, 140.

terms of physical comfort and the structures of care and affection
that it symbolizes, to all its children.[27]

Yet when the Stanford researchers surveyed school personnel to determine how high a priority they gave to aiding homeless children in
school, they found that school staff "did not see the issue of homelessness as any more urgent than the numerous other problems currently plaguing the school system" (*Stanford Studies*, 28). The studies
concluded that policy makers who urge that schools be the main providers of services for homeless children must work to ensure that additional resources are given to schools for these services. Yet, with the
decline of other liberal policies such as drug rehabilitation, youth employment, and gang counseling, the state has subsequently cut rather
than extended aid to schools. Simultaneously, in a proposition passed
by the voters, it also cut Aid to Families with Dependent Children.
Obviously, for homeless children, cutting AFDC is no less threatening
than cutting services provided by the schools. Rather than the structures of care and affection that a benevolent state bestowed upon Steedman, telling her that she "had a right to exist," that she "was worth
something," the state today offers little.[28] By 1995, one in every three
children in California, or roughly 2.7 million, were living in poverty.[29]

Contrary to right-wing demagoguery about "victim" mentalities
and feelings of "entitlement," the Stanford studies found, homeless
children expect very little. When asked to fantasize three wishes, more
than half wished for basic needs such as shelter and income and the
well-being of family members. A nine-year-old wished for a car, a bed,
and a kitchen for his family. A twelve-year-old boy said his wishes
would be

1. My father having enough to buy food.
2. Money to rent an apartment.
3. If there was money left over, a bike. (23)

27. Carolyn Kay Steedman, *Landscape for a Good Woman: A Study of Two Lives*
(New Brunswick: Rutgers University Press, 1987), 122–23.
28. For the perspectives of some homeless children themselves, see Judith Berck, *No
Place to Be.*
29. "California Children Poorer Than Ever," *San Francisco Chronicle*, 22 June
1995, A1. See also "California's Children Faring Badly," *San Francisco Chronicle*, 23
March 1992, A11. Nationally, child poverty rates increased about 22 percent between
1979 and 1990. After the largely youth-led Los Angeles rebellion of April–May 1992,
more than one publication (e.g., the *San Francisco Chronicle*, 2 May 1992, front page)
began its analysis with James Baldwin's words from *The Fire Next Time*, quoted as an
epigraph to this chapter.

An eight-year-old girl wished

1. That I had a big house.
2. Never to have to move again.
3. That I'll always be with my family. (ibid.)

Another twelve-year-old boy would only venture one modest wish: "I wish we could be less poor. Not rich. But have enough to eat" (22). When asked what jobs they would like to have when they were older, homeless children, like their privileged counterparts, talked about growing up to be dancers, athletes, and doctors, but they often told researchers that those things would never happen for them, that they were impossible. A twelve-year-old boy said he would like to be a lawyer, but when asked what job he expected, he answered "McDonald's" (24), naming a company whose "McJobs" have come to be the type of "low-pay, low-prestige, low-dignity, low-benefit, no future job in the service sector"[30] and some of whose locations have taken to blasting horrifically loud opera from their entrances as a way to discourage homeless loiterers and panhandlers (art as weapon in class warfare). Other children could not imagine jobs at all. A twelve-year-old boy said that when he grows up, "I'll do nothing, just sit around, if I have a place to sit around, if I'm not dead" (ibid.). Expressing skepticism about a future of any kind, a teenager living on the streets asked, "Why would I worry about dying from AIDS in the future when I don't know if I'm going to survive until tomorrow?" (31). Sixty-nine percent of the teens living on the streets had experienced the death or suicide of friends, and 62 percent of them had attempted suicide themselves.

Although their expectations are low, homeless children have, according to the studies, unusually high capacities for sympathy with the needs of others. The studies concluded that despite their problems, "homeless children were more likely to be compassionate than to be hardened. Their hardships seemed to give them a higher level of compassion for human suffering. Many of the children expressed a strong desire to help others in need and to create a better world" (22). In writing of the permanent "surplus," or un- and underemployed, population of London in *The Condition of the Working Class in England* (1845), Engels too had remarked upon the sympathy of the poor for the poorest: "The [beggars] perambulate the streets with their families, appealing to the benevolence of the charitable. It is very noticeable that such beggars . . . subsist almost exclusively on the charity of the working classes . . .

30. Douglas Coupland, *Generation X: Tales for an Accelerated Culture* (New York: St. Martin's, 1991), 5.

who know from personal experience what it is like to go hungry and who themselves may at any moment share the same fate."[31] Their sympathy may be contrasted with the curious phenomenon among the relatively affluent today of "compassion fatigue," a term made popular by the media in the 1980s. We read in the press and heard on television of this term. We were told that people with jobs and homes were "worn out" by feeling compassion for people on the streets.

Like Engels and Mayhew more than a century ago, the Stanford studies found that, contrary to past and present popular opinion that homeless families were made up of the mentally ill, drug abusers, alcoholics, undocumented aliens, and shifters—in Mayhew those "unwilling to work" owing to a mixture of personal problems and character deficiencies—the actual causes of homelessness are low wages, unemployment, and lack of affordable housing, with support from families and friends making the difference between families at risk of homelessness and those that are actually homeless.[32] Other findings failed equally to correspond with popular images: most families' homelessness was not the result of early parenthood, substance abuse, or recent immigration. The studies concluded in the neutral, affectless language of sociology that "homelessness was associated with social circumstances more than with personal qualities" (38), thus resisting the defamation of poor people that was a major cultural effect of the 1980s. Late-twentieth-century social science repeats the findings of Mayhew's work, as reported in his *Low Wages, Their Consequences and Remedies* (1851). Like Mayhew's ethnography, the results of the Stanford studies will have to compete with free-market ideology.

When homelessness was the number one issue in the San Francisco mayoral race, the two leading candidates, the incumbent and the former police chief, expressed opposite views. The mayor, Art Agnos, promised low-cost housing, job counseling, drug rehabilitation, and social work, and he let homeless people camp across the street from City Hall in Civic Center Plaza for more than a year, until the shelters opened. He resisted the modern trend of enclosure. The former police chief, Frank Jordan, proposed that a work farm be built near the city jail, as far out of sight of city residents as possible, to which homeless people might be sentenced if they rejected alternatives and "persisted

31. Friedrich Engels, *The Condition of the Working Class in England* (Stanford: Stanford University Press, 1968), 100.

32. Again, see Barak (1991) for the New Homelessness as a result of the specific conditions of postindustrial information society, esp. ch. 3, "The Political Economy of the New Vagrancy," 53–74.

[in] sleeping in the streets."³³ Jordan's strategy, according to the press, was "driven by the perceived need to rid the city's residents and businesses of a major nuisance that has tarnished its international reputation" (ibid.). Here we have the economics of the postmodern city in a nutshell: a growing homeless population, residents consumed by compassion fatigue, and merchants conceiving of the city not as a home for its citizens but as an object of consumption in the global market. In this climate, it was no surprise when the police chief was elected the new mayor of St. Francis's city. The early political economists took for granted that law was instituted to protect the haves from the have nots. Given the carceral dimension of the modern homeless-proof metropolis, it needs a police chief as mayor. (And this is to say nothing of the number of people actually incarcerated, in some cases as a response to their poverty. It is well known that the United States has the highest per capita prison population in the world. In California alone, the ratio of prisoners to residents in 1994 was 1 in 256. Given the anticrime legislation passed in the 1990s, especially the famed "three strikes" law requiring people convicted of felonies twice before to serve twenty-five years to life without possibility of parole if convicted a third time, predictions were that the ratio would be 1 in 146 by 1999. By comparison, Singapore, typically noted for a tough anticrime posture, incarcerates 1 in 452, and western Europe incarcerates 1 in 1,278.³⁴ Yet anticrime zeal does not extend to the [tax-supported] building of new prisons. Department of Corrections officers note that prison gymnasia have been made into dormitories, classrooms are currently being converted, and they soon expect to set up tents in prison yards.)

For alternatives to Mayor Jordan's work farms, we can look back to the nineteenth century. Unsettled by enclosure and industrialization, the poor quadrupled their numbers between 1780 and 1820, and everyone, from Edmund Burke and Robert Malthus among the free marketeers to Jeremy Bentham, Thomas Spence, and Robert Owen among the social planners, offered solutions to the social crisis. In 1820, Sydney Smith complained that "[a] pamphlet on the Poor Laws generally contains some little piece of a favourite nonsense, by which we are told this enormous evil may be perfectly cured. The first gentleman recommends little gardens; the second cows; the third village shops; the fourth a spade; the fifth Dr. Bell, and so forth. Every man rushes

33. *San Francisco Chronicle*, 25 September 1991, A17, A20.
34. "Prisons Brace for Flood of Convicts," *San Francisco Examiner*, 11 September 1994, A1, A7.

to the press with his small morsel of imbecility." [35] With very few exceptions, the proposals leading up to the 1834 Poor Law were paternalis-
tic, all telling an inaudible population how to live and die, arranging
paupers into ideal communities or giving them leave to die as they
were. The debate raged even after the New Poor Law centralized government control over the fate of the poor, institutionalizing those once
eligible for outdoor relief or forcing them on pain of incarceration and
dismemberment of their family units to work for less than a living
wage. This continuing failure to make progress against the problem
of poverty was facilitated by the failure of reformers to consider the
particular perspectives of the poor themselves. Put differently, they
continued to consider the poor as means in their own social planning
rather than as ends in themselves.

Dickens's immediate response in the pages of *Oliver Twist; or the
Parish Boy's Progress* (1837) is well known. Convinced that the poor
consume rather than conserve, the governing board of philosophical
gentlemen treat the orphan Oliver as an abstraction and thus cruelly:
this was Dickens's critique of Benthamism. Yet Dickens himself treats
the middle class (Rose Maylie's circle) as abstractions and thus sentimentally and the urban unemployed (Fagin's gang) as abstractions and
thus sensationally. That is, Fagin's boys are a different species from
Oliver, who was originally born into the middle classes and whose
birthright apparently protects him from the environmental effects of
the East End, just as the middle-class "utilities" of the political economists, such as domesticity, marriage, and self-interest, cease to be utilities when they are Nancy's or Fagin's. (Cobbett, among many others,
had pointed out—albeit romantically—similar contradictions when he
suggested that Parson Malthus's evil—sexual reproduction—was
the poor's good, "the greatest of all compensations for their inevitable
cares, troubles, hardships, and sorrows of life.")[36] Insofar as it turns
out that the real threat to Oliver is not Fagin's "surplus population"

35. Cited in J. R. Poynter, *Society and Pauperism: English Ideas on Poor Relief,
1795–1834* (London: Routledge, Kegan Paul, 1969), 330. Poynter's remains a masterful
compendium of the Poor Law debates. More polemical, but extending to the end of the
century, are Gertrude Himmelfarb's *The Idea of Poverty: England in the Early Industrial
Age* (New York: Knopf, 1984) and *Poverty and Compassion: The Moral Imagination
of the Late Victorians* (New York: Knopf, 1991). In *The Age of Atonement: The Influence of Evangelicalism in Social and Economic Thought, 1795–1865* (Oxford: Oxford
University Press, 1988), Boyd Hilton meticulously supports an original thesis that economic policy derived from rentier Evangelicals whose philosophy of self-help converged
with laissez-faire.

36. William Cobbett, *Advice to Young Men,* cited in Thomas Robert Malthus, *Essay on the Principle of Population* (New York: Norton, 1976), xxiii.

but rather his own legitimate brother, who wants his patrimony, what happened in the plot of *Oliver Twist* was what happened in the amendment of the Poor Law itself: in the efficient eradication of the corruption of the bourgeoisie, Fagin's orphans in the novel and the actual poor of England were treated as means, not as ends in themselves. In *Oliver Twist,* they are efficiently killed off or deported; in the amendment of 1834 their families were dismembered and they were incarcerated in workhouses.

In his expedient treatment of the underclass Dickens displayed the same ideological prejudices as the political economists he was purportedly attacking, yet the subsequent reception of *Oliver Twist* indicates that the poor whom Dickens intended as the means of Victorian moralism could at the right historical moment assume the role of ends in themselves. It is probably fair to say that, for most readers of *Oliver Twist,* the poor (Dick), the desperate (Nancy), the violent (Sikes), and the tormented (Fagin) are the imaginative center of the text, not the efficient middle-class Maylies and Brownlows. This was prominently conceded in Carol Reed's 1968 musical *Oliver!,* in which, in sporadic eruptions of the political Unconscious, the lower classes dance, the upper classes do not, and the police—the social mediators between the two—half-dance. No longer sacrificed to the needs of Victorian plot and morality, the Dodger and Fagin dance off at the end, arm in arm, aesthetic ends in themselves in the utopian 1960s. On the other hand, in the 1999 Alan Bleasdale/Renny Rye ITV production, the focus dramatically shifted to the corruption of the bourgeoisie.

Like that of totalizing narrative, the danger of utilitarianism is that it is liable to treat people as means to the end envisioned by the reformer rather than as ends in themselves. John Stuart Mill, the best of the utilitarians, attempted to formulate a policy toward the poor. In "On the Influence of Government," book 5 of his *Principles of Political Economy* (1848), Mill supports government assistance to the indigent, not distinguishing between the so-called deserving and undeserving poor. Although he maintains that energy and independence should not be discouraged by undue aid, he acknowledges that "[e]nergy and self-dependence are, however, liable to be impaired by the absence of help, as well as by its excess. It is even more fatal to exertion to have no hope of succeeding by it, than to be assured of succeeding without it. When the condition of any one is so disastrous that his energies are paralysed by discouragement, assistance is a tonic, not a sedative."[37]

37. John Stuart Mill, *Principles of Political Economy* (Middlesex: Penguin, 1988), 334.

The assistance should be public rather than private, first, because charity is inefficient, "lavishing its bounty in one place, and leaving people to starve in another"; second, because the state provides subsistence to criminals, so "not to do the same for the poor who have not offended is to give a premium on crime"; and finally, because if the poor are left to charity, "a vast amount of mendacity is inevitable" (335). Since the state owes no more than subsistence to the deserving, and can give no less than subsistence to the undeserving, it may leave to private charities the option of discriminating between them. By 1845, of course, Engels had already pointed out how such language tended to criminalize the poor.

Like Bentham and (implicitly) Dickens, Mill thought that the ultimate solution to the problems they perceived as overpopulation and scarcity would be state-supported colonization. And at this point we begin to see how even Mill fails to escape the tendency of utilitarianism to treat persons as means rather than ends in themselves. Colonization "involves the future and permanent interests of civilization itself" (336), and for that reason its costs should be born by the state, not the "surplus population" forced to emigrate for their livelihoods. Mill's view of colonization is efficiently economic, the motor of Progress: "The exportation of labourers and capital from old to new countries, from a place where their productive power is less, to a place where it is greater, increases by so much the aggregate produce of the labour and capital of the world" (337). The limited perspective of the trained political economist, the insensitivity to the domination of both indigenous peoples and emigrants, is perhaps clearest in Mill's bland reference to "unoccupied continents." He concludes the section on colonization with the necessity to keep the communication open "between the hands needing work in England and the work which needs hands elsewhere," with no acknowledgment of any costs but the pecuniary ones of shipping.

> There is hence the strongest obligation on the government of a country like our own, with a crowded population, and unoccupied continents under its command, to build, as it were, and keep open, in concert with the colonial governments, a bridge from the mother country to those continents, by establishing the self-supporting system of colonization on such a scale, that as great an amount of emigration as the colonies can at the time accommodate, may at all times be able to take place without cost to the emigrants themselves. (341)

Both the indigenous peoples and the poor who are forced to emigrate are treated merely as means to Mill's economic expansionism, part of his abstract plan of universal progress.

Marx was equally Progressive in his attitude toward colonization but considerably more self-critical of the brutality it entailed. In two essays on British rule in India (1853), he argued that "England has to fulfill a double mission in India: one destructive, the other regenerating—the annihilation of old Asiatic society, and the laying of the material foundations of Western society in Asia."[38] Both missions were terrible, and Marx does not, like Mill, pass over the violence and the sorrow, but he nonetheless claims that only when a great social revolution of indigenous peoples shall have mastered "the results of the bourgeois epoch" and "subjected them to common control" or communism, only then will human progress begin. In order for the poor at home and in India to be ends in themselves they must first be the means of revolutionary progress.

By way of more traditional Christian rhetoric, Ruskin attempted to treat the poor as ends in themselves by focusing on the responsibilities of the rich. In *Unto This Last* (1860–62), he replaced the principle of self-interest with that of self-sacrifice and applied the principle of self-sacrifice not to the poor, like Malthus, but to the upper classes. He denies that he has sympathy with socialism, or the redistribution of property, for the fact of wealth is strength, the rich are strong, and they should not be made weak. Yet they should employ their riches and their strength in the service of others. Appealing to a natural hierarchy and the demands of paternalism, he concedes this much to Malthusianism:

> Say that it is continually the fault or the folly of the poor that they are poor, as it is usually a child's fault if it falls into a pond, and a cripple's weakness that it slips at a crossing; nevertheless, most passers-by would pull the child out, or help up the cripple. Put it at the worst, that all the poor of the world are but disobedient children, or careless cripples, and that all rich people are wise and strong, and you will see at once that neither is the socialist right in desiring to make everybody poor, powerless, and foolish as he is himself, nor the rich man right in leaving the children in the mire.[39]

38. Karl Marx, "The Future Results of British Rule in India," in *The Marx-Engels Reader*, ed. Robert C. Tucker (New York: Norton, 1978), 659–64; quotation is on 659.
39. John Ruskin, *Unto This Last* (Middlesex: Penguin, 1985), 223 n.

Ruskin demands moral restraint not, like Burke or Malthus, on the part of the poor, but on the part of the rich, asking that they limit their consumption of luxuries until the day when they will be available to all alike: "Luxury at present can only be enjoyed by the ignorant; the cruelest man living could not sit at his feast, unless he sat blindfold" (228).

Although *Unto This Last* was largely an attack on Mill, the earlier author had already supplied the best answer to Ruskin. In "On the Probable Futurity of the Labouring Classes," Mill had exposed the sentimentality of paternalism, whether in relation to class, gender, or age, with a clear analysis of the dynamics of power:

> All privileged and powerful classes, as such, have used their power in the interest of their own selfishness, and have indulged their self-importance in despising, and not in lovingly caring for, those who were, in their estimation, degraded by being under the necessity of working for their benefit. . . . The so-called protectors are now the only persons against whom, in any ordinary circumstances, protection is needed. The brutality and tyranny with which every police report is filled, are those of husbands to wives, of parents to children.[40]

While Mill and Ruskin reflected on the comparative scope of rights and responsibilities, the most sublime plan for social welfare, one that could encompass them both, was still to be articulated. In "The Critique of the Gotha Programme" (1875), Marx envisioned two stages of socialist society. The first would give what capitalism had promised but failed to provide: compensation equal to one's contribution. In the second stage, when the narrow horizons of bourgeois rights would have been transcended, then each would contribute according to ability and receive according to need—need not simply in the sense of necessities but in the sense of the needs of developing humankind. Sketchy as it was, it aimed to treat each as an end in herself, not as a means in another's story of Progress, paternalism, or domestic peace.

Less imaginative than Marx, Mayor Jordan of San Francisco, with a plan called "Matrix," dispatched vans to round up homeless people and transport them ("voluntarily") to shelters that were already so crowded and tuberculoid that they were turning people away. Given the ungrateful response of homeless people to the mayor's invitation, we can expect that this latest attempt at enclosure and efficiency will

40. Mill, *Principles of Political Economy,* 120–21.

also fail. Of more interest historically, however, is his administration's increasing insistence that homelessness be seen as an economic rather than a social problem, meaning that the cost of homelessness to the wealthy, rather than to the homeless themselves, becomes the focus of policy. The mayor's office estimated that "public annoyance at the highly visible presence of street people is costing San Francisco roughly $170 million a year in sales." In a measure that is being eagerly watched by other metropolitan areas, voters approved the mayor's proposal for $500 fines and six-month prison sentences for "aggressive soliciting" by homeless persons on the streets ("how on earth are they going to pay it?"). The new economic conception of society was revealed in the campaign's reference to homeless citizens as "a menace to the common good"—those whose only space is the public space are by that fact itself excluded from the commonality, and the good that under the utilitarians designated the welfare of all now means the comfort of the propertied.[41]

Departing from the twelve-year standoff between advocates of homeless people and government officials, the Clinton administration raised the national figures from 600,000 homeless on any one night (the previous official number) to seven million homeless at some time in the 1980s. It also raised the politically sensitive issue of the middle-class subsidy, the home mortgage interest deduction, which cost the federal treasury $41 billion in 1993. Of that amount, 85 percent went to the richest one-quarter of Americans, who made more than $50,000 per year. The Clinton plan suggested that government was misdirecting its resources.[42] In 1994, Secretary of Housing and Urban Development Henry Cisneros suggested that the federal government use surplus military bases, but he also acknowledged the "delicacy" of using "precious real estate" for homeless people.[43]

Since Matrix was established in August 1993, the city has attempted to enforce laws against what the mayor calls "quality of life offenses," cracking down on homeless people, whom he calls a public nuisance. By the end of the program's first month, the police commander in charge was able to report "an immediate *visual* impact. Those areas certainly haven't become totally aesthetic overnight, but it is an improvement."[44] By mid-September civic officials in Berkeley, across the

41. See "Limits on Begging Could Set Trend," *San Francisco Chronicle,* 3 August 1992, A1.
42. *San Francisco Chronicle,* 17 February 1994, A3.
43. *San Francisco Chronicle,* 5 March 1994, 2.
44. *San Francisco Chronicle,* 1 September 1993, 1, A13, emphasis supplied.

Bay, were complaining that homeless people driven out of San Francisco by Matrix were moving on Berkeley streets,[45] and Jordan and his critics were said to be locked in a "struggle for the city's character," viz., Jordan's "tougher city" versus San Francisco's "reputation for tolerance."[46] Police crackdowns in the form of tickets and arrests have made Matrix the subject of national attention. In the summer of 1995, Matrix was enlisted to clear "campers" from Golden Gate Park, amid considerable publicity and protest. Since the mayor was up for reelection at the time, many suspected political motives for the highly visible "purge."[47]

Both historically, then, and in the present, social planners and politicians have used the poor for their own ends, while novelists and ethnographers have shown that it is more comfortable to meet the Other in the relative privacy of print than on the pavement (and some economists have argued that this confrontation, in print or on the pavement, causes pleasure to the most advantaged). In Seattle, the public library has once again surfaced in relation to homeless people, this time not as a barrier but as a partial solution. Homeless men there, it seems, spend the entire day, every day, plugged into the Internet, finally finding a home—at least in the daytime—in cyberspace.[48] This link between history's richest man—Bill Gates—and his country's poorest is surely a testament to human creativity under conditions of necessity.

Attempting to give homeless people a voice, the Theatre of the Homeless has returned to the public space of the stage, between the private bourgeois space of reading, the postmodern impersonality of the Internet, and the anomie of the streets. In contemplating the Theatre at the end of this book, I do not propose it as a solution to economic inequality or as representative of the aesthetic life: like all aesthetics discussed in this book, it is a practical intervention into the issues of moment. I do, however, value it precisely as an intervention in *public* space, in the older sense of *public* as the space of dialogue, debate, interpersonal contact.

Theatre of the Homeless is a theater group from the San Francisco Peninsula whose roster varies on any given night according to the fortunes of the homeless actors themselves. The cast includes men, women, and children who are now, or have recently been, homeless. They are all amateurs, and they "perform" by telling their own stories and the stories of others they know who are on the streets but unable

45. *San Francisco Chronicle*, 10 September 1993, 1.
46. *San Francisco Chronicle*, 24 September 1993, 1.
47. *San Francisco Chronicle*, 4 March 1994, 1, A6.
48. *San Francisco Chronicle*, 17 July 1994, A8.

to address audiences. Part of their impact on audiences derives from their being local (non)"residents": they are all homeless in the same space as their audience. I first saw them at my university, where they were brought in to raise awareness of homelessness among a comparatively affluent student body. It was an example of the aestheticization of poverty par excellence: persons whom the students might avoid on the streets were now being paid to stand on stage and "entertain" them. Further, students who might not give money on the streets were now paying to listen to persons they might not listen to on the streets. The audience treated the Theatre of the Homeless just as they would any play: the encounter between the two—dare we say—*classes* of people was only allowed to take place because there was a stage. The "actors" knew this: they introduced their performance by saying that normally they were the invisible people we passed by as we went about our daily business. But tonight it was different; we were listening. (Whereas politicians find homeless people all too visible, they themselves, reasonably enough, take the opposite view.)

Then they told their stories, which were unpolished and unremarkable. That night in the 1990s they included a former businessman who hadn't held a steady job since 1983; an old woman who temporarily joined the ranks of the homeless when she was visiting the University Medical Center for a serious health problem and her purse, with money, credit cards, and identification, was stolen; a teenaged victim of abuse who had run away and was living in her car and attending college (she could not bring herself to talk about the abuse, but she alluded to it); a veteran who said that he had "lost his soul" in Vietnam the night he bayonetted a pregnant woman; and three children between the ages of seven and twelve who had never known a permanent address, only the names of parks and shelters they had passed through. Like all nervous children in performance situations, they spoke quickly and inaudibly, so that the audience missed most of what they said; but we did hear that the white girl loved God and that the two black boys usually performed with their father, who "couldn't be there that night." In any case, the children, at least, were not less effective because they were unpolished. Their inexperience, like the banality of the stories, effectively diminished the Theatre's potential to sensationalize or aestheticize homelessness—a problem that social explorers of the nineteenth century, including Mayhew, often had in commodifying their research for print.[49]

49. For an extensive discussion of the conflict between sensationalizing and providing information in Mayhew and other Victorian social explorers or reformers, see chap-

Although Theatre of the Homeless is reviewed in the morning papers just like any other commodified entertainment, it was precisely the banality of the stories—unemployment, the breakdown of the healthcare system, wife battery, child abuse, unassimilated veterans of recent wars and war technologies—and the storytellers' lack of polish that deaestheticized the popular cultural images of homelessness. This lack of controlling narrative, sensational depiction, or aesthetic distance (like the privacy of reading) permitted the contact between performers and audience, in which their pain and our responsibility—in both Ruskin's paternal and Mill's economic or systemic senses—made for the discomfort and humiliation of both. Before aesthetics was forgotten as a social force or a handmaiden of the good, the Fabian socialists thought that disgust—distaste—at poverty and violence would be a progressive force for its amelioration. To counteract the extreme glamorization of wealth in the 1980s and the equally extreme objectification of poverty, the Theatre of the Homeless attempted an aesthetic space, a stage, where ordinary people could view each other across the abyss of property.

That such a situation is barbarous, and has nothing to do with the aesthetic life as Burke in the eighteenth century, Wilde in the nineteenth, or Woolf in the early twentieth knew it, goes without saying. Yet the Theatre founders had adopted as their slogan "Theatre of the Homeless—Rebuilding Community from the Street Up." Although I am mortified to be a citizen of a state where contact between "the two nations" can only happen through the mediation of a stage—that is, our contact must be "staged"—that aestheticized space functions as aesthetic spaces have always functioned when they have meant something more than cultural capital: as a space of freedom, a space free to imagine the community that does not exist. The imagined community of the homeless actors and the "symbolic analysts" of the Silicon Valley is but a symbol of the morally good, not the good itself. But it is a symbolic answer to the great enclosures.

---

ters 2 and 3 of Gagnier, *Subjectivities* (1991), esp. 62–93 and 99–138, "Henry Mayhew's Rich World of Poverty" and "Representations of the Working Classes by Nonworking-Class Writers: Subjectivity and Solidarity."

CONCLUSION

■ ■ ■

The sociologist J. Urry describes contemporary global culture as images, language, and information flowing through "scapes" of geographically dispersed agents and technologies.[1] This cultural flow gives rise to a cosmopolitan civil society that "precipitates new modes of personal and collective self-fashioning as individualization and cultural formations are . . . combined and recombined" (1980). Urry insists on the importance of culture in understanding the global economy: "Increasingly economies are economies of signs. . . . [T]his has implications for the occupations structure and hence for the increasingly culturally constructed preferences of taste" (1981). Urry is pointing toward a global aesthetics in which many cultures, in Hegel's phrase, "represent themselves to themselves and thereby construct their identities" in a global market. While the ideology of individualism has grown stronger, the culture that informs individuals has grown more diverse, more global, and more commodified. We "symbolic analysts" need an aesthetics that can analyze not only cultural and art objects that are inevitably commodified but also political, legal, health, and education systems that, because they are commodified, are aestheticized. We also need an aesthetics that can provide critical distance from, and alternatives to, the forces of the market. In showing the changing features of Economic and Aesthetic Man and Woman over the past two centuries, this book has been committed to this tripartite task: analyzing art objects, analyzing the aspects of everyday life that have been aestheticized for the consumption of citizens or subjects, and providing critique and alternatives. It may be that future work for both economists and culturalists will be in analyzing the cultural construction of, and constraints on, taste and preference, and for some

1. J. Urry, "Is the Global a New Space of Analysis?" *Environment and Planning A 1996* 28, no. 11 (1996): 1977–82.

of us in studying the moments when aesthetic knowledge enhances the quality of life for everyone.

When Holbrook Jackson wrote his chapter on William Morris and the Arts and Crafts movement in *The Eighteen-Nineties* (1913, dedicated to Max Beerbohm), he noted the commodification that threatened the progressive development of taste. What began as a great movement toward the liberation of humankind through pleasure in creative labor "was in danger of ending as an empty fashion with the word 'artistic' for shibboleth."[2] Yet Jackson nonetheless named the 1890s "a decade singularly rich in ideas, personal genius and social will" whose "central characteristic [was] a widespread concern for the correct—the most effective, most powerful, most righteous—mode of living" (12, 17). There is no doubt that at the end of the twentieth century, Economic Man and Woman were rich in ideas and personal genius. Whether Jackson's "social will" can survive them into the twenty-first may depend on our aesthetics, or on different cultures' capacity to represent themselves to themselves and to others creatively, productively, and with a just mode of living. In 1949, George Orwell feared that the image of the future would be a boot stamping on a human face forever. If we are prepared to say that Marxism is dead, and that Smith's sympathy and Mill's progressivism are discredited, are we also prepared to make the image of our future the stage of *Salomé* or the picture of Dorian Gray, Fukuyama's "infinitely diverse consumer culture" or Pater's "flood of external objects," or just the solipsistic individualism of "each mind keeping as a solitary prisoner its own dream of a world"?

2. Holbrook Jackson, *The Eighteen-Nineties* (New York: Mitchell Kennerley, 1914), 306.

APPENDIX

■ ■ ■

TASTE, OR SEX AND CLASS AS CULTURE

What one's ordinary self likes differs according to the class to which one belongs. . . . Barbarians like field-sports and pleasure; the Philistine likes comfort and tea-meetings; the Populace likes beer.
—Matthew Arnold

I remember Luton
As I'm swallowing my crout'n.
—John Hegley, "A Poem About the Town of My Upbringing and the Conflict Between My Working-Class Origins and the Middle-Class Status Conferred upon Me by My University Education"

How do the roles of producer and consumer in the broad anthropological senses we have considered map onto social class? We may approach this question through a comparison of the analytic categories of gender and class. Gender is a much clearer concept today than class. Gender is a role, masculine or feminine, or a relation of inequality between things that might not on the surface have to do with "masculine" or "feminine" (as in "These are *gendered* categories"). Thus we are gendered as male or female, or with respect to social power, aesthetics is gendered female, economics, male. We also increasingly distinguish gender from sex and sexuality. Gender is a role or an abstraction concerning a relationship, whereas sex pertains to biology or at least reproductive functions. Work on cross-cultural biology (for example, in the enormous variations in the onset of puberty) and on transsexualism has certainly complicated any essentialist no-

An earlier version of this appendix appeared as "The Functions of Class at the Present Time" in *Women: A Cultural Review* 11:1 (2000): 21–28 (© 2000 Routledge).

tions of biology and sex.[1] Today, when we ask what it means to be female, we hear a variety of answers. We meet a woman. Long before her operation, when she looked like a man, she *felt* like a woman. Is she a woman because she *feels* like a woman or only when she *looks* like a woman? Another has been *socialized* as a woman, that is, she has had the *experience* of being treated like a woman, which has included certain experiences of oppression and subordination that people who have only recently become women may not share. Is she a woman because she has *experienced* being a woman in a society that discriminates against women? Another always *felt* like a woman, but she only became a woman after surgery, at which point she tried to play professional sports and then found that genes or chromosomes alone could make her a woman. The assignation of sex, as experience, as socialization, as genetics, today is certainly contested. Nonetheless, it is generally distinguished from gender and sexuality and linked to reproductive function.

Sexuality, on the other hand, is now largely relegated to two domains, although such assignments may be limited to postindustrial consumer societies. First, sexuality refers to pleasure liberated from reproduction, or even the roles that were historically associated with reproduction; witness sex clubs that currently advertise that "We don't do gender." This notion of sexuality as *mere* pleasure, or in extreme cases—"We don't do gender"—as mere performance, accounts for the way most consumer societies understand sexuality, as fungible, as about pleasure, as deriving from individual tastes and preferences. Or, second, in a radical feminist analysis of the same consumer cultures, sexuality refers to pain. Catherine MacKinnon and Andrea Dworkin have developed a famous analogy: female sexuality under current conditions is to women what labor under current conditions is to workers, or what black culture under current conditions is to black Americans: it is alienated, constructed within a relationship of domination and subordination.[2] MacKinnon and Dworkin have argued, and proposed

1. Ruth Hubbard, "The Political Nature of 'Human Nature,'" in *Theoretical Perspectives on Sexual Difference*, ed. Deborah Rhode (New Haven: Yale University Press, 1990), 63–73; Anne Fausto-Sterling, *Myths of Gender: Biological Theories About Women and Men* (New York: Basic, 1985); Marjorie Garber, "Spare Parts: The Surgical Construction of Gender," in *Theorizing Feminism: Parallel Trends in the Humanities and Social Sciences*, ed. Anne C. Herrmann and Abigail J. Stewart (Boulder, Colo.: Westview, 1994), 238–56; Suzanne J. Kessler and Wendy McKenna, *Gender: An Ethnomethodological Approach* (Chicago: University of Chicago Press, 1978).

2. Catharine A. MacKinnon, "Feminism, Marxism, Method, and the State: An Agenda for Theory," in *Feminist Theory: A Critique of Ideology*, ed. Nannerl O. Keohane, Michelle Z. Rosaldo, and Barbara C. Gelpi (Chicago: University of Chicago Press,

legislation on the basis of these arguments, that we will not know what female sexuality can be until we live in a society free of sex and gender domination—just as Marx and Engels argued that we will not know what creative human production is until we are free of class relations.

MacKinnon's and Dworkin's views have been controversial even within the feminist community; if one does reject the view that women as a class are dominated as workers are exploited, then we must ask further questions. If sex is distinguished, as a biological or reproductive function, from gender as a role, and from sexuality as pain or pleasure, then class is clearly not like sex, not biological. Is class like gender? That is, can class be performed like a role? Is class like sexuality? That is, is class both a pain and a pleasure?

In trying to analyze how class functions in late-twentieth-century market societies and how it relates to gender, we are not playing word games. In asking how class is an objective condition, a role, a pain, or a pleasure, we have hit upon the main usages of class in social theory today. The usages we might consider are class as subjectivity or identity; as an objective relation to the economy or division of labor; as a discourse or myth, in Roland Barthes's sense of myth as a historical construction that conceals its own contingency, depoliticizes, and naturalizes;[3] as a postmodern hyphenization with race, gender, or sexuality (as in "I'm a white working-class lesbian"); and as a performance. We shall explore the scope and limits of each of these contemporary uses of class, especially in their relation to gender. The essence of class and gender is precisely the relation between the classes and between the genders, and the relation of class to gender. As Marx said of capital, "capital is not a thing, but a social relation between persons," so class and gender are essentially social relations rather than essences.[4] Too often critics speak of only one class or gender, reifying what is essentially a social relation.

Probably the least time need be spent on identity, for the problems with class identity politics from the perspective of gender have been documented and analyzed. They have led to labor aristocracies that marginalize women and women's work, less skilled workers, and people of color. They have tended toward heavily masculinist political methods; they have distinguished production from reproduction and

---

1981), 1–30, and MacKinnon, *Only Words* (Cambridge: Harvard University Press, 1993).

3. Roland Barthes, *Mythologies,* trans. Annette Lavers (1957; reprint, London: Vintage, 1993).

4. Karl Marx, *Capital,* ed. Frederick Engels (New York: International, 1967), 1:766. See also the section on Wilde in chapter 5 above.

thereby promoted a gendered division of labor and separate spheres; they have emphasized production and reproduction over desire and have failed to account for subtle or complex forms of subjectivity, such as envy and shame. Identity politics, that is, is about will and rationality—I will my solidarity with women or workers—but subjectivity may be irrational—I may feel shame or envy even when I most loudly assert my solidarity—just as feminists may find to their confusion that their patterns of desire are not so correct as their principles. Here the work of Pamela Fox in *Class Fictions,* in which she applies the shame theory of Helen Merrell Lynd to working-class writing, or of Carolyn Steedman in *Landscape for a Good Woman,* in which she critiques radical politics from the perspective of her working-class mother's desire, are exemplary in exposing the conflict between traditional masculine class politics (based in "the relations of production") and the politics of desire to share in the good things of the world.[5] This is not to say that one may not have a visceral, nonrational identity with one's class, as in the way that generations of Americans have come to express the feelings we associate with our "Grandma's hands," but only that identity *politics* as a politics may be in tension with subjective feelings. Subjectivity in its deeper forms may also conflict with objectivity, where objectivity means the convergence of opinion of others. I may feel like a king but I won't be treated like one at the bank. I may feel like a woman, but if I walk like a man, talk like a man, and look like a man, I will for all practical purposes be a man.

Let us return to the subtle cases in which subjectivity conflicts with identity. This may point to the strongly *cultural* aspect of class. Taste—or class as *culture*—may disincline middle-class people to share anything but political solidarity and economic resources with the working class. Put differently, a good leftist will willingly share the *pains* of working people, willingly redistribute the wealth, but will she share in their pleasures? The issue arose in chapter 2 in the case of John Stuart Mill and his mother. Mill understood the pains his mother suffered on his behalf and therefore supported women's cause, but, precisely because she was oppressed, he could not sympathize with her pleasures. A number of nineteenth-century feminists of both sexes remarked on the gulf between men's and women's sympathies and the impossibility of bridging it unless their material conditions were made more equal. The critic Helen Blythe has written extensively on emigration to New

5. Pamela Fox, *Class Fictions: Shame and Resistance in the British Working-Class Novel, 1890–1945* (Durham, N.C.: Duke University Press, 1994); Carolyn Kay Steedman, *Landscape for a Good Woman: A Story of Two Lives* (New Brunswick: Rutgers University Press, 1987).

7   nd in the nineteenth century and the place that the Antipodes
      ɹ the British cultural imagination.[6] The cases she discusses of
      ·class emigration are illuminating. Thomas Arnold, not the
      ʳter of Rugby but his son, Matthew's brother, dreamt of New
      as an alternative to British society, a place of beautiful, cre-
      ɹ, in contrast to the sordid deprivation he saw in London as
      to and from his job at the Colonial Office. But that dream
      ʰen he followed it to the colony, owing to his inability to
      ɔurgeois taste; he liked the work they did, but he found
      ...ɪng their leisure, taking their pleasures, New Zealanders dis-
gusted him. Mary Taylor, a close friend of Charlotte Brontë, also went
to the Antipodes in pursuit of a society that would dignify labor. Giving herself to hard physical work in the colony, engaged in tense correspondence with Brontë on the latter's ambivalence toward women
working, Taylor nonetheless missed the middle-class *culture* of Britain
and ultimately returned to the society that had formed her tastes. Arnold and Taylor did not balk at sharing the pain, or labor, of the
people, only at sharing the people's pleasures. Marxists and other pro-
gressives have always supported the working classes around issues of
labor or production. But especially in relation to global labor forces,
it remains to be seen whether alliances will extend across the diversity
of pleasures.

The argument that class is culture, or taste, is based on evidence that
pleasure is not transitive across class. Most of this evidence, however, is
limited to the testimony of the upper middle class, who are usually the
ones who write about it. It may be that such conservative ideas of taste
are giving way in consumer society to more random, mixed patterns
across social groups. John Hegley's "I remember Luton / As I'm swallowing my crout'n"—and the irony of its title—suggest as much, especially in comparison with the anxiety or "shame" expressed by earlier
generations of writers and poets, as in Fox's study. Hegley seems as
comfortable with croutons, the mere representation of bread (in which
taste marks sophistication in the realm of representation), as with the
working class whose history has been so profoundly dependent on the
real referent, bread.

This higher tolerance of diversity in taste and pleasures would be
consistent with consumer ideology, to which I shall return below. But
to the extent that taste, or class as culture, is constitutive of class feel-

6. Helen Blythe, "A Victorian Colonial Romance: Conjuring up New Zealand in
Nineteenth-Century Literature," Ph.D. diss., English Department, Stanford University,
1998.

ing, a gender analysis would demand to know specific gender valences of taste, as in *Women and British Aestheticism,* edited by Talia Schaffer and Kathy Psomiades, in which women's particular contributions to late Victorian Aestheticism are compared to men's and the Decadence is seen to be both gendered and class-specific.[7] There is also a gender valence of class as taste or culture in another sense that I think is crucial: the *reproduction* of taste or class as culture. Although there are exceptions, the main way in which taste or class as culture is reproduced is by birth. (Academics are often the exceptions, those "educated" out of the tastes of their parents, which probably contributes to their emphasis on the cultural aspects of class.) Economists typically treat the wealth that is transferred through taxation or social services; yet by far the largest wealth transfers in history are from parents to children. Just as children are born into economic classes, so are they born into taste or class as culture. The gender politics of the reproduction of class as culture is evident in the recent call from education authorities in Britain for fathers to read at home with their sons, so that reading might not be gendered female.

The issue of class as taste has come to the fore as social theory has debated productivist versus consumption models. Early on, Max Weber distinguished between status and class. Whereas Weber took class to express objective relationships of production, status groups expressed the distribution of prestige through relationships involved in specific *styles* of life.[8] In modern market societies, these styles related to specific practices of consumption. Yet neither class nor status was a matter of individual will or capacity but rather was one of broad social relations, so that status had to be conferred by a community. The relation of class to status, of position in the forces of production and reproduction to taste or style or consumption patterns, is central to any sociology of culture. Obviously, just as women's class positions have to do with the gendered relations of production and reproduction, so women's statuses are also gendered: consider women's styles in relation to taste and power.

Here we should also recognize the potential of the work just beginning on addiction. Above I cited some economists' work on addictive tastes:[9] just as one can be addicted to heroin, so that, contrary to di-

7. Talia Schaffer and Kathy Psomiades, eds., *Women and British Aestheticism* (Charlottesville: University of Virginia Press, 1999).

8. Max Weber, *Economy and Society,* ed. Guenther Roth and Claus Wittich (New York: Bedminster Press, 1968); see also Anthony Giddens, *The Class Structure of the Advanced Societies,* 2d ed. (London: Hutchinson, 1979).

9. Gary S. Becker, *Accounting for Tastes* (Cambridge: Harvard University Press, 1998) and Gianfranco Mossetto, *Aesthetics and Economics* (London: Kluwer, 1993).

minishing marginal utility, the more one gets the more one wants, so one can also be addicted to music, or art, or literature, or wine, or food with certain real or imagined distinctive characteristics, so that one may not be able to go "back" in one's taste to enjoy what was once perhaps enjoyable. In the section of his *Confessions* (1821) called "The Pains of Opium," the great anatomist of addiction Thomas De Quincey represented himself as equally addicted to "ruby-coloured laudanum" and "books of German metaphysics."[10] Above we saw how an elite literary education gave Wilde the resources to surmount the abjection of imprisonment. Probably the most important work to be done on taste will be the convergence of economic and cultural theories of addiction. This future work may well explain the intractability of hierarchical tastes (the "cultured" reader or consumer) as well as the long-term effects of education in providing life-supporting, or even life-saving, human resources, heretofore too crudely conceived as human "capital."

If identity, which is largely political, and subjectivity, which deals in less rational forms such as taste, envy, and shame, have been much discussed, what about class as hegemony, where hegemony is defined as an ideological bloc that deprives other ideologies of their full development?[11] In much New Historicist work, identity categories such as class and gender are eschewed in favor of the supposed discursive grounds of their production. Thus in *Making a Social Body* Mary Poovey claims that the "social body" as predecessor to "the masses" was "made" in debates on education, poor law, sanitation, and health, and that the grounds of class lie in the discursive and institutional production of class.[12] Here class is a form of social control, not totalizing, to be sure, but nonetheless a formation—Poovey's subtitle is *British Cultural Formation*—of the masses through the discursive and institutional practices of the generators of discourse. Poovey is not interested in the identity, or subjectivity, of the poor, nor in their positions with respect to the labor process, but in their status as discourse or myth: "the social body."

I have criticized Poovey's work elsewhere, largely on methodological grounds.[13] Here we should distinguish between textualists such as

10. Thomas De Quincey, *Confessions of an English Opium Eater,* ed. Alethea Hayter (1821; reprint, Harmondsworth: Penguin, 1971), 95–96.

11. Ernesto Laclau and Chantal Mouffe, *Hegemony and Socialist Strategy: Towards a Radical Democratic Politics* (London: Verso, 1985).

12. Mary Poovey, *Making a Social Body: British Cultural Formation, 1830–1864* (Chicago: University of Chicago Press, 1995).

13. Regenia Gagnier, "Methodology and New Historicism," *Journal of Victorian Culture* 4, no. 1 (spring 1999): 116–22.

Poovey who study dominant discourses that arguably "produce" social formations such as class and gender (the social body or the wom-
en's sphere or, in her more recent work, "facts" themselves)[14] and the
materialists who treat the cultural aspects of class more critically, exploring their limitations as well as their scope. The newer "culturalist"
labor historians, for example, have traced the cultural construction of
what have heretofore been perceived as economic categories, such as
class. Eric Schocket (1998) has recently employed performance theory
in general and Marjorie Garber's work in particular in the development
of what he calls "class transvestism," that is, when middle-class writers
of the late nineteenth and early twentieth centuries showed their comradeship with the poor, the social body, by literally costuming themselves in the garb of poverty.[15] Schocket shows how the comradeship
was born of simulation and created a "culture of poverty." Yet whereas
Garber sees transvestite logic as working toward progressive ends by
destabilizing gender, class transvestism occludes economic relations
and reconstructs class as culture, but culture as voluntary rather more
than, as in taste, a product of one's particular history and environment.
Then, Schocket shows, class culture can be read as difference and absorbed into "pluralism." This is, of course, the problem of multiculturalism when it is treated as a mere celebration of diverse cultures rather
than as cultures also embedded in political and economic inequalities.

Gender performativity exposes the constructedness of gender,
showing that it is not an essential or natural category but a social one.
Class performativity, in contrast, may obscure economic inequalities
and reconstruct class as culture or choice. In many ways, such notions
of class as performance are entirely compatible with the ways in which
mainstream economics conceives of class today. The methodological
individualism at the core of mainstream (neoclassical) economic theory precludes consideration of class, though it does allow for special-
ized niche markets. That is, class in contemporary economic theory,
which goes back to the shift after 1871 that began this book, amounts
to market behavior, where "behavior" equals actual market performance or consumption patterns. Class equals taste equals consumption.

A view not based on methodological individualism would argue
that in order for there to be individuals who assert their class by asserting their tastes through their consumption patterns, there have to

14. Mary Poovey, *A History of the Modern Fact: Problems of Knowledge in the
Sciences of Wealth and Society* (Chicago: University of Chicago Press, 1998).

15. Eric Schocket, "Class Transvestite," *Representations* no. 63 (fall 1998): 109–33.

be social processes whereby surplus labor, including women's unpaid labor, is performed, appropriated, distributed, and received. These social processes constitute individuals, their needs, and to a large extent, their choices. An adequate method would need to recontextualize the idea of individual needs and choices within the social constitution of individuals.[16] This social constitution is indeed objective and, at least for most people, relates to the kind of work they do, or, alternatively, the kind of work they do not do, or are prevented from doing.

Objectively, one's class is one's position in the labor process, although one's political identity and subjectivity may be in ambivalent relation to one's class. One may perform a class identity, but the performance is subject to material limits. Hegemony may posit a class, but objective classes are reproduced by material processes, such as one's birth, one's position in the labor process, and one's effective demand (or capacity to consume), as well as by hegemonic institutions and discourse. The introduction of consumption models of taste and status draws together both class and gender, for consumption and leisure, the realms of pleasure for most wage laborers, are as significant in the formation of identity and subjectivity as production, as in Carolyn Steedman's example of her working-class mother's desire for a New Look coat.

We shall do better today to take from the history of political economy a focus on the division of labor, the kinds of work people do, including unpaid labor at home, and the ways that work structures identity and subjectivity, than on more abstract class identity (for example, wage laborers and capitalists), and to see that both local and global divisions of labor or work patterns are made along race and gender lines as much as along class lines. Equally important, consumption patterns (or taste, or pleasure) may be as significant as production, or pain, so we should account for people's pleasures and desires as well as their pain and their place in narrowly conceived "productive" relations. Class is no less significant than it always was, but future work should disaggregate the concept along these lines, mindful of gender salience in the division of labor and in the reproduction of class. And it should include *critical* analysis of the realms of taste, pleasure, consumption, leisure, and status.

16. David F. Ruccio, "The Merchant of Venice, or Marxism in the Mathematical Mode," *Rethinking Marxism* 1, no. 4 (winter 1988): 36–68, esp. 60–64.